OPEN VISTAS

OPEN VISTAS

Philosophical Perspectives of Modern Science

by HENRY MARGENAU

New Haven and London: Yale University Press

Originally published as Volume 3 in
the Trends in Science Series.

PREFACE

It can hardly be said that this little book was written; it was born, and born without much labor. By fortunate chance, and by the generosity of the Louis W. and Maud Hill Foundation, I was appointed to teach at Carleton College in 1953 where a triune combination of scholarship, science, and statesmanship in the remarkable person of President Laurence M. Gould, first stimulated me to prepare a lecture on "The New Faith of Science." Thus launched, my thinking moved farther afield, and the more ground it covered the stronger grew the conviction that modern science, when properly understood, can be of tremendous help to the searcher after philosophic, moral, and, indeed, political truth. In particular, it seemed that the most salient elements of recent physical science, namely its progressive dynamism implying a disavowal of stagnant truth and its surrender of the doctrine of mechanistic determinism, when translated into moral and social terms, mean precisely the same as the word democracy.

Fed by occasional invitations to lecture, the book thus wrote itself. The incident of its publication was a Sigma Xi lecture at Yale, which involved the signing of a publication contract. However, some of its contents formed the subject of a most enjoyable series of National Phi Beta Kappa talks under the auspices of that organization in 1958. Parts of the book have been published, although in different form, in a number of journals, and it behooves me here to express my indebtedness to their editors for permission to use some of the material already set forth in their columns. They

are: *American Scientist,* Brown University Press, Carleton
College Press, *Centennial Review of Arts and Science,
Christian Register, Discourse, Key Reporter, Main Currents of Modern Thought, Philosophy of Science,* and *Physics Today.*

Natural evolution is not a systematic process. Hence it
is to be expected—and it calls for apology—that this booklet will not present highly coordinated, rigorously reasoned
arguments. While I hope that substance and a measure of
cogency are here, the intent is to transmit in these pages
the spirit, and not so much the detailed substance of modern theoretical physics. Nor can I imagine a single reader
whose interest will attach itself uniformly to all sections.
There are discussions, especially in Chapter VII where particular views cherished by the author are elaborated at
possibly undue length. For this I ask the reader's indulgence. The sections concerned are indicated by footnotes;
they may be omitted without interrupting continuity of
treatment. Chapter I, it should be noted, is a summary of
an earlier book.

Finally, I should confess to, and atone for, a major sin.
The sin is the introduction and use of an uncommon word,
which will doubtless be resented by scientists whose creative contact with elementary particles reserves for them the
privilege of baptism. My proposal of the word *on* (plural,
onta) for elementary particle is made in all humility for
private convenience. It seems appropriate as the simplest
word for "that which is," the neuter of "being," a noun in
its own right and at the same time the ending of the names
of all elementary particles save one.

For much of the clerical work incurred in the preparation of this manuscript I am gratefully indebted to Mrs.
Ethel Himberg; to the small but growing circle of science

vi

students who have acquired an interest in philosophy and given me a critical appraisal of my thoughts I express my special acknowledgments.

HENRY MARGENAU

New Haven, Connecticut
October 1960

CONTENTS

Preface   v

Chapter I.   *Introduction*   1
              1. Scientific Method
              2. Meaning of Existence in Science
              3. The Role of Intuition in Science

Chapter II.   *Science and Human Affairs*   27
              1. The Nature of Facts: Their Glory
                 and Their Impotence
              2. Two Movements
              3. Philosophies of Our Day and
                 Their Scientific Roots
                     Mechanistic Materialism
                     Empiricism, Logical Positivism
                     Existentialism

Chapter III. *The Inner Light of Reason*   59
              1. The Tentative Nature of Postulates
              2. The Logic of Scientific Reasoning
              3. The New Faith of Science

Chapter IV.   *Esthetics and Relativity*   77
              1. The Idea of Invariance
              2. The Idea of Relativity
              3. Inertial Systems
              4. Newtonian Relativity
              5. Einstein's Special Relativity
              6. The Empirical Consequences of
                 the Lorentz Transformations and
                 Their Confirmation

Chapter V.   *The Decay of Materialism in Our Time*   103
1. The Sublimation and the Vanishing of the Material Ether
2. From Atoms to Elementary Particles to Singularities in Space
3. "Elementary Particles"

Chapter VI.   *The Fade-Out of Concrete Models*   129
1. Classical Mechanics
2. The Microcosm
3. The Dualism in the Nature of Onta
4. Waves of Probability

Chapter VII.   *Reality, Determinism, and Human Freedom*   171
1. Scientific Law in a Random Universe
2. Reality in the Microcosm
3. Probabilities, Continued
4. The "Bankruptcy" of Modern Physics
5. Historical Reality
6. Causality and Determinism
7. Human Freedom

Chapter VIII. *Open Vistas*   215
1. Looking Outward: Cosmology
2. Looking Inward: The Common Denominator of Science, Ethics, and Religion

Bibliography   243

Index   249

Chapter I

INTRODUCTION

1. Scientific Method

This book deals with a variety of topics, each of which has scientific and merits philosophic interest; their aggregate hangs together rather loosely, suggesting an arbitrariness of selection which was in fact not intended. I thought at first that the manner of treatment and the spirit of discussion would provide the necessary measure of coupling and unity, expecting the topics themselves, along with the context, to do their own integrating. On second thought, however, and at the friendly advice of a helpful reader, I decided to prefix an introduction that might focus thought and state a philosophic view which underlies and unifies the substance of this book. It exposes the connection between science and philosophy, testifies to the generality, the simple and universal humanity of the scientific approach, and allows certain traditional philosophic problems to be seen in a contemporary setting.

The initial hesitation which disposed me to omit this introduction arose from a sense that its contents could not be new. Hence, in overcoming this hesitation I must warn the reader that the present chapter offers merely a synopsis of a view and a terminology originally published in several articles in the *Journal of Philosophy of Science*[1] and worked

1. "Meaning and Scientific Status of Causality," *Journal of the Philosophy of Science, 1,* 133–148 (1934); "Methodology of Modern Physics, I," *Phil. of Science, 2,* 48–72 (1935); "Methodology of Modern Physics, II," *Phil. of Science, 2,* 164–187 (1935).

out more fully in an earlier book.[2] Its central concern is the scientific method, which is regarded as a refinement and a systematic extension of the ordinary knowing process.

Many competent scientists claim that there is no method of science: there are only sciences, each evolving its own method as it proceeds. This workaday view of the toiling scientist is a natural reflection of his daily experience. For as a specialist he is concerned with a multitude of diverse tasks requiring many different methods for their solution. Unless his mind soars above his daily pursuits, it is fairly natural that the working scientist should characterize his business as a welter of different and incompatible techniques. In the same spirit the woodsman might claim that there are only trees but no forests.

Even for the generalist and the philosopher of science, common features among the various scientific disciplines are not easy to perceive. Unifying traits will always escape one's view so long as it is focused solely upon the *subject matter* of the scientific disciplines. The factual fields of physics, biology, and psychology are completely different. When content is made a principle of classification, there will indeed be only sciences. However, when one asks the more penetrating questions, "What is a scientific problem and when does science regard its problems to be solved?", certain features common to physics, biology, and psychology spring into view. A sense of unity arises only through this *methodological approach* to the meaning of science. Hence it is this approach I now wish to sketch, for it shows science to be an important part of our human concern for the validity of knowledge or, some would hold, as that phase of

2. *The Nature of Physical Reality,* McGraw-Hill Book Co., Inc., 1950.

the cognitive process which to date has achieved its highest perfection.

Science is precisely what the etymology of that word suggests: it comprises what we know, that is to say, everything we "really" know. How often have we uttered in conversation the simple phrase, "Yes, I know." To lay bare its intention is our present task, for the meaning of this innocent sentence reveals the method of science.

Since knowing is only part of human experience, science is limited. For our total experience includes, besides knowledge, such components as feeling, judging, willing, and acting as well. To recognize the peculiar relevance of science for knowledge, however, is not tantamount to admitting that science has no application whatever to the areas of feeling, judging, and acting. For it may be that purely affective states of mind, insofar as they are objects of knowledge in addition to being immediate experiences, are indirectly tractable by the methods of science. But I wish to ignore this complex of problems here in order that the central features of scientific method shall not be obscured by inessential details.

Let us denote by the term *experience* the broad expanse of all matters that can possibly enter our consciousness. Experience thus means more than it does in the language of the strict empiricist, who wishes to limit the term to that which is directly perceived. Its present usage includes sensing, reasoning, feeling, judging, acting, and all the rest. From this universe of experience we now select what is called the *cognitive component*. While it may be difficult to define this with analytic precision (the contents of our experience do not fall into neat pigeonholes, and to define an isolated part of it is always an arbitrary matter), we are all subjectively aware of the ingredients of the knowledge

3

process; it usually involves having some sort of sense impression, remembering similar impressions, interpreting the impression or awareness in terms of external objects, relating these objects to other objects of a similar kind, reasoning about that class of objects, etc. In another form, the process of knowledge may start with a question which is heard or read, a question which sets us to thinking, to recalling facts, to analyzing a situation in order to arrive at an answer. Loosely, the faculties which bring about cognition are known as the senses, memory, and reasoning. But these are psychological terms, which suggest distinctions perhaps not altogether supportable in the face of the ineffable facts of experience.

Among the elements that go into knowledge, two extreme types can be recognized. Representative of one type is a mathematical idea such as that of a *number* or a *function* or a *group,* a pure concept, very abstract and rationally manipulatable, whose meaning does not flow from the accident of its "existence." The other type is represented by what are commonly known as *facts,* such as the circumstance that you now read this book, or that the light is shining through your window. Pure concepts and pure facts are the names which our language attributes to these two polar types of experience. Yet I hesitate to use these words, "concepts" and "facts," because they convey impressions of obviousness and of finality which obscure many intricate and important problems of science. This is particularly true about the word fact, which covers many sins. Hence at the risk of annoying the reader, I shall introduce a different terminology which I now proceed to explain.

What is factual about a fact is that it is independent of our control: it is simply there; it clamors to be recognized by us as such. A fact is what cannot be denied, what obtrudes itself into the process of knowledge whether we wish it there or not; it is the last instance of our rational or cognitive appeal. A fact is spontaneous in our experience, often unexpected and practically never merely the consequence of some chain of reasoning. It is often in the form of an immediate perception, or a sensory datum, or an observation. Most significantly, facts function as *protocols*[3] against which scientific theories and all other kinds of conjectures are ultimately tested. Let me simply use the letter P (which may stand for protocol, perception, or for primary) to designate this kind of experience. As examples I offer the seeing of this shape called desk, the hearing of a sound, the awareness of a pain, or indeed that combination of many such immediacies which we call an *observation* in science.

Contrasted with these P-elements are thoughts, ideas, mental images, fancies: in general all those rational entities which go by the more sober name of concepts. Concepts are the results of human processes of abstraction, sifting, reasoning; they emerge at the end of a long chain of activity in which man feels himself intelligently involved and responsible. Their genesis is perhaps best described by the term construction. Therefore, I propose to call them *constructs* to indicate the active part which our reason plays in their establishment. Whether and in what sense they are "pure" constructs having no relevance at all for more factual types of experience is not of interest at this moment.

The polarity of constructs and P-data should not be construed as implying that these two classes of entities never

3. The word protocol, despite its current legal and diplomatic usage, is taken here in its original meaning as a "public record or registry," a "first draft" of an experience later to become formalized knowledge. It meant literally a leaf glued to a manuscript suggesting the contents of the manuscript.

mix. In fact any cognitive experience involves elements of both classes, and it is only through an effort at methodological reduction that the two components can be separated at all. Practically any statement, any sentence about a factual experience, already involves interpretation, conceptualization, and therefore constructional elements. The latter clearly abound in our experience, and it is difficult to point to a kind of experience of which it may be said that it is a pure P-fact. Suppose I analyze the experience which is communicated by the phrase, "I see this lamp before me." What is incontrovertible and must be taken for granted is my awareness at this moment of a luminous yellow patch, with well-defined geometric contours, coupled perhaps with a tactile sensation of something hard, and a feeling of warmth in my hand as I touch it. All these are immediacies which must be assigned to the P-domain. But the sentence, "I see this lamp," asserts far more than what I have just described, for it alleges that there is present outside of me in three-dimensional space an object called a lamp with many features which I do not now perceive, and many which I could never perceive. I assume that it has an interior which I cannot see, a backside which is not now in view, that it is present whether I am looking at it or not, that it consists of molecules and has an internal structure of a very complicated sort, and so forth. In assuming this I have constructed out of a complex of P-data an essence containing far more than was immediately given. Strictly speaking, the lamp as a three-dimensional external object is a construct which points to many P-facts, for instance those which have given rise to it in the present sensation, but also to many possible ones which may have been experienced in the past or which may be expected to be experienced in the future. As has often been pointed out by

6

psychologists, it is not correct to say that the lamp is immediately given in sensation, or that it is itself part of the P-domain.

The distinction becomes both clearer and increasingly necessary when more abstract concepts are considered. It is generally conceded that the concept number, while relating to P-experiences, has nevertheless the dominating character of having been constructed. We could arrive at the concept number even if there were no concrete things to count. This becomes particularly evident when we consider such entities as the concept of infinity, which by its very nature can have no direct P-counterpart.

There is a sense in which facts are immune to treatment by reasoning: they are simply there and have to be reckoned with. Indeed it is their lack of internal order, their refusal to follow an obvious rational pattern, which constrains our mind to engage in the process of constructing rational counterparts for them, counterparts which are governable by rational rules and which can be made to fulfill our desire for order and coherence in experience. A heard noise, for instance, at once suggests the presence of a sound source somewhere in space; we look for it, and if this search ends in another P-type experience in which we see the object, our desire for rational coherence in our experience is satisfied. Coherence has not been established directly between the two P-facts; an essential third element within this coherent scheme is the constructed object.

To speak of the intervening object as a construct may be offensive to many. "The streetcar or the fire, or the tree," you will say, "were not constructed by me. They are objects of which I *become aware* through what has been called P-experiences." Now I am the first to admit that the distinction here made is in this instance a highly academic and indeed a perfectly useless one; nevertheless I would insist that it is logically sound even if artificial. But I would add that it is very important for us to learn to recognize the difference between P-type facts (or data) and constructs even in so simple an experience as this, for if we go on blindly ignoring this distinction, we shall never be able to understand fully the more recondite and involved excursions of modern science.

As an example, consider the sentence: This desk consists of atoms. If both desk and atom are taken to be data, i.e., P-facts of experience, the statement raises no difficulties. But a little reflection shows that, while the desk may in some sense be given directly in sensation, the atom certainly is not, and the statement thus seems to imply rather awkwardly that something given in sensation has smaller parts which are not given in sensation. In the present terminology, we would have to say with equal embarrassment that a set of P-experiences, called the desk, is spatially composed of a set of constructs. There are two ways in which this dilemma can be avoided: one is to deny our distinction and to claim, in addition, that atoms are P-facts, like the desk. The denial would be proper if the claim were just; every consideration of modern physics, however, refutes the claim; the desk has visual size, shape, color, position, i.e., all the attributes of sensation, whereas the atom, in a basic sense, has none of them. The other remedy is to make the distinction between sensory facts and constructs and to note that the term desk, as it appears in the statement under examination, is already something other than a set of P-experiences, that it is in fact a construct. The statement then indicates how one kind of construct is related to another kind by spatial inclusion; it involves no passage from one realm of discourse to another. We accept this latter way of avoiding the dilemma.

If practically any cognitive experience already contains constructs, what can possibly be meant by a pure P-datum? My answer is this: it probably does not exist. Yet whenever we analyze a scientific experience, we sooner or later come to a place where we say: This we accept, or this is incontrovertibly true. Here we have reached the P-domain. It forms a sort of limiting plane bounding the unlimited domain of constructional experience. Because of this I like to speak of the P-facts as forming the P-plane and to picture the P-plane as a sort of boundary, without thickness as it were, of the constructional domain to which I shall refer as the C-field. The latter is rich and large; it contains most of the interpretations featured by science, excluding only that "direct appeal to nature" called observation or empirical verification which the scientist uses to "validate" his ideas about nature.

From the point of view of the psychologist, a P-plane fact is neither simple nor unanalyzable. Only methodologically does a given observation form the last instance of appeal for the physicist; he either cannot or does not wish to analyze it further. According to the standards of his science this set of facts, this observation is to be taken for granted, is to be taken as a test stone for his reasoning about the world. To him it is a P-plane fact. The psychologist, on the other hand, may not wish to take this complex of psychological data as ultimate. He may, for good reasons of his own, wish to dissect it further, and he may actually come to the conclusion that a sensation is further analyzable in a psychological way. If this be true, the existence of a P-plane in my sense is nevertheless guaranteed, for it is a necessity for every

9

science to regard certain data as incontrovertible; and even the psychologist, in denying the ultimacy of the physicist's P-experiences, must somehow fall back upon unanalyzable primitives of his own. If science gives up the premise of a P-plane, it loses the very basis of its competence. Let us remember, however, that a P-fact for one science may not be a P-fact for another.

We have separated the elements of cognitive experience into two classes, P-facts and constructs. Strictly speaking, the assemblage of sensations, visual, tactile, kinesthetic that assails me as I look before me is not the desk but the P-experience which leads me to postulate the three-dimensional object I call desk. The construct is not identical with the P-experience: it somehow *corresponds* to it. Ordinary language is often confusing; when it speaks of a force it may refer to a certain muscular sensation (P-fact) or, indiscriminately, to a highly refined idea used by the physicist and defined by certain mathematical symbols. When it speaks of light, it may mean a sensation of brightness and color or, on the other hand, a sinusoidal variation in an electromagnetic field. As experiences, the two are clearly not identical, but one *corresponds* to the other. When pressed for precision, ordinary language permits us to speak of light in its subjective and its objective or scientific aspect: this amounts to admitting the difference between P-plane and constructs I have tried to sketch. The correspondences between them form an important subject of epistemology but will not be dealt with in this brief account.

Further examples of the relation between P and C can easily be cited. When I have the experiences which normally occur when I turn my gaze in this direction, I postulate the existence of a lamp; when I hear a certain noise, I postulate the existence of an airplane; when I note a certain acceleration, I assume the existence of a force; when I observe a certain track in a cloud chamber or hear a click in a counter, I postulate the passage of a charged particle; when I see a person behave in a manner I call reasonable, I endow him with an intelligent mind—all these are instances in which a P-experience calls into play specific constructs via certain rules of correspondence (which for the present will not be further analyzed).

Now there are right and wrong constructs in terms of which we can make experiences of the P-sort understandable. Even though the sensation as such is undeniable, one may be mistaken in supposing that what he sees is truly a lamp, for it may be an optical illusion that beguiles the mind. The noise may come from a stage prop and not an airplane; the thing I have seen behave intelligently may have been a robot and no conscious being at all. Such queries lead to the important consideration of the conditions under which the assignment of constructs to P-facts is scientifically valid. The business of science might be supposed to be the mapping of individual P-experiences in a unique and simple way upon the field of constructs, a mapping which is regulated by principles of convenience and of economy of thought. If this were the entire truth, then perhaps the simplest and most acceptable scientific theory would be one proposed by Berkeley, who believed that every factual experience is but the manifestation of a thought in the mind of God. His thesis, which is here oversimplified for the sake of the argument, creates a simple and indeed a convenient correspondence between the facts on the P-plane and the constructs of the C-field. Yet it is unsatisfactory. The reason is not that it is wrong, for clearly it could never be shown to be wrong. Its fault lies in its very generality. For it lacks a property which I like to call *logical fertility*. The whole

11

scheme is logically sterile, there is nothing that the scientist can derive from it, nor anything which he can test by empirical means. The theory states its case and is done; its acceptance or rejection makes no difference in our P-experience.

The lesson to be drawn from this consideration is that scientific theories must contain constructs which are in some sense logically fertile, and I shall mean by this the deductive quality which the Berkeleian theory so obviously lacks. Scientific theories differ in the degree to which they are logically fertile, some having a great deal of logical power, others very little. But in general they strive for a maximum of logical fertility; science avoids the use of ideas leading to sterile situations in which predictions cannot be made.

As another example, let us consider how lightning was and is explained. An old mythological theory associated with the visual fact of lightning the notion of an irate god throwing a thunderbolt. Modern theory connects it with the construct: "electrical discharge in the atmosphere." The mythological concept contains nothing which brands it as scientifically unacceptable per se; its appeal to an unseen god, for example, is not intrinsically objectionable, any more than the appeal to an invisible condition of ionization in the air. Nor is the mythological construct unverifiable, for it is clear that, if we assume some knowledge about the god, we can reason about his behavior and conclude, for example, that when a human being appeases him, he will be patient and throw no thunderbolts, whereas if he is offended he will cast a bolt. Not only has the mythological notion this theoretical degree of logical fecundity, it even exposes itself to direct test. For it is quite conceivable that man could experiment and see whether, if the god be offended, he will throw thunderbolts. This was in fact believed to be the case. The scientific explanation involving the concept of ionization is likewise verifiable. But it has one advantage over the mythological scheme: it applies to a *greater range* of P-plane facts. While the thunderbolt hypothesis could explain at most the phenomenon of lightning, the physical theory now in vogue leads one to understand not only this particular experience but also many others, as for instance the facts of electrical discharges in the laboratory and, as a further vast extension, almost all other manifestations of electricity. Thus it is seen that an advantage of the modern hypothesis (aside from the circumstance that we now believe it to be better confirmed by the facts) lies in its greater *extensibility*.

To summarize, the thunderbolt hypothesis is rejected in favor of the ionization hypothesis because the latter is more *extensible* (aside from other reasons, to be sure).

Why was the Ptolemean doctrine, which placed the earth at the center of the solar system, surrendered in favor of the Copernican heliocentric theory? Contrary to widespread belief, the Copernican theory was not better verified by astronomical observations; with very few exceptions these could be accounted for on the basis of either set of constructs. What gave the Copernican theory distinction above that of Ptolemy and finally led it to victory and general acceptance was its pervading *simplicity,* a quite formal characteristic of scientific theories which has little to do with empirical verification.

When the information drawn from the preceding examples and many other similar ones is systematized, it leads to the following conclusion: scientific constructs are regarded as valid representations of (P-plane) facts if they satisfy two large sets of requirements. The first set may be called methodological, or indeed metaphysical. It has to do

13

with the native fitness of the constructs themselves, with the manner in which they place themselves in formal relations, with their coherence and their logical range. It is possible to name the different criteria; I have tried to present a list of them in the book already cited.[4] Metaphysical requirements which the constructs of science have to satisfy are: *logical fertility, extensibility, multiple connection, causality, simplicity, elegance,* and several others. This enumeration should not be taken as naming a set of absolute and authoritative axioms, of unchanging categories of thought in the Cartesian or Kantian sense. It is simply an assortment of basic maxims of science which have grown through application and use during the history of science, principles which have proved their power and have now come to be generally accepted by working scientists who, sometimes without knowing it, employ them in their researches. They are not absolutely *necessary* principles of knowledge, and, as already suggested, they may change in time. But a survey of the history of science shows that changes in them proceed very slowly, and that a modification of the metaphysical requirements when it occurs (e.g., the present changing attitude with respect to the principle called causality) induces profound and extensive changes in the structure of science itself.

A set of constructs which obeys the metaphysical requirement does not for that reason alone become acceptable. Theories, i.e., sets of constructs, must also satisfy the requirement of *empirical verification.* The process of empirical verification is a circuit starting somewhere in the P-plane, swinging from there by means of some rule of correspondence into the C-field, where it propagates itself by

4. See footnote 2.

formal reasoning from one part of the field to another. Finally, the chain of experiences sweeps back from the C-field to the P-plane, pointing to another place than that from which the circuit started. In simpler language the scientist starts with an observation; this observation is then interpreted in terms of the constructs that are associated with it. These constructs allow him to reason, and he finally emerges with a prediction which says that if the original observation was true, then something else must also be true. This something else can usually be investigated empirically. If it is found to be true, the circuit is declared successful. Now the *requirement of empirical verification* demands that a set of constructs be traversable in many ways by circuits of the type I have described. If all these circuits have been found successful, that is to say if the theory has been tested in many ways, the scientist regards the constructs forming the theory as *valid*. What was originally an hypothesis has now become a satisfactory theory, the former constructs have transformed themselves into verifacts, and insofar as the constructs had the character of tentative entities these entities have now become realities, and they are said to *exist*.

The method of science can be schematized by means of a picture like Figure 1. The line P represents a section of the P-plane of science. To the left of it extends the field of constructs or the C-field. Some constructs, like those denoting the things of our daily experience, lie very close to the P-plane. Others like force, energy, valence, life, intelligence are more abstract and lie some distance away from the P-plane; but they are nevertheless connected with it by definite rules (drawn as double lines in the figure) which set up unique correspondences between constructs and P-plane facts. Very far to the left we find highly abstract entities such as field, numbers, groups, probabilities, psi-functions, and also such constructs as God and immortality. Meta-physical requirements endow the constructs with native fitness. They demand, for instance, that there should be a full set of relations (drawn by light lines) between the con-

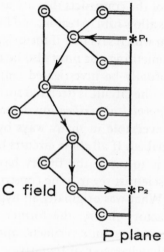

Fig. 1

structs in the figure. They demand furthermore that from every C lines must extend via other C's and end in the P-plane. A circuit of empirical verification (following the arrows in Figure 1) starts at P_1, goes through the C-field, and returns to P_2. P_1 might be the observation of the position of a comet at a certain time. That part of the C-field through which the circuit moves might be Newton's theory of universal gravitation, and the final transition to P_2 might be the prediction of the position of that same comet at some future time. When a set of constructs is traversed by a great number of such circuits, it is said to be verified, and the

16

constructs are said to correspond to reality, or even to compose reality.

The method of science is nothing more than an elaboration of procedures of common sense. Even the simplest instances of gaining knowledge are examples of the scientific process just described. Let us see, for instance, how we decide whether a given experience represented a true sense perception or a sensory illusion. There is nothing in an experience as a P-fact which allows this distinction to be made. A deception or an hallucination can be just as vivid and memorable as a bona fide perception. It is only when we *interpret* the experience, that is to say when we set up a correspondence with constructs and test the internal coherence of these constructs, that a decision as to the validity of the sense impression can be made.

Suppose I conclude that the vision in question reveals an actual object. This means that a transition from the P-plane to the C-field, a very brief and obvious transition to be sure, has been made. The construct encountered, the external object, satisfies all the metaphysical requirements, and the question is only whether in this instance it embeds itself properly and in a sufficient number of successful circuits of empirical verification. In the present simple instance, this elaborate phrase means nothing more than the possibility of my testing the hypothesis: this is an external object. A modicum of reasoning would lead me to expect that if I reached out to touch the object, I should have a tactile impression. If I do reach out and fail to have this impression, the circuit has not been successful; and I conclude that while the experience as an experience was real enough, it was nevertheless a sense illusion because the construct I associated with it did not turn out to satisfy the requirements for validity which we have previously estab-

17

lished. In highly developed sciences like atomic physics, organic chemistry, psychology, or theoretical economics, such circuits of empirical verification take on very elaborate forms.

2. *Meaning of Existence in Science*

In view of the problems that will later arise, it may be helpful to analyze a few scientific sentences which involve the word existence. What, for instance, does a scientist mean when he says, "Electrons exist"? He certainly does not imply that they are present within his experience in the same simple manner in which he encounters ordinary external objects. This is at once clear from the fact that electrons can never be seen or apprehended in the direct manner in which we assure ourselves of the existence of large visible things. Furthermore, according to modern physics, electrons do not even have positions at all times nor some other visual attributes ordinarily assigned to objects, for they partake of the renowned dualism (cf. Chapter VI) which makes them sometimes appear as particles and sometimes as waves. These are qualities unheard of in ordinary things. Evidently the electron is a physical construct which does not lie very close to the P-plane but is something rather abstract, not to be conceived intuitively in a simple imageful way.

The claim that electrons are real means this. Suppose we postulate such entities, endowing them with a certain charge, a certain mass, and certain other qualities such as spin and Hamiltonian. These constructs now have the unique quality of being correlated with a variety of P-facts in a simple manner. Among these facts are observations on the flow of electricity in wires, observations on the flow of electricity in liquids or in gaseous conductors, the production of heat and light by currents, the peculiar appearance of certain cloud chamber tracts, the behavior of photocells, and a host of other physical facts. In terms of the diagram of Figure 2, the electron, together with its qualities and properties, corresponds to a small set of constructs some distance

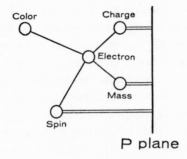

Color
Charge
Electron
Mass
Spin

P plane

Fig. 2. (Note that the construct "color of the electron" is not multiply connected, fails to satisfy the metaphysical requirements, and is therefore uninteresting, indeed rejected by physicists.)

from the P-plane, and from this set there emerge heavy lines connecting the set with many parts of the P-plane. Because this compact theoretical structure is logically fertile, allows so many successful circuits of empirical confirmation, we have no hesitation in declaring the set of constructs—i.e., the electron together with its mass, its charge, etc.—part of physical reality. That is the sense of the statement: the electron exists. In particular, no claim is made that the electron is directly perceptible, or that it has the qualities of ordinary things, e.g., that of occupying a definite point of space at every moment of time.

Let us now turn to another proposition which may be called scientific: namely, the statement that man has a mind, or that human minds exist. Here the meaning of existence is even less obvious than in the foregoing example. For what

19

it asserts, if anything, is this: Man is capable of simple sensations like seeing a tree, or hearing a sound, or being engaged in a reasoning process like doing arithmetic, or of pondering over a construct like a number. These are *simple* experiences in the sense that we normally have them without being conscious of them. But we can also reflect upon them while engaged in them; we can be aware of being aware of the tree, we can be aware of thinking about numbers, and so on. Thus it seems as if in every phase of our experience we can somehow reflect upon this experience and pronounce it ours; we may not only have the experience but we can also be aware of having the experience. This circumstance, this possibility of reflection which represents a given experience to us as peculiarly our own, is what the reference to mind exposes. On this interpretation of the meaning of mind, the construct establishes a universal reference, setting up a logical relation between itself and every possible experience. If it did nothing more than this, if its usefulness could not be tested in any other way, I suppose it would occupy the status of the Berkeleian god, and the idea would be logically sterile. It is conceivable, however, and I believe it is true, that this vague construct may also be endowed with organizing qualities which make for the unity of our entire experience and thus allow it to assume a role in which it becomes logically fertile. If this is true, mind becomes a valid construct of science and the statement that it exists is perfectly meaningful. But again this existence has no necessary relevance to anything substantial or material existing in space.

The story becomes even more complex when we analyze such statements as the one alleging that other people have consciousness. As far as my own experience is concerned, it is perfectly meaningful for me to say that I am conscious, or at least that I am conscious of something. There is a direct, introspective way in which this construct of consciousness can be empirically tested. It is part of everyone's P-plane. But when consciousness is assigned to others, every avenue of *direct* testing is closed. In a sense the definition of consciousness then changes from its previous, first-person meaning; it becomes a construct, takes on an indirectness which deprives it of *immediate* significance and transfers what residue of meaning the concept retains to the manner in which it relates itself to other constructs. The consciousness of others does not enter into immediate correspondence with our P-plane under any circumstances, but the idea makes plausible why other people behave as I do under similar circumstances. The construct, while immune to direct verification, renders coherent a host of other constructs and provides logical fertility for a set that would otherwise be barren. It is only in this more circuitous sense that the consciousness of others can be maintained, and that this construct can be said to be valid or to exist.

Perhaps it is clear from these examples that existence, even in science, is not a simple thing to comprehend or to demonstrate. The meaning of terms like existence, validity, and truth may be very far from anything that common sense conveys.

3. *The Role of Intuition in Science*

Since the claim is sometimes made that non-scientific knowledge is based upon intuition, while science uses the inductive or the rational approach, it may be helpful to discuss briefly the role played by intuition in science. The word intuition requires clarification in order that misunderstanding be avoided. It seems to me that it has two meanings which I shall set forth as meaning *a* and meaning *b*.

As we have seen, the process of scientific explanation aims at setting up correspondences between valid constructs in the C-field and data on the P-plane. To attain this goal, a scientist can move in either of two directions. He can start on the P-plane and drive his inquiry into the C-field. This is called the *inductive* approach. Alternatively, a scientist may begin with the postulation of some conjecture involving simple or otherwise appealing constructs, derive from them their implications and see whether these implications, with the use of certain rules of correspondence, are verified in P-experience. This is called the *deductive* approach. Historically, significant discoveries have attended either process. Which approach works better in a given problematic situation is a psychological question; it cannot be answered in general and depends largely upon the personal disposition or endowment of the investigator. Some minds are given to induction. They are able to survey with minute care a set of data or facts, abstract from them with the use of Baconian or other inductive rules their residue of significance, and connect them successfully with certain constructs which the data in a sense "suggest." Another type of mind, more rationalistic in its aptitude, will begin with speculations about certain abstract constructs, perhaps certain particularly simple and beautiful differential equations. It will solve these equations, will develop the implications of its initial abstract guesses, and see whether or not they have any significance with respect to P-experience. When the connection between the C-field and the P-plane has been made it can be traversed in either direction, and the question as to deduction or induction and their relative merits has ceased to be important.

Now there are scientists who have an uncanny ability. By training or natural endowment they have come to possess the faculty of contemplating a set of P-plane facts, pondering over them, and then arriving at once at a valid set of constructs which, they would say, are "suggested" by the phenomena. The ordinary scientific mind would have to go painfully and slowly through all stages of the process of linking constructs with P-experiences. The person having cultivated this remarkable faculty, however, is capable of performing what has been called the "inductive leap," a passage which seems to soar over the intervening gap between abstractions and facts with an ease not given to the ordinary mortal. This "inductive leap" is often spoken of as *intuition* in science. It is what I referred to as meaning *a* of that word. There is something striking, incomprehensible, psychologically miraculous about this leap, something akin to revelation in religion. In the terminology of Pitirim Sorokin, it involves a supraconscious act.

While this kind of intuition is strange and perhaps remarkable to the psychologist, it creates no difficulty for the method of science. For although it generates scientific correlations in a marvelous and maybe unorthodox way, it does not set itself above the ordinary criteria of validity in science. When the leap has been performed, the creative investigator, or at any rate his contemporaries or successors, will set to work filling in the details of the intuitive process; and if the details are contradictory, or if the results of the completed process of explanation fail in other respects to conform with the maxims of scientific validity (i.e., with the metaphysical requirements and the requirement of empirical verification), the inductive leap is declared a failure.

Less spectacular instances of intuition in this sense *a* also occur in ordinary cognition, where they are called instinctive guesses, or successful conjectures.

There is also meaning *b* of intuition: it designates a certain kind of introspection for which the claim is made that it delivers insights and truths. The advocates of this mode of obtaining knowledge often hold that true knowledge, scientific or otherwise, is somehow lodged within our mental makeup, is hidden in nuclear form within our own mental faculties and lies there ready to be grasped. Thus it has been maintained, for example, that the properties of space and time need not be discovered by painstaking investigations concerning the behavior of actual bodies in space and time; they may be revealed by "intuition," by a careful analysis of the ideas of space or time as they present themselves to the unindoctrinated mind. This was in part the view of Kant, who held time and space to be pure forms of intuition and used that term approximately in the sense *b* here under scrutiny. The character of space thus determined was Euclidean, as is well known; any doubt concerning the validity of Euclidean space would, in view of the unerring powers of intuition that revealed this truth, be a challenge to the very essence of human understanding.

In a similar way Husserl and the phenomenologists have advocated the use of intuitive knowledge obtained by what they call *Wesensschau*. This is supposed to be some sort of principle of introspection leading to indubitable truth or, to use their favored term, *eidetic* truth. Such intuition is said to reveal the laws of logic, the principles of the human mind, and even some of the basic knowledge of the physical world. It is what I have called intuition in its meaning *b*.

When claiming validity independently of the requirements of valid constructs, intuition *b* brushes aside the main controls of the method of science. Its results become promiscuous and untrustworthy, as can be seen from the elementary fact that on the basis of this kind of intuition a bona fide sense perception is indistinguishable from an hallucination. Both proclaim themselves to be eidetically true, and unless one seeks for validity in terms of pervasive logical coherence and empirical testability, both deliverances, the true and the illusory, must be accepted without discrimination. Even on a higher scientific plane the faults and errors of intuition in its meaning *b* are quite apparent. So far as the concepts of space and time are concerned, this intuition proved entirely deceptive, for they are not Euclidean, and it is now well known that doubt as to the Euclidean nature of space and time does not constitute a basic challenge to all human understanding. The mind of the modern scientist, trained in non-Euclidean geometries, can very well have intuitions quite different from those of Kant and Husserl. We thus see that intuition in the mere sense of clear discernment of introspective facts does not provide the safeguard which scientific methodology requires.

What has been said is that intuition alone does not guarantee scientific truth. There is nothing in the methodology of science which ostracizes intuition, even in sense *b*. Psychology should and largely does regard it as a kind of P-experience to be reckoned with, as providing data which must somehow form the termini of associations with constructs, ruled by the methodology of science, in terms of which the facts of intuition themselves become understandable. It may also be that intuitions of type *b* form a P-plane for introspective psychology. But if they do, and if psychology is to have the structure of a science, it must provide in addition to these intuitions rules and criteria in terms of which they may be consistently judged to be valid or false. The very general conception of method outlined in this introduction is basic to the reasoning that follows. In the main body of the book, however, we shall not take occasion to relate explicitly every detail to the foregoing epistemology; problems will be treated in less technical language and in the natural setting in which they arise.

Chapter II

SCIENCE AND HUMAN AFFAIRS

1. *The Nature of Facts: Their Glory and Their Impotence*

Science is said to deal with facts,[1] and with facts exclusively. In the popular mind, science is the compendium of all certified or certifiable facts, its goal is the creation of a universal encyclopædia of factual knowledge. The precise meaning of "fact" in phrases of this sort is perhaps not obvious, but its accent is on the immediately given in human experience, on matters which can be ascertained objectively by all careful searchers after truth, on the discoverable in contradistinction to what is invented. Behind this preoccupation with facts one sees the shades of Francis Bacon denouncing the idols of the market place and of the theater, of David Hume insisting on the primacy of perceptions, of John Stuart Mill attempting to achieve trustworthy knowledge by his principle of induction. The entire Anglo-Saxon scientific tradition seems to be summed up in the flavor of these men's teachings, and students in our schools today are taught that reliance on verified fact is the distinguishing feature of modern science that finally succeeded in overcoming the obscurantism and authoritarianism of mediaeval thought.

Over against fact stand theory and speculation, and in the minds of many scholars and most practical persons theory falsifies. That science is best which relies least on interpre-

1. To establish continuity with the Introduction we note that facts are common experiences lying on or very close to the P-plane.

27

tation, just as an account of history or a newspaper report attains quality through avoidance of theory, through complete reliance on facts. According to this popular view, science is like an enormous picture puzzle; the scientist discovers the pieces and trusts that benevolent nature or providence has shaped and adjusted them so that they will fit together. When enough piecemeal facts are available and put in their proper places, a recognizable pattern results, and a problem has been solved. That problem or pattern is then finished once and for all and a new one in some adjacent field is started. Coupled with this favored interpretation of science is often the expectation that some day, when all facts are known and the world pattern is finally assembled, man will be able to regulate his affairs in ideal fashion, the golden millennium will arrive, and happiness will blossom everywhere.

It is not hard to see that such a view commits grave errors. First, it takes facts as given and significant in themselves and, second, it mistakes knowledge, the encyclopædia of certifiable facts, for understanding. Yet it is evident to every scientist that a bare and isolated fact, an unrelated experience, a single observation, commands no one's sustained attention; it is inherent in the nature of an isolated fact to be *un*satisfying, to clamor for context and fulfillment. But a set of *related* and *suggestive* facts, a significant experience, a set of observations called an *experiment*—these are the building blocks of science and of philosophy of science. And what is it that makes a fact related to other facts, makes a perception suggestive, an experience significant, a set of observations an experiment? Clearly they require a certain background of interpretation to take on meaning, a medium of expectations which they confirm or confute, a texture of theory which they illuminate. A forest of facts unordered by concepts and constructive relations may be cherished for its existential appeal, its vividness, or its nausea; yet it is meaningless and cognitively unavailing unless it be organized by reason. Reflection upon this matter leads to this somewhat paradoxical and startling conclusion: facts are not interesting or important ingredients of science unless they point to relations, unless they suggest ideas combined into what is called a theory.

The second error made by the advocate of the factual picture puzzle lies in his mistaking knowledge for understanding. True science is not a two-dimensional affair lacking depth and vertical perspective as the picture puzzle implies; it has a third dimension where facts take root in rational constructs. A surface array of facts may constitute *knowledge;* the very word understanding, however, suggests a stratum beneath that of facts, a stratum where ideas, laws, and principles unify factual experience and inspire it with scientific significance. It is a telling observation that the Hall of Fame in science contains the names of few men who discovered facts but a host who made facts significant by providing pervasive and integrating explanations. Certain noteworthy properties of a right triangle are named the Pythagorean theorem after the man who *proved* them, i.e., gave them rational status; we do not even know what practical genius discovered these properties as facts and taught the Egyptian surveyors to use them in their work long before Pythagoras. The errors we are endeavoring to expose originate in a disregard of theory, in a belief that facts have feet on which they can stand. Actually, they are supported in a fluid medium called theory, or theoretical interpretation, a medium which prevents them from collapsing into insignificance.

The arithmetic of facts which inclines us to expect a

finite sum of total knowledge and thereby promises heaven on earth, reveals itself as a fraud in every scientific discovery. No discovery ever terminates an inquiry; it may answer a question of fact, but in doing so it raises further problems because it progresses into a continuous field of logical relations studded with kernels of fact, and when a fact is conquered the relational web beyond it suggests further facts as challenges to further progress. Science has no boundaries; it has an horizon which widens as science advances, placing in view more and more unknown terrain but never heaven.

Having noted and deplored the glory of facts in our thinking, let us hasten to assess their proper function. For in spite of what has been said they are the alpha and the omega of science. They are precisely that: the starting points for theory and interpretation as well as the crucial termini conferring validity on all ideas. We have counseled against the omission of the rest of the alphabet.

The fact-bound bias, the hypnosis induced by the fixation of our gaze on the obvious and the immediate, has unhappily crept into larger areas far too important for haphazard attention: among them are the teaching of science and international politics.

As to the former, the teaching of physics in our colleges may serve as an example. Most of the upper-class courses are well taught. They are largely handled by men who teach their specialties and therefore inject into their work the enthusiasm that inspires their researches. They maintain a proper balance between facts and interpretation, and the pace is moderate, allowing for reflection. Furthermore, the students who take these courses have already survived the ordeal of their initial exposure to the facts. On the whole it seems as if the going was smooth for students who have passed the barrier of the elementary science courses.

Let us now consider those who have not. The typical freshman or sophomore course in physics begins with mechanics and ends with a conglomeration of facts frequently called "Modern Physics," winding its devious way through such topics as heat, thermodynamics, hydrodynamics, sound, electricity and magnetism, geometrical and physical optics. An elementary course in physics has come to embrace all these things; if anything is omitted the course is regarded as incomplete. The unsuspecting student is forced to take this entire mélange or nothing.

Physics teachers have developed an unshakable reverence for the sanctity of the subject matter in an elementary course. A suggestion that part of the material be omitted tends to be treated as heresy, and responsibility for fullness of the course is imputed to deans of engineering schools and medical schools, who, it is said, insist that candidates for admission to their institutions be exposed to all the items of this potpourri. Yet interrogation of these august officials leads invariably to the assurance that medical schools and engineering colleges make no prescriptions as to the selection of the subject matter in any elementary course in physics and chemistry, that they leave this entirely to the discretion of the science teachers. Perhaps this point needs emphasis, for it demolishes the one and only reasonable argument which the propagandist for completeness of subject matter in an elementary course can use to support his position.

The point is that these courses are crammed with a super-abundance of uncorrelated facts, uncorrelated at least in the mind of the student who leaves the course. Within one year no professor can teach and no student can absorb such an overwhelming avalanche of material together with its conceptual connections. But the attempt is made, even if it

31

is painful to both student and teacher, in deference to the rigor of science and often with the avowed intention of showing that science is difficult. The teaching method consists in presenting first all the facts. They are often skillfully introduced by ingenious lecture demonstrations and thus made memorable to the students. The second stage of the method aims to induce students to remember, correlate, and learn to use these facts. And the third is an attempt to develop a modicum of theory so that the facts are illuminated by the light of principles. Since time presses there is usually very little opportunity for this last phase of the process; what happens, therefore, is that theories, laws, and mathematical equations are again treated as though they were facts to be memorized. Conceptual illumination is put at the end where, since teachers are forever rushed because of the fullness of their courses, it is slighted. Sometimes the fault lies with the instructors in charge of the elementary courses. Being experienced teachers, they are often relieved of the necessity and of the opportunity for doing research. In time their knowledge grows eclectic; their approach to their subject becomes general and indiscriminate. Somehow they develop a feeling that in their one yearly contact with an elementary student they must teach him all they know, and in their enthusiastic but massive embrace the student's love for the subject is killed.

The remedy for this situation is obvious. Above all it is necessary to ease the superabundance of detailed facts in the elementary sciences courses. Whole segments like thermodynamics, hydrodynamics, and indeed optics, could be omitted from an elementary physics course without destroying either the continuity or the value of it. This would leave time for proper digestion of the facts presented, would give an opportunity to discuss, with student participation, the meaning of the new things learned, would open vistas into other fields, such as philosophy and history of science. These are minimum remedies whose desirability seems beyond question. But there may be reasons to doubt whether they alone will be sufficient. Perhaps they need to be coupled with a shift of emphasis from induction to deduction in the teaching of elementary science. For it is deductive reasoning which allows the premises, the postulates, the principles that unify our thinking about the world to be placed most clearly in evidence, and it is unfortunate that in our elementary teaching a proper balance between induction and deduction is not often achieved.

The error of mistaking science for an exclusive catalogue of facts is symptomatic of a bias in other parts of our thinking, for it results in an underestimate and a disparagement of the power of theory to convince in the realm of international affairs; indeed, it may prove to be a tragic handicap in our struggle for supremacy in a world that probably no longer dares conduct military wars.

In the words of a far-seeing Belgian journalist, Marcel Gregoir, we have entered an era in which "Il faut non seulement vaincre notre adversaire, mais le *con*vaincre; de plus en plus, la lutte se transforme en croisade." The correlation between fact and theory has thus become of vital importance. For facts alone never carry conviction, and in the ideological warfare between East and West it is of utmost importance that we carry convictions. In this struggle we have evidently experienced reverses, and a frank analysis of the circumstances surrounding our failures might involve the following reflections.

The ideology of the East is a dogma, a teachable creed. Youths in all lands but ours argue heatedly about the correctness of the theses of Hegel, Marx, Engels, and Lenin.

SCIENCE AND HUMAN AFFAIRS

They often pride themselves on being able to prove in a rational and convincing way that the concepts of capitalism suffer from internal inconsistencies, and that for this reason, and no other, this form of society cannot survive. Those who have lived in foreign lands, even before the era of so-called cold wars, know the fervor and enthusiasm of the communist expounding his creed, know the absolute conviction with which he believes in the logic, the ideal supremacy of his point of view. He is an avowed rationalist with perhaps one weakness: he ignores many facts, but unfortunately he does not ignore enough to make him an easy mark.

Let us be equally frank about our own attitude. We are convinced of the superior value of our economic views, our democracy, our freedom. Our image of these, however, is immediate, is factual, our love for them so deep and unquestioning as to blind us to the need for defending our view in theoretical terms. Yet it is true that a person who has not lived our democracy, our freedom, a person to whom the immediate facts of our existence are not available, can have no comprehension of them. A foreigner coming to our shores is perfectly sincere when he ridicules our slogans; he is bewildered much like a trusting child steeped in fairy tales when it confronts the facts of life. Ours is a way of life, a set of facts, and not a doctrine; we are setting it against a doctrine which is not a way of life. This was not always true. At the birth of our nation the philosophic concept of freedom, the idea of human rights swept across oceans and inflamed the minds of men like Voltaire; unfortunately, these same convictions, to which we still give unreasoning lip service, have now sunk to the level of factual expediency.

The inference to be drawn from such considerations is clear: we must fill our voice, which is heard across the globe, with theoretical appeal. On the side of empirical apprehension, in the sphere of facts, our case is excellent, and everybody knows it; but we forget that facts by themselves never carry ultimate conviction. For the other side can always argue, and does incessantly argue, that correct concepts will in time engender superior facts and that a correct social and economic doctrine, which in their opinion is already moving on the economic and technological scene with an acceleration impressively high, will in time make our facts of life seem crude and worthless. Our error of overemphasizing facts is made more grave, and it easily escapes detection, because of a very general empiricist philosophical tradition in which at this juncture we happen to be caught. More will be said of this in later sections. The important mandate now seems to be that we recognize our bias and correct it by supplying a teachable doctrine of democracy which elevates this philosophy from the status of a feeling in our bones to a defensible thesis that commands conviction. And a shift of emphasis from facts to reason, which is necessary in the ideological conflict, should not be difficult to effect. For our scientists, including economists, have indeed been theorists for many decades; they are frequently taken to task for their supposed theoretical bias. Whatever their failings are, they have produced magnificent rational arguments for our political philosophy. Open any treatise on economics and you will find ample material for argumentation and debate, material that will beautifully document the positive theoretical and logical aspects of our point of view. We need to pull this material out of research treatises and college texts and float it abroad; we must forge every available theoretical element of the logic of western science into a piece of shining armor and enlist it in ideological warfare. Ideas are as potent as economic operations, and we have neglected them. Ideas, like satellites, may be launched and put into orbit; they are needed to tell the missing part of our story.

In returning from this diversion, which an effective exposure of the dangers of the picture puzzle view of science seemed to require, I suggest another simile which symbolizes more adequately the central meaning of science. It is the process of crystal growth.

Teachers of elementary physics sometimes show an interesting classroom demonstration. A certain substance, heated to a temperature just above its melting point, is poured into a glass container with flat faces placed between plates of polaroid. One then shines light through the arrangement and projects a pattern on a screen. What is visible is chaos, irregular bits of liquid, random motion. The phenomenon is interesting in its caprice, in the completely unpredictable nature of its detail; it may be likened to the rhapsodic dance of facts.

Then suddenly, as the liquid cools below its melting point, crystallization begins. At a certain point within the molten mass, where chance decrees that it should happen, a little regular edge will form and become the seed of a pattern of regularity and beauty. One crystalline facet is added to another, and a strange kaleidoscopic design penetrates what was previously a volume filled with chaos. The penetration is erratic, proceeding sometimes along a narrow channel, sometimes over a broad expanse. But wherever it goes, the material interior to the crystallized domain is resplendent with colorful beauty and geometric order; symmetry, pattern, design, and all the circumstances which make prediction possible are present everywhere.

Human experience in its immediacy, in its factual character, is like the liquid matrix before the crystal grows—

unorganized, irregular, and largely bare of meaning. This is true of the sensory data, the perceptions, the simple and instrumental observations which ultimately, when interpreted, produced the body of science; it is equally true of introspections, feelings and other states of consciousness which, when properly organized, give rise to non-scientific kinds of human concern. Every day we confront new and unexpected impressions and sensations rising from the fertile ground of being. The fact that they are unorganized and uncharted does not detract from their importance in our lives; indeed, the most momentous problems confronting us have to do with this amorphous part of our experience, with the whirl of facts, sensations, feelings, and volitions. Art, religion, many of our social attitudes, fall into this class of experience.

But somewhere in the interior of this shapeless volume special kinds of experience take an orderly or, if I may use the metaphor, crystalline form. Science transforms some aspects of randomness into understandable patterns, makes occurrences seem regular and predictable. The substance of our earlier experience is still there, but it is now informed with design and has become clear in its meaning. Where the crystal of science begins to form is hard to say; its seed may be the genius of an individual or some unexpected chance discovery. But wherever the scientific process begins, it illuminates the space it covers and continues its organizing growth indefinitely. It would be folly to suppose that the crystal will ultimately include the whole of experience; for the amorphous matrix is unlimited in extent, and as science progresses more and more of it will come into view. In this respect the crystal analogue is inadequate to represent the function of science, for the liquid matrix is always enclosed in a container, always finite in its substance, whereas the raw material of science is infinite, is forever being created. There is no danger that science, like a cancer, will throttle, overwhelm, and absorb the entire domain of experience. Its progress is orderly, self-restrained, and furthermore it can never exhaust all experience. Science confers theoretic relatedness upon previously unorganized factual knowledge. Like the process of crystal growth, it does not change or degrade the substance itself—factual experience —which it comprehends; it informs it with design, connectiveness, and clarity, and it creates in our minds the power to predict.

Some sciences *are* perhaps correctly portrayed by the picture puzzle analogy, e.g., such purely descriptive disciplines as natural history, botany, zoology, and geography; others are not. To the latter category belong all the physical sciences. The interesting difference between these classes is in the manner of reasoning: the latter are able to conduct rational proofs, whereas the former are not able to do so. They can present factual demonstration, but not deductive inference. Botany, for instance, can show whether a certain plant exists, how it adapts itself to its environment, what its life cycle is; but this is an altogether different matter from proving, as we do in physics, that Kepler's laws are consequences of Newton's law of universal gravitation. The two classes of science are often labeled descriptive and "exact." These terms are not meant to imply value judgments for all sciences are originally descriptive, but they manifest an inborn tendency to become exact. Also, as noted, a science cannot be exact unless it has a descriptive factual basis. But what needs to be recognized is that the method of exact science continually and successfully invades descriptive science in a manner that improves and ennobles its content.

2. *Two Movements*

Henceforth we shall understand by science exact science, the method of inquiry which first discovers facts and then brings them under rational principles, due emphasis being given to the latter. The aim of this section will be to examine the effects of science, or scientific discovery in the larger sense, upon the society of men.

The obvious effect is technological; it is the visible and impressive movement from discovery through commercial development, production of new goods and devices, advertising and sale, toward the establishment of greater comforts of life. This causal chain, which in the end enhances, or at any rate modifies, our so-called standard of living, our external circumstances, will here for brevity be called the *obvious* movement, for it is this trend which is open and clear for all to see, and which earns the applause of people in our society today.

But every truly great scientific discovery launches also another trend, a trend much less apparent and more subtle in its progression from phase to phase through human culture. The discovery, acting as a *fact* in initiating the obvious movement, becomes the leaven of an idea in the other. It clamors to be understood, and the scientist must provide some sort of *theory* in terms of which the discovery takes on significance and organizing power. The requisite theory contains novel features, features contradicting what was previously regarded as true; and by virtue of this apostasy the discovery induces a rearrangement of thought in adjacent fields. Sooner or later the internal structural consistency of the science that was disturbed by discovery is restored, but in the process some cherished beliefs, some aspects of common sense, have had to be surrendered. In this

39

way Copernican astronomy destroyed the complacency of
the geocentric view; relativity theory repudiated the concept of absolute motion and, to some extent, the simple intuitions of geometry; quantum mechanics denies the continuity of motion; and a good deal of time will probably
elapse before men cease to feel that such theoretical consequences of discovery violate common sense.

Results as challenging as these cannot fail to have a profound effect on philosophic speculations. Indeed philosophy, in time, must and does take account of the ideological
consequences of scientific knowledge, first by changing its
cosmological beliefs and perhaps its theory of knowledge.
Changes in one branch will entail changes elsewhere, and
even though the sequence of alterations is uncontrolled and
haphazard (chiefly because we are less conscious of them
than we are of the technological sequence) they nevertheless
tend to embrace the entire structure of philosophic thought
before their course is run.

The chain of events ends in new views with respect to the
nature of the universe, the relation of man to the universe,
and the relation of man to man. Ethics, sociology, politics
are ultimately subject to infestation by the germ that is
born when a discovery in pure science is made. This movement, which terminates in a change of the cultural milieu of
man, will here be called the *obscure* movement. We note in
retrospect that there is a paradox in the fact that proponents
of Russian communism profess the supremacy of the obvious movement while disparaging the other, whereas the
western democracies reverse the declaration, pay lip service
to ideas but practice what Marxism professes.

Let us now cast a brief glance at the intervals of time
which elapse between discovery and the culmination of the
two movements, the obvious and the obscure. It seems rea-

sonable to postulate, and I believe history shows, that human society enjoys maximum stability when the two movements are in balance. This was often true, both in western and in eastern cultures during the ten or twenty centuries that preceded ours, and the balance resulted from the lumbering slowness of both movements. Gunpowder was discovered in the 12th century, used in warfare two hundred years later. Galileo and Newton found the laws of mechanics in the 17th century; the machine age arose in the 18th and 19th. Oersted discovered the magnetic field of electric currents in 1820, electric motors became industrially important nearly one hundred years later. Thus the technological gestation period, the time required for the obvious movement to be completed, was of the order of a century, and there is clear evidence already in the examples mentioned and in others to be cited, that it is continually decreasing. One of the stupendous technological developments of our time, the development of the fission bomb, lasted from 1939 to 1944. Whereas two centuries were required to convert gunpowder into a mildly effective military device, five years in our time saw the conversion of a scientific discovery into the most devastating weapon. The vast acceleration of the technological process has been well documented in a graph for which the author is indebted to Dr. L. R. Hafstad (see Figure 3), an impressive summary of recent inventions with dates of discovery and of resulting patents. The curious reader may find it interesting to compute from the graph by extrapolation how long it will take in the year A.D. 3000 for a discovery to be patented.

In extreme contrast with these examples is the snail's pace at which even today scientific knowledge transforms itself into philosophic understanding: The obscure movement proceeds at the same slow rate as in the past. One of

41

the best examples to illustrate this point is perhaps the quantum theory, discovered some 50 years ago. Its technical mathematical implications, the matrix theory, the Schrödinger equation, the transformation theory, are well known and have gone into the textbooks, yet the meaning of these

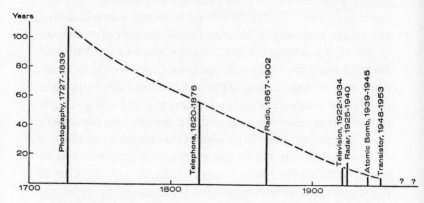

Fig. 3. From Discovery to Commercial Product: Acceleration of the "Obvious" Movement

formalisms in philosophic terms seems to be as obscure as ever. The literature on the philosophy of science is alive with controversies regarding interpretation of measurement in quantum mechanics, the causal qualities of that theory, and the ultimacy of its basic assumptions. The amazing fact is that precisely the men who are themselves the distinguished fathers of that discipline—men like Bohr, DeBroglie, Schrödinger, Heisenberg, Einstein in the last years of his life, and Born—feel the need for clarity in this area most keenly; they are the serious contributors to the researches in the field of the philosophy of quantum mechanics. The pity is that too many young physicists smile indulgently at these philosophical efforts, regarding them as senile and too far off the beaten track of their science to be worth serious attention.

The past is full of examples suggesting that periods of the order of a century or two were needed to bring the obscure movement to its fulfillment. To consider but one, take Kepler's laws of planetary motion, shown by Newton to be consequences of the principle of universal gravitation. The striking feature of that discovery was its claim to absolute accuracy, to universal validity, the cosmic applicability of pure mathematics. The best philosophical transcription of these aspects of scientific law was given by Kant 150 years after Kepler when he suggested that it is man's mind, not nature, which reverberates in syllogisms and mathematical equations. Man projects the limitations of his understanding, the pure forms and categories of his own reason, into the world at large and finds it behaving in accordance with his own reasonable precepts. Were it not for the supreme adequacy with which that philosophy reflects the apodictic character of celestial mechanics, Kant's success would be an enigma. The intrinsic appeal of so abstruse a doctrine is necessarily low, and it can only be its cogent scientific basis which made that doctrine sweep a continent and which propelled it, despite its common-sense implausibility, into the domain of ethics and religion. It is a far cry from Kepler's laws to the categorical imperative, but the obscure movement connected one with the other. And it required more than a century to do so. The same seems to be true today, whereas the obvious movement achieves its goal within a decade.

Historical instances of an imbalance between the obscure and the technological or obvious movements which proved destructive to society are not hard to find. The culture of ancient Greece suffered from a pathology which was the reverse of ours: the obscure movement was ahead of the obvious. As for an example of *balance* that proved stabilizing and beneficent, we need only look at our own constitution, a document unique in history for its longevity. It was based on a philosophy in accord with the science of its day, as the record shows. Locke's philosophy was a response to mediaeval science. Thomas Jefferson was a disciple of Locke. Hence, our constitution reflects the balance, composure, and maturity of a philosophic view solidly based on science. Jefferson himself said: "All its authority rests upon the harmonizing sentiments of the day."

But let us return to the present arena. Not only in the West, but indeed everywhere we see evidence of an imbalance between the two movements that started from scientific discovery. The obvious one has been vastly accelerated in all parts of the globe, the obscure has not found its goal. It flounders and gropes without rational guidance on both sides of the Iron Curtain, and the ideological cleavage between East and West is, in part at least, symptomatic of the failure of the hidden movement to have completed its course.

Scientific discoveries travel across all curtains. They cannot be contained very long when the world stage is set for them. Consequently, the discoveries themselves, and largely their technological results as well, become common knowledge in a short time. But they are partial knowledge unless their meaning is apparent in deeper ways, unless philosophic understanding of them is as clear as their factual entailments. Until that time each partisan can put his own arbitrary interpretation upon his science. This is what is happening now.

Admittedly, it is conceivable that a given scientific discovery be compatible with two conflicting philosophic interpretations, in which case contradictory understandings could be reached and reliance upon completion of the obscure movement would be of no avail. I am willing to discount this possibility as a highly academic one for the following reasons. First, philosophic indiscriminacy may be the lot of single discoveries in science—to be sure, but as their number in a given area increases, as groups and related complexes of discoveries appear, philosophic significance becomes more and more directed. Secondly, history shows that in the long run a single major philosophic view always wins out among the practitioners of science, even if superstitions continue in other quarters. I take it therefore that a common science will ultimately engender a measure of agreement in philosophic outlook across all artificial curtains when equilibrium between the two movements is finally established, when our intellectual atmosphere is congenial with our applied science.

Hence arises the suggestion, vague perhaps and insecure at this point, that two problems should be of very serious concern to the thoughtful student of science and history: how to speed up the obscure cultural movement so as to bring it into step with the obvious; and how to make the obscure movement less obscure. Both ends can be achieved by a shift in emphasis from technical science to the philosophical problems surrounding and pervading science, by consciously taking stock of the needs for philosophic digestion of discovery and of our patent failure to achieve it. Fortunately, this need is being recognized by universities and research foundations, though not very clearly as yet by government agencies and industry. The present book is meant to be a small contribution to the attainment of that goal.

Against the background of the preceding discussion the

purposes of the subsequent pages may now be set forth as follows. Denying the dangerous myth of the philosophical neutrality of science, we first endeavor to establish a few historical connections between scientific discoveries and philosophic views. Next we attempt, by showing the inadequacy of the science on which a given philosophic view is based, to discredit that philosophy. Finally, and this is our major task, we survey the principal features of contemporaneous physical science and try to envision the outlines of a philosophy that is in harmony with it. The last endeavor, however, is necessarily bound to be unwarranted and fallible prophecy. For we are unfortunately still in the middle of that century of gestation which present attitudes toward science seem to impose upon us.

3. *Philosophies of Our Day and Their Scientific Roots*

By making selections from the current philosophic scene we shall briefly sketch in this section how the obscure movement has worked in the recent past. The philosophies chosen for discussion had important scientific grounds but, as will be shown later, they have lost that ground today and must be regarded as inadequate. We include a review of existentialism. Although existential philosophy is rarely considered to derive from science, it nevertheless speaks truthfully about certain important aspects of modern physics and is therefore interesting. This thought will be developed further in Chapter VII. At present, existentialism will concern us primarily as a negative reaction to science, since negative reactions can be as powerful as positive ones in molding human attitudes.

One impression we wish specifically to avoid. According to the theme of this book, science appears to spawn philosophies. While true, this is not the whole story: philosophy has an equally important influence on science in setting the scene, in fashioning the environment in which science flourishes, or vegetates, or dies. Today, it is true, philosophy has little substantive effect on science, partly because of the slowness and hence the unimpressiveness of what we have called the obscure movement. But this is an anomaly, and the past presents numerous examples of an effect reciprocal to that which is here under consideration. The manner in which philosophies affect science is certainly worth careful study; however, it is deliberately ignored in this book.

Mechanistic Materialism

Materialism has many forms, the most plausible and influential of which, at least in the Western World, is what will here be termed mechanistic materialism. It is completely characterized by its two theses: (a) Matter obeys the laws of classical mechanics; (b) To be is to be material, i.e., nothing exists that is not material.

Because the laws of classical mechanics are differential equations which generate continuous functions, they commit materialism to the hypothesis of universal continuity. All changes occurring in matter must be continuous changes: objects change their sizes and shapes by infinitesimal gradations; they move along continuous paths in three-dimensional space. Succinctly, this character of motion may be said to mean that the position x of any object is a continuous function of the time, $x = f(t)$.

If it is felt that the continuity hypothesis is self-evident and logically necessary, let it be recalled that St. Thomas contradicts this allegation by insisting that continuity, far from being necessary, may or may not apply to the motion of his angels. "Motus angeli," he says, "potest esse continuus et discontinuus sicut vult. . . . Et sic angelus in uno instante

47

potest esse in uno loco, et in alio instante in alio loco, nullo tempore intermedio existente." We cite this passage merely to record that discontinuous transfer is at least not inconceivable.

Thesis (a), though sometimes questioned in the remoter past (for instance, in Zeno's paradoxes), became part and parcel of physical science through the work of Galileo and Newton. Forces are regarded as continuous functions of space and time; they are proportional to accelerations, and these assumptions define a differential equation whose solutions are continuous trajectories in space and time. Were it not for the success of this analysis, it might be questioned whether science would have embraced the continuity of motion so completely; our experience, especially when very refined, does not always endorse it. Our visual field is granular because of the limited resolving power of the eye; perception is not indefinitely keen, and the relation between stimulus and response is not always continuous. But classical theoretical physics and inherent plausibility established the continuity thesis and made it an integral part of that world view which followed Newton's science.

Thesis (b), the identification of existence with materiality, is likewise implied in Newton's work. It became a philosophic conviction at a later time, perhaps as the result of several further developments which increased its power and its certainty.

Early in the 19th century there arose a sweeping scientific conviction: beginning as a tentative disbelief in the possibility of perpetual motion, it developed into the principle of conservation of energy, the strong belief that energy can change its form but is basically indestructible. Yet this knowledge was nothing more than an inductive generalization of a multitude of facts, for no one had derived the conservation law from first principles concerning the nature of the universe.

Helmholtz succeeded in doing this. In 1847 he published a famous paper wherein he showed energy conservation to be a consequence of two simple assumptions. One, that nature consists of mass points, i.e., small particles of matter; the other, that the force between every pair of mass points is a central force, that is, a force acting along the line joining the two particles. Helmholtz' proof was a tremendous scientific achievement, acclaimed everywhere, and it induced many scientists, because of its dazzling brilliance, to believe the premises of Helmholtz' syllogism along with its conclusion. If conservation can be logically established on the basis of these two simple postulates, they *must* be true. Every logician knows full well, of course, that this reasoning involves the fallacy of "affirming the consequent,"[2] that the same conclusion may be deducible from different hypotheses—but few people bothered about the logic of the situation and few withstood the conviction that nature did, in fact, consist of nothing but mass particles known as matter.

A decade after Helmholtz this view was reinforced by a doctrine of quite a different sort. Darwin published his *Origin of Species,* a work which, on the face of it, seems unrelated to Helmholtz' contribution. But again its world-shaking significance led to an acceptance not only of its essential intent but also of the undertone and spirit that accompanied its presentation; the emphasis on the survival of the fittest, the tooth-and-claw behavior of all creatures, seemed to agree in its philosophic pattern with the physical materialism of the time. And toward the end of the century, fed by other tributaries much like these two, there

2. More fully explained in Chapter III.

arose the powerful stream of mechanistic materialism. Man believed that there was indeed nothing in the world that was not material, nothing that failed to obey the laws of mechanics.

Empiricism, Logical Positivism[3]

The strict, precise, and unconditional character of the laws of Newtonian dynamics or celestial mechanics with its suggestion that "reason applies to nature," the consequent rationalism of Kant and others, lost support in some quarters when physics turned its attention to the subjects of heat and thermodynamics. Here was a scientific field in which dynamic regularity was not the norm; its laws resulted, strictly speaking, as anomalies from the chaotic interplay of large numbers of molecules. Chance governs the individual; what appears as lawful behavior is merely a sequence of chance-produced composite states having abnormally large probabilities. The chief era of these discoveries began in the late 18th and extended through the first half of the 19th century, and the names associated with them are Lavoisier,

3. In strictest application the term positivism designates the philosophy of Auguste Comte (1798–1857) whose thoughts, worked out primarily in sociology, were based exclusively on the knowledge and methods of the physical or "positive" sciences of his time. In a wider sense, positivism extends its concerns to all the data of experience, still refusing to accept and use *a priori* and metaphysical principles. Metaphysical principles are regarded as purely verbal, and positivist philosophers have at times conducted great polemics against them. This form of philosophy is similar to empiricism, which started with David Hume (1711–1776). The interests of positivism today are primarily logical, those of empiricism epistemological, but aside from this slight difference in approach the two doctrines are identical. The claim of the *Encyclopædia Britannica* that physical scientists generally view the universe from the positivist standpoint is inaccurate.

Black, Count Rumford, Davy, Mayer, Joule, Carnot, and Clausius.

Thermodynamics is the most empirical of the physical sciences. Its theorems are relations between an excessive number of experimental variables; it thrives in a situation spurned by other branches of physics, namely, one in which more variables are used in the description of material systems than are actually needed. Because its measured quantities are not logically independent, thermodynamic formulas exhibit that well-known disfigurement by subscripts added to partial derivatives, an outward indication of its earthy stature, of its factbound significance. There are no neat and elegant second-order differential equations with solutions representing the unique history of a thermodynamic system. Nor are the basic laws very simple. The most embracing "law" (law in the sense of mechanics, i.e., an equation connecting variables of state) is the equation of state; it is different for every substance and has extremely complicated forms for all real bodies. The contrast with Newton's law of universal gravitation is remarkable and is philosophically suggestive.

Furthermore, even the greatest generalizations encountered in this branch of science, the so-called laws of thermodynamics (which everywhere else would be named principles), entered the scene as inductive inferences from a large mass of experiments and not as deductive consequences of some simple and pervasive conjecture. Much ingenuity has been lavished on the question whether they are as true as the laws of mechanics, or whether they permit exceptions, and even now textbooks sometimes say that water can freeze on a hot stove if you wait long enough.

The reason for this wary and circumspect approach to the validity of thermodynamics lies partly in its history and its formal structure, but primarily in the reformulation which its discoveries induced within the science of mechanics itself. For in the process of readjustment enforced by the discrepant new knowledge regarding heat, as described earlier, the ideas of mechanics were enlarged to include the subject of statistical mechanics. This contains all the theorems of Newtonian mechanics plus special postulates concerning the probabilities of molecular motions. Only with the use of probabilities can theory account for observed thermodynamic behavior. And the need for probabilities, a novel feature in the explanatory scheme of physics, puts the imprint of looseness and ambiguity, which only actual observation can resolve, upon the basic theories of thermodynamics.

The philosophic implication of all this is perfectly clear. Even if theory says water will boil, one must not trust that prediction completely. For experience *may* show that it will freeze. It is all a matter of probabilities. Laws are approximate, and the childish amazement expressed by those who hold that "reason applies to nature" actually marvels at a fairy tale. Nature fundamentally defies reason; she goes her own erratic way, producing regularity through the law of large numbers, by sheer exhaustion of alternatives for aberration. Law, strictly, is an illusion. And in the midst of this universal play of chance, man is a creature endeavoring successfully to make the best of things, betting on the basis of probabilities.

The preceding account is not an accurate description of the present views of men (Carnap, Hempel, Feigl, Frank, and others) who call themselves positivists or empiricists. What I intended to sketch is empiricism as it first arose, and as it ought to be if it had remained unmingled with other considerations. Its emergence was inevitable, for it is the unique terminus of that obscure movement which started from the basic discoveries in the science of heat and thermodynamics.

Existentialism[4]

There are scholars who deny the claim of existentialism to be a philosophy; few indeed will recognize it as a world view developed in response to science. It is in the first place a working attitude of artists, a pervasive mood which passionately seeks to justify the sordid as well as the magnificent contingencies of existence; it includes Nietzsche's joy over the death of God and Tillich's quietly pious "courage to be." With Kierkegaard it is the resolution, brought on by irritation at the static concepts of traditional philosophy, to progress from the habit of understanding backward to one of living forward. In Malraux the accent is on the absurdity of life and on the need to endow it with significance through adventure; the heroic gambler is the object of justifiable admiration. The works of Sartre, a "widower of God" according to his own testimony, express and portray the nausea of existence. But all these men, whether they admit it or not, stage a revolt against science. Their attitude

4. The philosophy of existentialism, insofar as it acknowledges any debt to science, leans upon anthropology, centers its concerns about the nature of man and thence projects its findings into the universe. Chief among its tenets is the belief that man's essential character and distinction do not rest in his universal character, in some sort of universal essence, but in his individuality, his particular person, his unique existence and his historicity. It opposes spontaneity, possibility, and freedom to the notions of generality and necessity. Everywhere, it decomposes universality and coherence into a pluralism of many independent centers. Notable recent proponents of existential philosophy are Kierkegaard (1813–1855), Marcel, Sartre, Jaspers, Buber, and Camus.

is a response to science, albeit a negative one; their philosophy is, so to speak, a result of the obscure movement jumping its track.

Before I attempt to demonstrate this seemingly unsympathetic assertion, I should say in all fairness that it is an overstatement and not wholly true. For there is an element in the attitude of existentialism that reflects a deep insight of very recent science; I refer to the fact that theoretical physics, by its last appeal to probability reasoning, especially in quantum mechanics, has again relinquished its hold upon individual events, on single observations. In a sense these are left untreated by most recent doctrine, and so a special appeal for attention to what is existentially given and scientifically fatherless is just. It may be, however, that this is an ex-post-facto conjecture, an artificial regularization of a philosophy which has fundamentally broken its bond with science.

For existentialism, when it speaks philosophically, declares war upon "essences," saying that existence comes before essence. What it means is that the unregulated contingencies, the bare and given facts and immediacies of our experience, take precedence over the regularities and constancies constructed or found by reason. The essences of existentialism, when freed of poetic disdain, are the constant entities and the laws of science. These are the citadel against which the onslaught of that movement is directed.

In our day the revolt broke forth openly and under philosophic generalship in the writings of Heidegger. He admits that science is a noteworthy attack upon truth or *Sein* or Being, but one not likely to achieve final and full success. For Being is, in his representation, an existential something that lives in the solitude of human experience and will not be caught alive in scientific traps. It is like rare game which man can espy, stalk, and observe quietly, but which will flee the noisy scene of science, and when the scientist does finally overpower and capture it, he comes to hold the corpse of truth and not living truth. Such a view, when stated more adroitly and without the use of metaphor, tends to assume a measure of persuasive plausibility sufficient to make it the stock in trade of many humanists and artists; it is the central creed of the hard-dying attitude which insists on a basic cleavage between science and the humanities.

The rebellion against science which has taken the name existentialism is aided and abetted by two significant facts. First, modern science has become increasingly and at times forbiddingly abstract, and the artist is repelled by it because in plain truth he cannot understand it. Hence, in curious reversal of that medieval attitude which led the scholar to scorn the craftsman because he spoke in his native vulgar vernacular, the existentialist now spurns the scientist because he uses an esoteric tongue called mathematics which, in the eyes of some, poisons Being before it is apprehended. The second fact giving strength to existentialism is the chaos of modern history which belies reason, order, and essence. Quiet desperation, probing the depths of human tragedy, contemplating death and coming up with the resolve to *be,* to *be* in the face of absurdity—those are understandable attitudes in the modern world of politics, natural to those who have severed their relation to science and to the order which science reveals.

Existentialism concerns itself with the nature of man more directly than any other modern philosophy. Through its commitment to the priority of fact, the doctrine is forced to portray man fundamentally as a creature cast out into a universe devoid of reason. Man engulfed by the abyss of being, finding himself alone, capable of anxiety and sure of death—such is the essential state of human existence. Relief is sought in diverse ways, by redemption in Kierkegaard and Marcel, by "gambling one's life on a stake higher than one-self" or by "transforming as wide an experience as possible into consciousness" in Malraux. Some, especially the novel-ists, seek to ameliorate man's prime state of irrational abjection by ethical and political manifestations; they activate, to quote Henri Peyre's excellent summary, "the desire not to remain unmoved by the anguish of other men suffering from the threat of war, by social inequality, or by economic injustice. Several of them have taken sides, usually with the extreme left, in political issues: but they have raised such issues to the height of metaphysical speculation and en-visaged evil as a cosmic phenomenon, though one which lies within the power of man to redress in part."

Freedom is a fact and a cornerstone of existential experi-ence; being isolated, unconditioned, and blind, it is a bur-den and a source of anguish. Still it compensates in a signifi-cant way for the forlornness of human existence and gives an active concern for the future to a creature whose past is meaningless. Man must make the best of freedom, his sin-gular and most cherished gift. But one gets the impression from reading the literature that its use, its unstinted and enthusiastic use, is also its complete justification. One finds neither a deep concern for the restraint of freedom nor a search for an explanation of this unusual phenomenon in a world that largely lacks it. Existentialism takes freedom as a fact not as a paradox and largely dismisses all scientific scruples concerning it. This is unfortunate, because modern science returns to the problem of causation and hence of human freedom, in a way that ought to interest the existen-tialist. This point will be developed in Chapter VII.

We have seen that both positivism and existentialism, two

doctrines which are philosophically much closer together than their advocates are likely to admit, spring from that complex of discoveries which forced science to shift away from infinitely certain and detailed laws to an account of positive happenings in terms of probabilities, probabilities which take on concrete meaning only in the face of actual occurrences—potentialities rendered meaningful by existences. But while positivism remains within the domain of science and acknowledges its indebtedness to science, existentialism repudiates this bondage, allies itself with rhetoric and art and often acts as though it never heard of science. Interestingly, however, both philosophies reached their culmination at about the same time, namely a century and a half after science made the shift in question.

Materialism, positivism, and existentialism are examples of philosophies springing from or created as reactions to past discoveries of science. We have suggested that they are no longer fully adequate to the science of today. Now, in order to perceive their defects, it becomes necessary to appraise current science for its philosophical implications. The author's limited competence requires that this appraisal be restricted to the physical sciences. And, here, three factors emerge as novel characteristics pregnant with philosophic significance. One is a new logical status of postulates, a radically altered assessment of the truth of first principles. The next chapter is to deal with it. The second factor is the deemphasis of what is loosely called common sense. Physics makes a very careful distinction between practical maxims which have become familiar and are therefore carelessly believed and the strict requirements of logic. Where these conflict it gives precedence to the latter. The area in which this is most clearly discernible is relativity theory; hence Chapter IV is devoted to that subject, albeit

57

in a context which is perhaps not wholly customary. Finally, modern science has largely relinquished the use of mechanical models and relies increasingly on abstract relations. The facts involved in this departure and their philosophical consequences are presented in the last four chapters of the book.

Chapter III

THE INNER LIGHT OF REASON

1. *The Tentative Nature of Postulates*

A radically new feature of today's philosophy of science is its unwillingness to accept a priori truth. It holds that all truth is subject to verification. Some types of verification make a direct appeal to observations and are very simple indeed; others are indirect and will be studied in some detail in this chapter. At earlier times truth was believed to adhere to *axioms,* that is, to certain very general rules of thought which lie at the basis of all reasoning, scientific and otherwise. From such basic axioms sprang more practical necessary propositions of lesser range and sometimes called postulates, and postulates entailed theorems. The truth of axioms, however, was thought to be open to inspection without proof, was guaranteed by the "inner light of reason" and was therefore indubitable.

No thoughtful student of science can fail to be impressed by the great scientific cogency, the usefulness, and the sweep of Euclidean geometry. It is one of the few scientific systems of thought, fully formalized and universally practiced, whose longevity rivalled that of the great historical religions. Its structure reveals beautifully the involvement of unproved axioms, and its partial abandonment shows clearly the change in question which has occurred in the philosophy of science. Let us therefore give a little thought to it.

Euclid begins his treatment of geometry with *definitions, axioms,* and *postulates*. The definition of a point, for example, reads "a point is that which has no parts." Among the axioms are such propositions as these: "Things equal to the same things are equal to each other." "If equals be added to equals, the results are equal." "The whole is greater than any one of its parts." "Things that coincide are equal."

The postulates are five in number. Among them we find: "A terminated straight line may be extended without limit in either direction." "It is possible to draw a circle with given center and through a given point," and so on. The famous fifth postulate, which is the interesting one in the present context, reads as follows: "If two straight lines in a plane meet another straight line in the plane so that the sum of the interior angles on the same side of the latter straight line is less than two right angles, the two straight lines will meet on that side of the latter straight line."

The detailed contents of the fifth postulate are of no importance to the sequel of our discussion. I have stated it in full because it has formed the focus of a series of inquiries that have given it historical importance.

First, it is interesting to note the classification of statements into definitions, axioms, and postulates. The definitions are presumably made for convenience and simplicity of speech, while the axioms are regarded as self-evident rules of thought and the postulates as necessary consequences induced by the axioms. Indeed the logical relation between the axioms and the postulates was a matter of controversy for many centuries, and numerous attempts were made to deduce the postulates from the axioms and the definitions. The chief endeavor was to derive as many of the postulates as possible from the axioms. Those postulates which were consequences could then be omitted from the list, while the remaining ones, which did not flow logically from definitions and axioms, would have to be regarded, like the axioms themselves, as a priori truths made valid by the light of inner reason.

The fifth postulate had a curious fate. It could not be derived from definitions and axioms, although many attempts to do so were made all through the Middle Ages. Hence men felt forced to look upon the fifth postulate as a true and needed axiom. But here an annoying logical difficulty arose, for it turned out that the method of *reductio ad absurdum* also failed; to speak more simply, it was shown that a *denial* of the fifth postulate which should have destroyed the validity of Euclid's system if the postulate were true and necessary, did not lead to inconsistencies and contradictions in the theoretical system. It was possible for the two lines in Euclid's axiom to satisfy the angle condition and yet fail to meet. This tantalizing situation was finally resolved by the works of three mathematicians, the Hungarian Bolyai (1832), the Russian Lobatchevsky (1835), and the German Riemann (1854) who announced the epoch-making discovery of non-Euclidean geometries. They deliberately modified some of the earlier postulates, denied the fifth, and succeeded in deriving systems of theorems quite as complete, consistent, and useful as that of Euclid. But the theorems were different. Thus, for example, in Lobatchevsky's geometry, the sum of the angles of a triangle is less than two right angles, and the defect (i.e., the difference between 180 degrees and the sum of the angles) varies directly as the area of the triangles. And the most surprising thing happened in our century, when Einstein was able to show that one of these non-Euclidean geometries, Riemann's, probably fits our empirical astronomical universe better than Euclid's.

Thus the inner light of reason had been shown to be empirically false so far as Euclidean geometry was concerned. The concept of a priori truth had been destroyed in at least one crucial instance (for what is a priori cannot possibly be false!), and a scientific mood was thus engendered which, in universal skepticism, required every basic proposition of an axiomatic sort to establish and sustain itself in the face of, and sometimes against the onslaught of, empirical evidence. Other developments in physics and in pure logic reinforced the empiricist attitude and led to a view which characterizes the method of all science as follows.

Science starts with unproved tentative assumptions; from these, with the aid of definitions and the formal devices of logic and mathematics, it derives theorems; it then tests these theorems in observations and concludes that the tentative assumptions, still called postulates by many scientists, are "true" in a new sense if all theorems agree with experience. The logical rigor of this process will be further examined below.

When this logical movement is performed in the opposite direction, it is said to be an explanation. To see this, consider for a moment what the physicist means and does when he explains the falling of a stone. The proposition to be "explained" is: this stone falls with an acceleration of 32.2 feet per second-per second near the earth's surface. The explanation is the process of including that statement in a statement of greater logical scope, from which it is seen to follow as a consequence. The more general proposition in this instance is a conjunction of Newton's laws of motion with his law of universal gravitation. When carefully analyzed, this procedure amounts to assuming that certain premises, in this case the law of universal gravitation, are true. The physicist is then able to deduce, by a series of logical or mathematical steps, the less general sentence concerning the free fall of the stone from these premises.

Indeed, the physicist may not be satisfied with this instance of reasoning, feeling that the premises are not sufficiently evident and that they, too, should be viewed as consequences from even larger or more basic postulates. That is to say, he may wish to answer the question why is Newton's law of universal gravitation true? This amounts to an explanation of the law of universal gravitation, and it is again an act which immerses the statement to be explained in a more general statement of larger logical scope from which the former follows. The physicist may appeal to general relativity and regard the law of universal gravitation, albeit in a slightly modified form, as a consequence of the metric of space. What he has thus achieved is a further generalization of the initial premises, a generalization which now takes the form of a postulate regarding the structure of space. At the present stage of science we cannot ask why the law of the metric is true. This is because that proposition stands at the very frontier of physical theory, and it must therefore be regarded as a postulate. It is possible, of course, and indeed seems probable, that some day, when the crystal of science grows further, this proposition, which now functions as a postulate, will be derivable from more embracive propositions which will then be called postulates.

The new view regarding postulates, i.e., the rejection of "the inner light of reason" as an absolute criterion of truth, is thus seen to affect the meaning of explanation. An explanation, as we have shown, is a series of deductions whose last member is the proposition to be explained, or as one sometimes says, it is a "reduction" of a particular statement (fact, observation) to general principles. In the past these general principles were thought to be certain, ultimate, and indubitable; today they are regarded as tentative and changeable premises. Only trivial matters are self-evident. The truth of postulates, in this modern sense, increases with confirmation of their specific consequences.

But surely, the reader will say, the theorems of arithmetic, e.g., two times three is six, are doubtless true and are not tied to any assumed postulates. This, I fear, must be denied; all forms of arithmetic are conditioned upon certain assumptions concerning the meaning of integers. Postulates regarding these integers are the premises from which such propositions as two times three is six will flow. As to the indubitability of this particular theorem, it may seem shocking to assert that it frequently fails, even in our ordinary experience, but this is nevertheless the case. As Jeans pointed out, the theorem does not hold for drops of water on a windowpane, some of which can at any moment merge into one. It is not true for volumes of liquid that are being mixed, as for instance, three gallons of water and three gallons of alcohol, which yield less than 6 volumes of liquid. The vast domain of ideas is wholly foreign to the laws of arithmetic; ideas are not countable—they may merge and annihilate one another in most curious ways. It must be recognized that even so fundamental a discipline as arithmetic has its own limited range of application, and that its truth is contingent upon the acceptance of certain premises called postulates which by virtue of their generality and our familiarity with them, frequently take on the semblance of self-evidence.

Modern physics has exposed the failure of arithmetic in a very special way, or, to put the matter less offensively, has shown that the laws of arithmetic do not apply to certain very fundamental quantities of nature. In quantum mechanics, one deals with operators which cannot be combined in the way of the equation $2 \times 3 = 3 \times 2 = 6$. For they are not permutable, i.e., if the two operators are designated by a and b, a times b is not equal to b times a.

The new view with respect to postulates may with perfect propriety, though perhaps with some caution, be related to the typical mode of reasoning in non-scientific fields, where the need for reliance on unproved convictions has always been recognized. Because of its logical structure, because of its need for fundamental postulational commitments, science now joins in particular two other areas of human concern, ethics and religion. The basic assumptions are called ideals or norms in ethics, faith in religion; in science they go by the prosaic name of postulates or axioms. When analyzed logically, the scientific equivalent of the act of dedication to ideals in ethics, of the act of faith in religion, is the tentative yet wholehearted acceptance of basic postulates at the very beginning of the scientist's quest.

Lest I be misunderstood as saying that there is nothing secure in this world, that our lives are shipwrecked and without anchor, adrift on a sea of uncertainties, I hasten to add that I can conceive of nothing surer than a tried scientific postulate, or indeed an ideal that lights my way, or a fervent religious conviction. True, the certainty of all these grows with effective use; they start as tentative maxims and finally, in a mature and integrated personality, they attain unconditional power over thought and action. Ultimate, absolute, and therefore static knowledge is never necessary in settling human affairs.

To demand ultimate certainty is tantamount to insisting that a sailor who wishes to moor his boat needs a fixed submarine object to which he can tie his craft. Our lives are such that fixed submarine objects are not available. We require an anchor of sufficient weight to prevent uncontrolled motion of our ships, and we supply the anchors ourselves. Items of faith, whether they belong to religion, the field of action, or of cognitive understanding, form anchors for the ships of our lives, and science is no exception to that general rule.

2. *The Logic of Scientific Reasoning*

For the sake of clarity and emphasis we shall restate the main considerations of the previous section in a slightly more technical way. This is done advantageously by focusing attention upon the meaning of "demonstration in science," because demonstration is the final act through which postulates are given their standing. Ordinarily the word demonstration is used in a great variety of senses; it connotes methods of conviction or persuasion ranging all the way from deductive mathematical proof to incidental exhibition of specific bits of evidence. Literally the word means "showdown," and its primary meaning centers in the presentation of crucial or striking sensory confirmation of a proposition.

Let us first accept the wider sense of the word, allowing it to stand for any experience that has a large measure of suasive power or evidence relative to a scientific proposition, supposing however (a) that the experience is of the direct or perceptory type (not merely the recognition of logical or mathematical consistency) and (b) that the proposition is sufficiently general to be called a hypothesis, or a law, or a theory. Under these conditions one perceives the occurrence of two large classes of demonstrations in a science like physics. The first may be called inductive or, better, correlational, the second deductive or, for reasons which will soon be given, exact. Correlational demonstration is practiced in the descriptive sciences; deductive demonstration in the sciences called exact.

Let Boyle's law be such a proposition: pressure times volume of an ideal gas equals a constant provided the temperature is constant. To demonstrate this law may mean making a very large number of measurements of the pressure and the volume of a gas at a given temperature, showing that they all very nearly satisfy the law. The logical situation here is this. An experimenter has obtained n values for the pressure P and n correlated values for the volume V. Except by an unwarrantable and logically illicit extrapolation, these $2 n$ experimental values cannot establish a belief that in every possible measurement, past and future, P will be equal to c/V. What they do imply is that a certain quantity called by statisticians the correlation coefficient, k, of the P_i with the c/V_i is very nearly 1, and this entails, via laws of induction which are progressively being clarified, that future observations will satisfy Boyle's law with a computable probability, a probability which is a function of both n and k.

Here then is the character of an *in*ductive demonstration: it changes n into $n + 1$, thereby increasing the probability in question. The psychological force of an inductive demonstration, however, is enormously greater than its logical force. If a student, to whom the law is a novelty, sees a few positive instances of the correlation between P and $1/V$, he is greatly impressed and takes the demonstration as final proof in the same vein and with the same satisfaction as a proof of Pythagoras' theorem. This immediate response is partly justified for the probability is raised from zero to a value not far from 1 by only two or three positive instances, whereas many further confirmations make it crawl toward 1 very slowly. But it is also partly wrong because the novice mistakes the element of surprise for cogency.

For the more advanced student a demonstration of

67

Boyle's law requires a great deal more. He will think of the law as implied by, or as a special case of, a more general proposition called the perfect gas law, or as a consequence of the equation of state for real gases, and he will even see this in the framework of the kinetic theory or of statistical mechanics. Having already confronted situations which led him to accept the validity of the laws of particle mechanics, and regarding the passage from particle mechanics to statistical mechanics as a simple and reasonable one, he thinks of the analytic consequences of that theory as true, and his a priori expectation, when confirmed by a very small number of positive instances supporting Boyle's law, engenders in him an assurance concerning the outcome of future experiments that is far beyond justification by the inductive probabilities mentioned. The point is that the coherence of the logical texture in which the proposition to be tested is embedded produces its own evidence, and this evidence makes reliance on correlations less severe and less important. Never, of course, does a scientist dispense with empirical confirmation, nor can a theory create empirical data out of purely rational ingredients—Eddington was, in my opinion, quite wrong methodologically when he suggested that the constants of nature are reflections of epistemological human procedures. What the physicist entertains here is a healthful respect for the positive feedback that takes place between purely inductive evidence and the a priori expectation which flows from the logical entailment of a given statement by more general propositions already confirmed. In practice, he couples correlational demonstration with deductive demonstration. A science which has attained success and stability between these procedures is called exact, and for this reason we have labelled the deductive method itself exact. Let us now study it more carefully.

Its use amounts to what is ordinarily called an explanation, a feat which is characteristic of the deductive process and has no meaning in any correlational pursuit. Explanation begins, as we have seen, with some very general affirmation, such as is contained, for example, in Newton's laws together with the ergodic hypothesis. Let me call this set of premises S_0. They alone do not imply Boyle's law. Hence, one introduces a set of further assumptions of a less general sort concerning which there is some empirical evidence. They might be the supposition that the forces acting between individual molecules are additive, or central, or indeed zero. These will be called S_1. From the conjunction of S_0 and S_1, theorems $T_1, T_2 \ldots$ can be derived by logical procedures; among these theorems is the general gas law and, as its special case, Boyle's law. But as a theorem the statement is still indefinite and empty, for it merely contains the symbols P and V whose reference to observation needs to be inserted. It is at this place that operational definitions enter, and by their intervention empirical manipulations can engage the symbols in concrete fashion, leading to a climax which logicians call confirmation of disconformation.

In symbols: $S_0 \cdot S_1 \supset (T_1, T_2, T_3 \ldots)$. One of these theorems, say T_1, functionally relates P and V. P and V in turn are connected to numerical values P' and V' by rules of correspondence of which operational definitions are a special and important class. If P' and V' are found in observation, T_1 is said to be demonstrated and to be true (with certain reservations). And if all T_1 are confirmed, preferably many times and by numerous observers, S_0 and S_1 are demonstrated.

Some may feel that the word "demonstrate" in this connection is ill chosen. I confess to some sympathy with this sentiment because the manner in which the S's are verified is rather indirect and lacks the "ad oculos" quality expected of demonstrations. Nevertheless, no more direct way to ascertain the truth of abstract propositions is available, and if the word demonstrate is to have any significance at all with respect to such general principles as the basic laws of mechanics, of thermodynamics, or the ergodic hypothesis which enter into our example, it must reside in the transition from S to P' and V' which has been sketched.

Accepting this meaning of demonstration, we ask what measure of certainty it confers upon S_0 or, to be more specific, upon $S_0 \cdot S_1$. In common language, $S_0 \cdot S_1$, henceforth simply written as S, is called the explanation of, or the reason for, Boyle's law. Every explanation in science is an act of logical inclusion—a chain of reasoning which allows a particular proposition known as a fact to be seen as the consequence of a more inclusive set of propositions. There is often a series of explanations as in the case of gravitational motion, where a "fact," like the fall of a stone, is explained by Galileo's "law" of constant acceleration; this itself can be explained in terms of Newton's law of universal gravitation; that law may be explained by being viewed as a special case of Einstein's law of gravitation. Here, at the present stage of physics, we have to stop, for there is no more general theory which yields Einstein's (or some other perhaps more successful formulation of general relativity) as a deductive consequence. A proposition forming the logical starting point of an explanatory chain is called a postulate or, as a carryover from the days when first principles were regarded as indubitable, an *axiom*. In our example of Boyle's law the chain has but a single link; at least one may think of it in that way. Strictly speaking the number of links is not countable: as in all deductive situations, one can interpose between first premise and final conclusion an arbitrary number of intermediate though usually uninteresting steps. Here, for simplicity, we shall regard the passage from S (basic principles) to T (Boyle's law) as one.

The demonstration in question has this form:

S implies T. T is true.
Therefore S is true.

$$S \supset T$$
$$T$$
$$\therefore S$$

Every student of elementary logic will recognize here at once the famous form of the fallacy of affirming the consequent. One is really not entitled to affirm S if its consequent, T, is true. The physicist knows this, too, for he is aware of the circumstance that Boyle's law may very well be also the consequent of postulates, quite different from S, perhaps not yet discovered.

The history of science is full of instances where accepted implication relations of the form $S \supset T$ have had to be abandoned. This may happen for several reasons, among them the following. First, it often occurs that refined experiments prove a given consequence, T, false. In this case S has to be changed. This change is uninteresting from our present point of view, for it could have been effected even if the reverse relation were true, if $T \supset S$. The usual case, however, is this. Further experimentation shows that T remains true, but new observations become possible, observations expressible, let us say, in the form of a theorem T'. Now T and T' may be quite compatible since they deal with different sorts of phenomena, but T' is usually not implied by S. If the relation $S \supset T$ were reversible, so that

T ⊃ S and T′ ⊃ S′, S and S′ would contradict each other, and we should be developing a kind of physics in which each set of phenomena must be explained by its own set of theories, simplicity and cohesion being lost. It is the irreversibility of the implication relation, S ⊃ T, which saves the day; for T and T′ can both be implied by a different and presumably wider set of postulates. This irreversibility, however, forces science to affirm the consequent.

Hence follows the important methodological result that physics never can be certain of its postulates. This is the price it pays for its dynamism, for its facility of self-correction, for its impressive rate of growth. And as for deductive demonstration, we see that it, too, can never reach certainty of its premises.

Yet the lack of certainty encountered here is altogether different from that which afflicts correlational demonstrations. The latter could be expressed in terms of probabilities. By probability the physicist means a relative frequency in some well-defined ensemble. Such an ensemble is available when Boyle's law is tested empirically: one can clearly specify and observe the relative frequency of volume measurements falling into a range about V_1 when the pressure has the value P_1. But what about the relative frequency of a theory (postulate, hypothesis) S?

It seems to me, in view of the practice of scientists and in view of the logical situation, that a search for a probability index of uncertain theories is unprofitable. We do not speak of theories and postulates as probable or improbable, but as correct or incorrect relative to a given state of scientific knowledge, or perhaps as approximations to a more exacting theory either known or not yet known. In applications of a theory we make allowance not for probabilities of hypotheses but for errors of numerical results. There is no ensemble of theories in which favorable and unfavorable ones can be counted, and this is because theories, like ideas, are not subject to arithmetic; two theories may be one, or many, or indeed none, if they are contradictory. Hence we conclude: *Inductive* or correlational demonstration involves uncertainties capable of numerical test as probabilities. *Deductive* demonstration of theories involves a different, intrinsic, logical kind of uncertainty which arises from the inevitable fallacy of affirming the consequent inherent in it.

3. *The New Faith of Science*

The word "faith" was used in an earlier context, not in the sense of belief in certain facts or dogmas, but in the sense of man's commitment and dedication to great principles of which he can never be absolutely sure. Facts are never subject to faith, or even ultimately to belief; they can be ascertained with sufficient effort by the method of science. It is their meaning that is continually held under vigilant animadversion, reflection, and censure. This meaning is always incomplete, but also always in the process of completion and fulfillment.

As we have seen in some detail in the foregoing section, scientific truth is necessarily tentative, subject to correction. The history of science exhibits instances where an increasing measure of tests and observations enforce a reassessment of tenets previously held. Nor are these incidents of reassessment rare happenings which form exceptions to the sure forward march of knowledge; they are in fact the rule. They characterize the best that man can do. To admit this is not to disparage science; it is to recognize the fallibility of man. To state the issue boldly, I would say that despite such inadvertencies, science is still the safest method of inquiry we possess, and I would urge caution against sources of knowledge which claim ultimacy and perfection. There is a modesty in science as we shall see below which makes man humble before ultimates; cocksureness and inflexibility are not attitudes of working scientists. Yet the modesty of which I speak conveys tremendous power, conveys facilities for self-correction. In science an error does not remain undetected or forgotten; the theoretical, ideal relatedness of all discoveries brings it to light in the course of further progress. Again, like the growing crystal in the picture we have previously suggested, it heals its flaws as it expands. Scientific truth is a dynamic truth, carried in a spirit of continual self-correction toward an ideal limit of understanding which is forever approached and yet never fully attained.

In one of Lessing's plays there occurs a beautiful parable in which man confronts the deity in his quest for truth. God's left hand contains the virtue called eternal search; his right holds final, absolute but static truth. After some soul-searching moments, man makes this humble plea: "God, open your left hand for me; let eternal truth remain a divine possession. I could neither comprehend nor use it." This, it seems to me, was the scientist speaking.

The modesty induced by the change in our attitude toward ultimate propositions in science takes other forms. Notably, the confidence of the nineteenth-century physicist who pronounced definitive judgment on what was possible and what was impossible, scientific and unscientific, who made a very clear distinction between the natural and the supernatural—this arrogance is gone from modern science. Certain problems that were taboo in physics a generation ago, researches in which a physicist indulged at the risk of losing his reputation, such as paranormal perception and clairvoyance, are now more widely regarded as worthy of consideration, and what is being criticized today is not a scientist's preoccupation with them, but the inadequacy of the methods employed. We know that present science is not the whole of science, and the surprises we have experienced in respect to novelty and strangeness of recent developments have engendered a degree of humility in our attitudes that is unprecedented in the history of scientific man.

It thus develops that a certain faith, a kind of voluntary, reasoned commitment must attach to the starting point, to the postulates of the scientist's method. Then it becomes clear also that his labors cannot produce ultimate certainty or static truth. On realizing this, one is likely to feel a degree of disappointment, an inclination to regret what appears to be the final disintegration of the scientific task. There might be cause for such pessimism were it not for the fact that here, at the very end of the scientific enterprise, another and over-arching faith appears: the scientist does not regard his quest as piecemeal, proliferous, and divergent. He holds with the fervor of a religious conviction that his task is meaningful, that the history of science does converge in the limit upon a set of knowledge, laws and principles that are unique, categorical, and all inclusive. This conviction again is not subject to logical and empirical proof; yet it inspires his researches, gives him a feeling of participation in a meaningful universal process; for example it sustains the nuclear physicist during periods like the present, when he sees little but chaos in the realm of elementary particles. That faith in the ideal convergence of the scientific adventure assures him that his present, seemingly futile labors are not in vain, that there will some day be a unifying theory in terms of which our present fragments of knowledge make elegant sense.

THE INNER LIGHT OF REASON

Were I to set down a creed which expresses the new faith of science, such a catechism would include the following articles:

I believe that the search for truth is a never-ending quest; yet I pledge myself to seek it.

I will not recognize or accept any kind of truth that pretends to be ultimate or absolute. I will consider and weigh all claims as provisional conclusions. If examination shows them to be stop signs on the road of inquiry, I will ignore them; if they are signposts, I will note them and move on.

I recognize no subjects and no facts which are alleged to be forever closed to inquiry or understanding; a mystery is but a challenge.

I believe that new principles of understanding are constantly created through the efforts of man, that a philosophy which sees the answers to all questions already implied in what is *now* called science is presumptuous and contrary to the spirit of science.

I believe in the convergence of the scientific laws upon principles that are all embracive, though they may never be completely within our reach.

And finally, it should be added that scientific illumination of human experience is not confined to the area of inquiry about nature. As later chapters of the book may suggest, scientific understanding can be made to penetrate, not only the dealings of man with nature, but likewise the dealings of man with man.

Chapter IV

ESTHETICS AND RELATIVITY

1. *The Idea of Invariance*

Figure 4 below is an arbitrary pattern drawn on paper; it shows a bit of complicated, perhaps interesting design but is largely without esthetic appeal. Figure 5 is the result of cutting the same pattern into a piece of paper folded in

Fig. 4

such a way that the figure is repeated 8 times when the paper is unfolded and smoothed out, after the fashion in which children make Christmas tree ornaments. Somehow, the repetition of an intricate but artless pattern engenders the esthetic qualities inherent in simple ornamental design.

77

The natural beauty of snowflakes resides in their "symmetry," which is only another word for the quality in question,

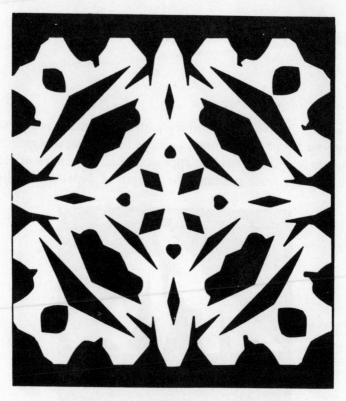

Fig. 5

demonstrated in Figure 6 below. This figure represents in a schematic way all known elementary types of snowflakes. Repetition of pattern is manifest in every one of them.

But a mere repetition is hardly responsible for beauty in any of these instances, for if repetition were to occur in a random manner—if Figure 4 for instance were strewn over the page in different orientations at random spots—the result might be considered beautiful as one sometimes endows a discord with capricious beauty, yet it would lack the

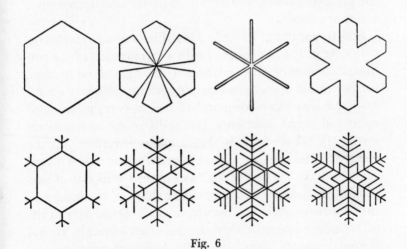

Fig. 6

stateliness of a major chord. Esthetic elements introduced, not by mere repetition of pattern but by orderly repetition, have been the object of scientific study; they are succinctly described in science under the heading of "invariance." The meaning of this term and its relevance to the figures under discussion will now be explained.

In ordinary language invariance means constancy; we say, for instance, that human nature is invariant, or that a clock which keeps good time runs at an invariant rate. If pressed for greater precision, we would qualify these statements by adding that, though human nature is not the same everywhere and at all times, human reactions are the same under *certain specifiable conditions,* and that the clock rate, though not constant under all conditions, is the same regardless of the *temperature* or perhaps the *degree of humidity* of its surroundings. One thus comes to realize that, when asserting invariance, one should for the sake of clarity state the presumed changes of condition under which invariance is meant to hold.

Strictly speaking, then, the idea of invariance remains incomplete unless it is coupled with a specification of the permitted changes or, if the changes are brought about by man, the permitted operations that are without influence on the quality asserted to be constant. Hence, in every meaningful statement about invariance, two things must be clearly set forth: (1) Whatever it is that remains invariant, (2) the changes, operations, or transformations under which invariance holds. In the case of our clock, item 1 is its rate of running, item 2 might be temperature changes, or changes in the moisture content of the air, or both, or changes in the surrounding magnetic field. In the other example, item 1 is human nature, item 2 might be change of geographic locale, or passage from one historical period to another, or differing race, or any combination of these. Let us speak of item 1 as the invariant property and of item 2 as the "transformations" with respect to which invariance is said to hold.

In this terminology, the beauty of Figure 5 lies in the fact that its shape (1) is invariant with respect to (2) all rotations in its plane about the midpoint through an angle of 90° (or multiples thereof). The shape of the snowflakes is invariant with respect to rotations through 60° and multiples of 60°. Item 1 is the shape of the figure, item 2 is the transformation: rotation about certain specific angles.

The Greeks called the circle a perfect figure. The reason is simple. The circle is the only figure whose shape is invariant with respect to all rotations, not merely multiples of 90° or multiples of 60°. Regular polygons derive their esthetic quality from their invariance, since a regular polygon of n sides is invariant with respect to rotations through $360°/n$. Rotational symmetry is another term for invariance against rotations.

There is another, slightly more analytic way to describe this state of affairs. For we may equally well employ algebraic language in place of our geometric exposition. Let us take for our example the last proposition: The shape of a circle is invariant with respect to all rotations. Now the algebraic representation of (the shape of) a circle of radius a is

$$x^2 + y^2 = a^2 \tag{1}$$

The reader may perhaps recall that the transformation, rotation through an angle φ, is represented by the pair of equations

$$x = x' \cos \varphi - y' \sin \varphi$$
$$\tag{2}$$
$$y = x' \sin \varphi + y' \cos \varphi$$

The understanding here is that x and y form a set of rectangular coordinates, while x' and y' are a similar set rotated through φ, so that x' makes an angle φ with x and likewise y' with y. In this new language invariance means that the transformations (2), when inserted in equation (1), yield an equation of exactly the same form in the "primed" coordinates. It is indeed easy to verify with the use of simple trigonometric formulas that substitution of (2) into (1) results in

$$x'^2 + y'^2 = a^2$$

Equation (1) retains its form when subjected to the transformations (2), whose physical significance is a rotation through an angle φ.

I shall not trouble the reader with the proof that the equation of a square (four straight lines at right angles) when written in algebraic form in the manner of eq. 1, does *not* retain its form when expressed in the x' and y' coordinates conformably to the transformations (2), *except* when φ is given the values 90°, 180°, or 270°. An exercise, easy for the connoisseur of analytic geometry, will prove this statement true. One may prove similarly that the equation of a hexagon retains its form under transformations (2) when $\varphi = 60°$, 120°, 180° or 240° or 300° and so forth; finally, even though the algebra entails terrific labor, the equation for Figure 5 can be shown to be invariant under eqs. 2 when $\varphi = 90°$ or multiples of 90°.

To summarize: when invariance is represented by means of equations, it requires that a given equation (e.g., eq. 1) retain its form provided a transformation of the variables (e.g., eqs. 2) is performed. The invariant equation is often called a *law,* and we shall henceforth follow this convention. Physics features many laws, and mathematics knows of many transformations. One should therefore expect a large range of applicability for the invariance idea in these sciences. The expectation is correct as will be seen. But before going farther afield, we shall examine the reverse side of invariance, which is called *relativity*.

2. *The Idea of Relativity*

Imagine you look at a scene through a cylindrical telescope tube. Then rotate the tube about its axis. Now look again! The scene will be as before; its appearance will not reveal the fact that the telescope tube has been rotated. But imagine you look at the scene through a tube of square cross section. A rotation of this tube about its axis will be evident because after it has been performed all lines which previously made a right angle with one of the tube edges will now slant differently: the shape of the tube serves to discriminate between the previous and the later orientation. That is, provided the angle of rotation is *not* 90° or a multiple of 90°. Expressed in geometric language, a shape which is invariant to a given set of transformations cannot be used to discriminate between conditions that differ by such transformations; or again, in the language of laws, a law which is invariant to a given set of transformations is indifferent to the conditions connected by these transformations. Still more formally: given a law L; L is invariant with respect to the transformation T. Let C_1 and C_2 be conditions such that T transforms C_1 into C_2. Then one cannot tell, on the basis of L, whether C_1 or C_2 is present. In our example L was the circle, T was a rotation about its axis, say through ϕ degrees; C_1 and C_2 were orientations of the circumference of the circle which differed by ϕ degrees. As we have seen, these could not be distinguished.

The indiscriminacy existing between C_1 and C_2 because of invariance, the fact that in view of L all C are equivalent and none can be said to be in essence different from the others, is technically called *relativity*. Different C are said to be relative to one another. In our example of the circular tube we might arbitrarily mark off the 360 degrees of a circle on the rim. Yet the procedure of rotating the tube and looking through it would never apprise us of the "true" position of the zero mark on the scale, and if a question arose as to which of several such scales were the right one our "law" would provide no answer. We can tell the angle *between* such scales, i.e., their *relative* orientation, by looking at them, but absolute orientation remains an empty concept.

This kind of relativity is generally associated with invariance; its meaning will become clearer and more interesting as we proceed to physical examples. Here we note that invariance always demands a price. The price we pay is relativity, a surrender of facilities for determining absolutes. This is often true in esthetics, too, for beauty generated through symmetry entails indiscriminacy of position. If someone turns a snowflake picture through 60° you are unable to tell. But if Figure 4 is turned, the result is evident.

Invariance with its implied relativity is at least as important in science as it is in art, for in science it introduces not only elegance in the formulation of laws but also a large measure of simplicity and convenience. For suppose a physical law, like the law of gravitation, were *not* invariant with respect to transformations between a large class of conditions. It would then have a different form, would indeed be a different law, under different conditions. Galileo's law of falling bodies might be written

$$\frac{d^2y}{dt^2} = g$$

Here g is the constant acceleration of gravity at the earth's surface, and d^2y/dt^2 is the instantaneous vertical acceleration of a falling body. Concerning this law one may ask the following questions.

Does it hold at all heights (near the surface of the earth)? The transformation that changes the height y into $y + h$, where h is a constant, is simply

$$y' = y + h$$

and it is clear that $d^2y'/dt^2 = d^2y/dt^2$. Hence the law is invariant with respect to all displacements along the vertical direction.

Does it hold at all times? The transformation which changes the present time t into a later time is

$$t' = t + T$$

where T is a constant. Again it is clear that $d^2y/dt^2 = d^2y/dt'^2$, and this assures invariance against displacements in time.

To be sure, these considerations are trivial and are always taken for granted. But if they were not true an awful situation would arise, the "law" would be different at different heights, and it would change its form as time goes on. Nobody would speak of it as a law under such circumstances and if the relation were written, it would amount only to a casual description of a fleeting phenomenon without general import. To be a law, a mathematical equation is expected to possess invariance at least with respect to space and time displacements, and it is desirable that its range of invariance be even greater.

3. *Inertial Systems*

We have asked whether laws hold at different points of space and at different instants of time, and have cast our inquiry in the form of mathematical equations. Much more interesting is the question whether physical laws are independent of the *velocities* with which bodies subject to these laws are travelling, and it is important to express this new concern likewise in mathematical form. First, however, let us probe its meaning in more concrete ways.

We know the law of fall of a body released from a position of rest relative to the surface of the earth. How about a body released from a position of rest relative to a moving train, or a rocket ship? Does it obey the same law? Does a clock run faster or slower when it is transferred from the ground to a moving vehicle? Do electric charges attract or repel each other differently when they are moving together at a certain velocity? To make these questions precise, we shall first introduce the idea of *inertial systems* and then formulate the transformations against which the laws must be invariant in case these questions have affirmative answers.

Figure 7 represents a two-dimensional system of rectan-

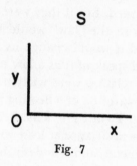

Fig. 7

gular coordinates, x and y, often called a Cartesian system or frame. The point of intersection of the two axes, 0, is called the origin. This reference frame, S, is assumed to be at rest, relative to the center of our galaxy. Let us call it the *primary* system. Figure 8 designates a second Cartesian frame whose axes are parallel to those of the primary system, but whose origin 0' moves with a constant velocity v relative to 0, and the motion is always along the x-axis. The axes in Figure 8 are labelled x' and y'; the system itself will be denoted by S', and we shall call it an inertial system. If v were variable in time, system S' would not be an inertial one.[1]

1. The word *inertial* makes reference to the "law of inertia," Newton's first law of motion, which holds only for systems here called inertial.

Let us suppose furthermore that S and S′ are sufficiently large to provide room for many people, and—horrid thought—let these people be scientists equipped with yardsticks and chronometers, capable of observing events in the outside world and of measuring the places and times at which the events occur. The time and place of a given event, when measured by someone in system S′ relative to his co-

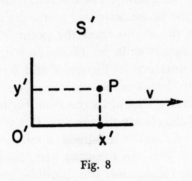

Fig. 8

ordinates, will of course be different from the time and place of the same event as measured in S. To see this more clearly, imagine an explosion at the point P in Figure 8. Notice that the full meaning of any event may be characterized by the answers to the following three questions: What happened? Where did it happen? When did it happen? The answer to the first cannot be represented in mathematical form; here even the scientist is forced to speak plain English. The second question asks for the x and y components of the point P in system S, and for $x′$ and $y′$ in system S′. The third requires a statement of the time t, measured on some clock or clocks, at which the explosion took place. In the sequel we pay no further attention to the content or nature of the event (remembering that it was an explosion) and concentrate upon its *kinematic aspects,* i.e., upon the answers to the last two questions.

Here, however, a slight difficulty appears, because people in the two systems must use different yardsticks and different clocks and these must first be compared. Let us imagine a comparison to have been accomplished, with the result that all yardsticks have the same length and clocks run at the same rate. All quantities of interest, namely x', y', x, y, t and t' can now be measured, x' being the distance of P's projection on the x'-axis from the point $0'$, x the corresponding distance from 0, etc. However, with the information already contained in Figures 7 and 8 there ought to be relationships between these measured quantities. In the first place, y and y' should be the same because the x- and x'-axes have been chosen to coincide. But what is the connection between t and t'? It depends upon the way in which the clocks in S' were *synchronized* with those of S. If, at a moment when comparison was possible, these clocks indicated the same time, t and t' will remain the same at all later times.

A convenient moment for synchronization is the one at which the origins 0 and $0'$ coincided, that is, when S' just passed across S with its constant speed v. At this instant, we shall say, both sets of clocks, those in S and those in S', read zero o'clock (midnight). Hence we expect the following relations: $t' = t, y' = y$, and a third, connecting x and x', which we must now establish.

Figure 9 shows x', the distance of Q from $0'$. As indicated, Q is the projection of P and the x'-axis. By definition x is the distance of Q from 0; it is larger than x' by the distance between 0 and $0'$ and this, by our method of synchronization, is simply the path travelled by $0'$ since zero o'clock, or v times t. Hence the third relation is $x = x' + t$.

In retrospect, then, we have found

$$t' = t$$
$$y' = y \qquad\qquad (3)$$
$$x' = x - vt$$

With apologies to the reader, I wish to acknowledge that I have taken him far away from the subject of esthetics. But

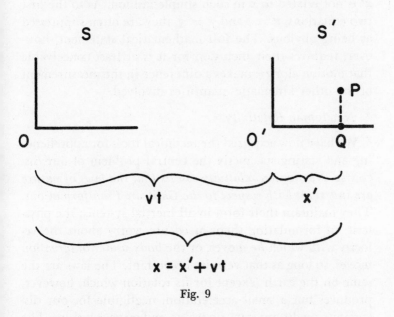

Fig. 9

we have now reached the point of maximum departure and I hasten to return to our basic problem. Esthetics, we saw, is largely founded on invariance. Invariance requires scrutiny of relevant transformations. And it happens that eqs. (3) are the transformations over which the historic battle of invariance in science has been fought. They are called, for no good reason (Galileo had no awareness of their importance), the *Galilean Transformations,* a term which will henceforth be abbreviated into G.T.

The G.T. indicate how one passes, mathematically, from one inertial system to another. They are the T's of section 2, which mediate between conditions C_1 and C_2, the latter being inertial reference frames. If two systems are not inertial, i.e., if v is not constant, eqs. (3) are incorrect because x' is not related to x in such simple fashion. As to the first two equations, $t' = t$ and $y' = y$, they are often suppressed as being obvious. The full mathematical statement, however, requires their inclusion for it is at least conceivable that motion along x makes a difference in the measurement of the other kinematic quantities involved.

4. *Newtonian Relativity*

We have now acquired the technical tools for apprehending and stating succinctly the central problem of our discourse. *Newtonian relativity asserts that the laws of nature are invariant with respect to the Galilean Transformations.* They maintain their form in all inertial systems; the physicist, in formulating them, need not worry about the velocity with which *he* moves, or the *body under observation* moves, so long as that velocity is constant. The laws are the same on the earth (except for its rotation which, however, produces but a small acceleration, negligible for our discussion), on distant stars, on trains, and on rocket ships. The passage from one inertial system to the other has no more effect than a rotation of a snowflake through $60°$. Students of physics ought to be thankful for this, as it relieves them of the necessity of learning different laws for different inertial systems.

Two points now require investigation. First, whether the assertion of Newtonian relativity is true, and second what

90

consequences of the sacrificial sort it entails. On the first, we shall dwell but briefly, contenting ourselves with a pair of examples and the mere observation that all laws in the branch of physics now called classical mechanics[2] are in fact invariant. The second point will receive due attention.

As the first example[3] we take again the law of free fall,

$$\frac{d^2y}{dt^2} = g$$

In view of eqs. (3), this may also be written

$$\frac{d^2y'}{dt'^2} = g$$

Nor does it matter whether we call the vertical direction y or x, for the equation $d^2x/dt^2 = g$ will be converted into $d^2x'/dt'^2 = g$ since v in eqs. (3) is constant.

The other example is the law of vibratory motion, familiar to most physics students from their introductory courses in that science. A mass m_1 located at x_1 is connected by a spring of stiffness K to a mass m_2 located at x_2. The law of motion for mass m_1 then reads

$$m_1 \frac{d^2x_1}{dt'^2} = K(x_2 - x_1)$$

On applying the G.T. to both coordinates, in the forms

$$x_1 = x_1' + vt, \qquad\qquad x_2 = x_2' + vt$$

2. It seems that physicists use the term classical to designate those parts of their science which are no longer valid!

3. The reader may omit these examples without detriment to an understanding of what follows.

and noting again that $t = t'$, the law reads

$$m_1 \frac{d^2 x_1'}{dt'^2} = K\left(x_2' - x_1'\right)$$

Hence it is invariant. The same is true for all other laws of classical mechanics, as already mentioned.

Now we consider the obverse face of the invariance coin: relativity. *If* the laws of nature do not discriminate between inertial systems, if no one can tell (by applying these laws) what is the value of the constant v appearing in the G.T., then there is no possibility of knowing which of the inertial systems corresponds to $v = 0$, that is, which of them is absolutely at rest. Hence the concept of absolute motion recedes into the same limbo of obscurity as the notion "absolute orientation of the telescope tube" in our earlier discussion. Only *relative* motions can be distinguished in nature, and this distinction is made by direct inspection or measurement, not by an appeal to the laws. It is this psychologically striking necessity of renunciation, man's inability to determine absolute velocity, which has given the theory of relativity its name, thus partly obliterating the logically far more important positive aspect of invariance which it contains.

We spoke of Newtonian relativity as comprising those laws of physics which are invariant to G.T. Again, Newton had no hand in it. The name has become attached to this part of physics because the most basic of all the laws within it are Newton's laws of motion. At this point the story of relativity would end or, to be truthful, it would perhaps not have been written, were it not for a most unexpected development that occurred at the beginning of the 20th century, a development which challenged the assertion made in the first sentence of the present section. Laws were discovered which were *not* invariant with respect to G.T. This led to a new form of invariance, a new form of relativity now usually connected with the name of Einstein.

5. *Einstein's Special Relativity*

The crucial discovery originating the new trend in physics was made by Michelson and Morley in a series of experiments designed to measure the speed of light in different inertial systems. Actually, their measurements were performed by allowing light rays to go at different angles relative to the motion of the earth in its orbit about the sun, and the apparatus used was most ingenious. The experiments are described in most textbooks on general physics and will not be reviewed here. Rather, I shall state the consequences or, to be logically precise, the possible implications of the Michelson-Morley experiments in terms which the preceding sections have made clear.

The experiments showed that the speed of light, *c,* which has the value 3×10^{10} cm/sec, approximately, is the same in different inertial systems. That is to say, if light were passing from left to right across S and S' in Figure 9, people in S' would find it to be moving with the same speed *c* as people in S. If this result is taken seriously, it permits the following interesting thought experiment to be conducted.

Let a luminous explosion occur at zero o'clock, when the origins 0 and 0' are coincident, and let its place be 0. Light will then be propagated with equal speed in all directions, and the observers in S will see it expanding in a sphere about 0, the radius of the sphere being *ct* at the time *t.* In the *x-y* plane depicted in Figures 7–9, the locus of the wavefront at time t will be a circle of radius ct. The law of this circle, the reader may recall, is

$$x^2 + y^2 = c^2 t^2 \tag{4}$$

But observers in S′ will likewise see a circular wavefront, because they too are in an inertial system. Hence their law of light propagation reads

$$x'^2 + y'^2 = c^2 t'^2 \tag{5}$$

In other words, the law of propagation is invariant. We have learned, however, that this statement is incomplete as it stands since it makes no reference to specific transformations. Common sense and previous experience make us expect that the relevant transformations are the G.T., and here is where trouble arises. As the reader can verify, substitution of equations (3) in (5) will not give (4)! To the physicist this is revolting, for it places in jeopardy the idea of invariance, that fundamental link of elegance which joins science and esthetics.

The difficulty, which engulfed the thinking of physicists around the year 1900, could in principle be resolved in two ways. One is to doubt the correctness of eq. (5), to question the validity of the Michelson-Morley results. The other is to doubt the G.T. The former way renounces the elegance afforded by invariant principles and blames inelegance on nature's inscrutable facts. For, after all, why should nature's laws be simple and convey esthetic appeal? The second way implies, not perhaps a disdain for facts but a strong tendency to rely on formal matters; certainly it disregards common sense, i.e., the kind of reasoning that underlay our derivation of the G.T. in section 3.

The efforts to find errors in the Michelson-Morley experiments were numerous but unsuccessful. An empirical quest of this sort can of course never be assuredly unsuccessful, for it is the nature of every inductive factual search that its completeness cannot be guaranteed. But people got tired of experimenting and turned with increasing readiness to the more challenging radical possibility of doubting the G.T. Einstein was their leader; his unconventionality and his boldness are attested not only by his scientific work, but also by his more incidental utterances. Common sense, he said, is merely the layer of prejudices which our early training in science has left in our minds. Many scientists of this period took the view that common sense is no infallible and innate *lumen naturale* but merely the residue which advancing science has left in its wake and which has penetrated popular thinking. They heeded D'Alembert's admonition, "Allez en avant, la foi vous viendra!" And they questioned the G.T.

Their question can be put in very simple mathematical form. It asks: given equations (4) and (5), what transformations, similar to but not identical with (3), will make them true? Now it happens that unless the word "similar" is interpreted very strictly, the question does not have a compelling answer. There is an infinite number of transformations compatible with equations (3) and (4). But if the additional requirement of *linearity* is imposed, if x, y, t, and x', y', t' are required to occur only in first powers,[4] the answer is unique. It had in fact been obtained before Einstein by Lorentz, who did not, however, recognize its full scope and significance. It goes by the name of *Lorentz Transforma-*

4. This requirement is a most natural one, for if squares and higher powers were permitted the resulting transformations might assign two or more events in system S′ to one event in system S. Insistence on linearity prevents the absurd possibility of multiplying events by going to another inertial system.

tions (L.T. hereafter). To derive them is a simple algebraic exercise which many readers will wish to perform but need not be reproduced here. The results are again expressible in three equations:

$$\left.\begin{array}{l} t' = k \left(t - \dfrac{v}{c^2}\, x \right) \\[2mm] y' = y \\[1mm] x' = k \left(x - vt \right) \end{array}\right\} \tag{6}$$

provided the symbol k stands for

$$k = \frac{1}{\sqrt{1 - \dfrac{v^2}{c^2}}} \tag{7}$$

One can easily retrace the steps of the omitted derivation by substituting these relations into eq. (5) and showing that one obtains (4). Equations (6) are the L.T., which must replace the G.T. if the invariance expressed by (4) and (5) is to be preserved. Accepting (6) means rejecting (3). Let us therefore see in what respects they differ.

The symbol v, we recall, is the relative speed of the two inertial systems, c is the speed of light (in vacuo). For ordinary everyday motions, performed by carriers of human beings, v/c is very small. In that case k is very nearly 1, vx/c^2 is negligible, and the L.T. "reduce" to the G.T. Is this perhaps the reason why the latter had always been found to be true? Evidently the difference between the L.T. and the G.T. becomes manifest only in motions whose speed is comparable to c, and such motions were not known until the present era. Atomic motions, and very soon the motions of rockets, belong to this category.

Teachers of physics are often asked whether the L.T. are

true. I find this a hard question to answer because of the peculiar manner in which the L.T. emerge. As our development shows, they make no claim to being true. They are the analytical consequences of our insistence on the invariance of the law of light propagation. Their truth is hypothetical: if eqs. (4) and (5), then (6). The latter provide, as it were, a dictionary which allows translation of the language spoken in system S into the language which ought to be spoken in system S', but the existence of the dictionary does not guarantee the reasonableness of language S', nor does it certify that this language is actually spoken. Textbook writers are not always aware of this; they sometimes pretend to derive the L.T. from "observations" involving light rays, clocks, and yardsticks, apparently unaware of the logical absurdity of such operational procedures. In fact the L.T. have no operational handles, for coordinates x, y, x', y' and instants t, t' are intrinsically unmeasurable. One can measure only lengths of physical objects, which are *differences* between coordinates, and durations which are *differences* between instants, and about these the L.T. remain discreetly silent.[5]

Nevertheless the L.T. can be confirmed empirically in an indirect manner. For they entail certain consequences with respect to lengths and intervals which are derivable from them in purely analytic fashion. One verifies the consequences, as we shall see. To put the logical situation aright, however, let us record the fact that he who claims to prove empirically the L.T., commits the logical fallacy of "affirming the consequent." The practical success, to be sure, is independent of such considerations; it vastly en-

5. For a more detailed philosophical discussion of these matters, the reader is referred to H. Margenau and R. Mould, *Phil. of Sci.*, 24, 297, 1957.

hances our confidence in the correctness of the entire scheme, the special theory of relativity, inspiring admiration for its magnificent sweep from abstract principle to empirical verification.

6. *The Empirical Consequences of the Lorentz Transformations and Their Confirmation*

Simple mathematical manipulations involving eq. (6), coupled with the customary interpretation given to coordinates and instants of time, leads to the prediction of five observable effects, some which will here be presented in mathematical form. The detailed derivation is omitted in all cases. If the L.T. are accepted, then the following empirical results must be expected.

1. Moving objects contract in the direction of their motion. If the length of a rod placed along x' and moving with S' is l' as measured by an observer in S', its length as measured by an observer in S is

$$l = l'/k \qquad (8)$$

Notice that k, defined in eq. (7), is always greater than 1.

2. Moving clocks go slow. If a clock in S' indicates a period T' for the interval between two events, a clock in S will record for the interval in question

$$T = T'/k \qquad (9)$$

It is this retardation effect which will keep a twin travelling through space with high speed younger than his brother. For some strange reason, a few writers regard such an outcome as paradoxical and disbelieve it on logical grounds. The suggestion may be strange or shocking to classical sensibilities, but it contains no elements of contradiction.

3. Velocities are not added as ordinary vectors, but in a

somewhat more complicated manner. Thus, if a rocket moves along x' in system S' with speed V, the velocity of the rocket as observed from S will not be $V + v$ but smaller. In particular, a light ray moving with speed c in S' will not acquire speed $c + v$ in system S but only c.

4. The mass of material objects increases as they move. If m_0 is a body's "rest" mass, its mass when moving must be $m = km_0$.

5. The increase in mass described under 4 is evidently equal to the increase in energy of the moving mass divided by c^2. Apparently, therefore, mass and energy are proportional. This is rigorously and universally true; indeed if m is the mass of any object whatsoever the associated energy is

$$E = mc^2 \qquad (10)$$

The last equation is often called Einstein's formula for the equivalence of mass and energy.

We now indicate briefly in what manner the five effects were verified. Physical confirmation is rarely direct. In the present instance, special experiments sometimes provide full evidence for one, sometimes more hypothetical evidence involving two effects.

Fairly direct is the test of the lengthening of time intervals in moving systems. During the last 20 years nature has supplied the physicist with particles carrying "clocks" and moving very fast. They are the mesons. The clocks mark off only two instants of time, namely their birth and their death; for these particles have a finite mean life period that is observable, and thus the particles themselves act as clocks. In one of the earliest experiments Rossi and Hall found that the mean life of fast and slow μ-mesons differed by a factor 3. This discrepancy disappeared when the retardation of the "meson's clock" was taken into consideration in accordance with equation (9): with this correction all μ-mesons have the same mean life span regardless of their speeds, and this must be regarded as strong confirmation of the retardation effect 2.

Even more direct is the observation of the *relativistic mass increase,* first accomplished by Bucherer and now a commonplace in every accelerator laboratory. It involved sending swift charged particles through a magnetic field and observing their deflections. Effect 4 is now so firmly established that the design of every synchro-cyclotron costing millions of dollars is based upon it.

Confirmation of the *contraction of lengths* is most easily afforded by a study of the Doppler effect. The formula for this effect is well known and is confirmed in numerous observations. Its theoretical derivation, however, involves two assumptions: retardation of clocks and contraction of space intervals. The first of these, unless coupled with the second, leads to an empirically erroneous answer. Since the first assumption is independently confirmed, the Doppler effect serves to confirm the second.

In 1851 Fizeau measured the velocity of light through moving water. His result did not conform to expectations based on Newtonian mechanics, i.e., on the ordinary vector-addition formulas for velocities. Hence, Fizeau concluded from his observation that the flowing water partially "entrains" the luminiferous ether in which light was supposed to be propagated. Today we know this conclusion to be erroneous, indeed the ether hypothesis of Fizeau's day has been abandoned; but Fizeau's observations are exactly those required by the relativistic *formula for velocity additions.* This is an amusing historical incident in which reinterpretation of an old experiment that had lost all status because of the erroneous ideas on which it was founded succeeded in making it demonstrate a brand new theory. There are many other, more recent confirmations of effect 3 in atomic physics.

Effect 5 is corroborated in so many instances, from the early Compton effect to the release of energy in nuclear explosions, that further comment on it in the present context seems unnecessary. Every nuclear reaction studied, every atom and hydrogen bomb and many astronomical observations justify equation (10). The theory of relativity, which originated with a call for invariance, received its final concrete approval in the hard and factual arena of experimental physics.

Thus ends one story in the book of miracles of science, a story which began with esthetic concerns over the form of nature's laws, passed through a stage of unbelievable predictions, shocking to common sense, and culminated in convincing demonstrations of the truth of its prophecies. That book contains many accounts of similar miracles, and others are being written at this very time.

In Chapter I we elaborated in a formal way how scientific explanation, and indeed scientific existence, depend on two basic principles: empirical confirmation and metaphysical fitness. Elegance and simplicity, we saw (Section I.1), contribute to this latter quality. These, however, are usually regarded as matters of esthetics and not of science. In the present chapter we have shown that they are relevant for science as well; we have seen them actually at work in modern physics, guiding thought and producing concrete results. Reliance on esthetic considerations (especially on the invariance of laws) and even on more embracive metaphysical visions is on the increase in recent researches. The movement is away from the limited forms of empiricism that characterized the earlier thinking in this century.

101

Chapter V

THE DECAY OF MATERIALISM IN OUR TIME

1. *The Sublimation and the Vanishing of the Material Ether*

In Chapter II we characterized materialism as a doctrine based upon the proposition: To be is to be material; only matter exists. A special form of this philosophy, called mechanistic materialism, has dominated the thinking of the West; it conjoins with the thesis above the further affirmation that matter, in all its aspects, obeys the principles of mechanics, and it is implied that these principles are the laws of classical mechanics, which are most simply cast in Newton's form.

In the present chapter we examine what happened to the first of these propositions. In the next, we describe the fortunes of the science called mechanics and follow the metamorphosis of the concept of "particle motion" from its Newtonian beginnings to its present quantum mechanical version.

Matter, according to an ancient well-established distinction, can exist in two forms. It may be continuous, as in the atmosphere that surrounds us, or discrete, as in the pebbles on a beach. There is a certain incompatibility in these two forms, and for this reason it is natural that science should attempt either to explain visual discrete objects in terms of an invisible continuum or the visible continua in terms of invisible discrete objects. Both endeavors are prominent in the records of the history of science. We are at present involved in the latter, in the attempt to resolve all matter into atoms or into even more "elementary" constituents, of which we shall speak later. The attempt was preceded, however, by another which sought to account for discrete forms by reference to a more fundamental continuous medium in which these forms arose as agglomerations, vortices, and other kinds of structure. The principal name for this continuous medium is "ether" and we now sketch in semi-historical fashion the features with which this medium has at different times been endowed.

First, let us see why the scientific mind was forced to focus upon it. The incentive was a remnant of Aristotelianism which has penetrated far into modern physics. When stated bluntly, as is done below, the argument seems trivial, but its effect on early science was far greater than its contemporaneous appeal. Aristotle had denied the existence of empty space; thus even what seems empty must, according to this supposition, be filled with substance. Coupled with the denial of empty space was the conception of *contact* forces— that is, forces capable of acting only when the agent is in *contact* with a body. Pushes and pulls between material objects are prototypes of contact forces, whereas the contrary class of forces, called *actions at a distance*, is exemplified by the pull of the earth on the moon. Clearly, contact forces are the only type compatible with Aristotelianism, and they are also most easily reconciled with the precepts of materialism; for if everything consists of matter, one might argue with Parmenides that empty space cannot exist. But empty space is necessary for action at a distance, and in its absence bodies must evidently be in contact.

104

Historically, the view that all forces are of this variety did arise with Aristotle, who denied existence of a vacuum, but clearly the notion itself can be held even in the presence of empty space. In that case there must be a material medium between bodies acting on each other by forces, and this must in some way transmit the influence. A domino block at one end of a row of upright pieces can exert a force on a block at the other end by falling against its neighbor, thus setting off a series of impulses which travel along the row until the last piece has been caused to topple. The ether theory, to which we now turn, started out as a continuum theory rejecting the existence of empty space; it later turned, at least by way of conjecture, into something like an atomic theory admitting empty space; throughout its life, however, it remained wedded to contact forces.

Gravitational forces were known to Kepler and others in the 16th century. Newton, some 50 years later, discovered their mathematical form, the famous inverse-square law of attraction. He succeeded, again without committing himself as to the nature of the forces ("hypotheses non fingo"), in showing that the motion of falling bodies, the motion of the moon and the planets, are necessary consequences of the inverse-square law.[1] Newton's reticence can best be under-

1. It is interesting to note why Kepler, whose imaginative mind had already seized upon the idea of an etherlike pervasive influence, failed to anticipate Newton's discovery. He deduced from the astronomical observations of his great friend and benefactor, Tycho Brahe, that the speed v of a moving planet is inversely proportional to its distance r from the sun ("law of areas"). But he entertained the old Aristotelian view according to which forces are proportional to velocities, and he therefore had to conclude that the force F is proportional to $1/r$, not $1/r^2$. This, he saw, is not compatible with the concept of an influence emanating from the sun, which ought to be dispersed through space in accordance with a $1/r^2$ law. Indeed, we find him wondering if per-

stood as embarrassment felt at the apparent necessity of admitting actions-at-a-distance. Though not a materialist at heart, he made a large concession to that doctrine.

The ether as such was introduced into science by Faraday in the early 19th century. Forces between electrically charged bodies had been studied, more or less as curiosities, by the ancient Greeks, but no reasonable hypothesis regarding their nature gained wide acceptance. Faraday's great experimental discoveries of electromagnetic induction and similar phenomena, by virtue of their strangeness and their clear importance, required a deepened understanding of the inductive influence for intellectual comfort. Faraday himself provided it by suggesting that an extremely tenuous, pervasive continuous medium fills all space and that this medium transmits electrical as well as gravitational forces in a manner vaguely reminiscent of the material domino blocks, but more particularly like an elastic body which can undergo stresses and strains. When a rubber fountain pen attracts a bit of paper, the charge on the tip of the pen puts the medium in a state of strain; the resulting stress forces, visualized as tiny stretched rubber bands extending from the charges on the pen and ending on opposite charges "induced" on the paper, are responsible for the attraction. This picture is a pleasing one and permits fanciful elaboration. One can draw these stress lines in the ether, indicate the strength of the forces by their degree of congestion and obtain a great deal of quantitative information

---

chance the solar flux is spread only through the plane of the planet's orbit, in which case a $1/r$ law would be expected. Here, it seems, is a lesson of how a mistaken philosophy (Aristotle's idea of force) can prevent an important discovery even when the essential facts are known.

from their use. The diagrams of lines of force one sees in today's texts on electromagnetism—indeed the terms line of force, bundle of force, and tube of force—are results of Faraday's fertile suggestion.

In these early days the ether lived a shadowy and secluded life; evidence for its existence was highly indirect and many scientists did in fact not believe in it. After all, it served the rather limited purpose of making gravitational and electrostatic attraction appear reasonable. But a major call was made upon it when Maxwell, another British physicist, discovered that light was an electromagnetic disturbance satisfying the same formal laws as do electromagnetic interactions. This discovery is all the more remarkable because it sprang from an examination not of the empirical facts about light, but of the formal laws regulating electromagnetic phenomena. It was a straight extension of the equations that describe Faraday's observations, joined by the expectation that the same set of laws, with an addition that made them more symmetric and elegant, ought to be applicable to light waves. And they were! The immediate result of Maxwell's extension was the prediction of radio waves, whose reality was soon established. Everything thus fell into line, and the theoretical basis of it all was the good old universal continuum, the ether, now called luminiferous ether because of its light-bearing quality. This second call upon its services became a *fiat;* men began to believe in its physical existence, and to wonder about its physical properties. For if it did exist, it should manifest its presence in other more direct, unmistakable ways. Convinced of this, physicists launched a search for the measurable properties of the luminiferous ether.

Naturally, thought at this point turned first to the mass, or the density, of the postulated substance. But this is hard to determine, for since we are inextricably immersed in it, we encounter all the difficulties of a fish trying to measure the density of the ocean, only worse, for the fish could conceivably learn to emerge from the water and weigh it, while for us this possibility does not exist in relation to the omnipresent ether. All we can do under these circumstances is to guess that its density is very small, smaller than that of the lightest substance known.

The density of a fluid is related to the speed of the *waves* which the fluid transmits. Scientists had measured the velocity of light, i.e., the velocity of the elastic disturbance propagated by the ether. They also knew in the last century how to calculate that velocity from the density and the elastic modulus or the pressure of the medium, for this is given by the formula

$$v = \sqrt{\frac{p}{d}}$$

If we take for v the speed of light, 3×10^{10} cm/sec, for the density d the density of the lightest known material substance (H_2) and solve for the pressure in the medium, p, we find a value of about one-thousand billion pounds per square inch. For lighter substances it would be even higher. This fantastic number is arresting and worrisome, and it makes one wonder about other properties which the strange ether might exhibit.

Can we be sure, for instance, that it is a fluid, i.e., a gas or a liquid? This should be easy to tell, because fluids differ from solids in the nature of the waves they propagate. A fluid transmits only longitudinal waves, an elastic solid, waves of both varieties, longitudinal and transverse. Now light is known to perform transverse vibrations, a fact established long before Maxwell's time. Two conclusions may immediately be drawn from these pieces of information: first, the ether can certainly not be a fluid; second, if it is a solid, there must be another kind of luminous wave of the longitudinal variety, or else the ether must be a solid different in character from all the solids we know. Longitudinal light waves have been sought but not discovered. Hence the ether has revealed its monstrous identity: it is a solid, but a solid which, unlike all other solids, does not sustain a longitudinal wave.

Let us postpone for a moment all concerns about the latter technicality. The jolt one receives from the idea that the universe is filled with invisible solid matter of extreme rigidity[2] is sufficient occasion to pause for a moment. How can the heavenly bodies pass freely through this solid medium? Ingenious men had answers. Sir George Stokes remarked that certain substances, such as pitch or shoemaker's wax, though rigid enough to sustain elastic vibrations, are nonetheless sufficiently plastic to permit other bodies to pass slowly through them. The ether "may have this combination of qualities in an extreme degree, behaving like an elastic solid, for vibrations so rapid as those of light, but yielding like a fluid to the much slower progressive motions of the planets."[3]

Hence the ether turned into a substance like shoemaker's wax. This seemed for a time to be a fortunate transformation, for it also accounted for the ether's failure to transmit longitudinal vibrations. Plastic substances like shoemaker's wax are found capable of both types of vibration, to be sure, but the longitudinal wave is very much faster than the

2. An application of the formula for the velocity of waves yields in this case a rigidity one million times that of steel!

3. E. T. Whittaker, *A History of the Theories of Aether and Electricity,* Longmans, Green and Company (1910).

transverse one, and it might be thought that in the ether the former travels so fast as to be unobservable. This was indeed supposed by Fresnel, but the hypothesis may now be disregarded in view of the fact that nothing has ever been found to travel with a speed greater than that of transverse light, and, as we have seen in the previous chapter, nothing ever will if the theory of relativity is true. The nonexistence of longitudinal ether waves therefore remains to be explained.

A mathematical theory to this end was advanced quite early (1839) by an Irish investigator named MacCullagh. He proved that a medium in which the potential energy depends exclusively on the rotation of volume elements will indeed be capable of only transverse vibrations. The trouble was that nobody could visualize such a medium except in terms of mathematical equations.

At this point Lord Kelvin, England's foremost theorist, who felt that all explanations in science must be in terms of visual mechanical models, triumphantly entered the scene. In 1889 he succeeded in designing a model exhibiting MacCullagh's rotational elasticity, and he claimed it to be a model of the ether. To quote again from Whittaker (op. cit.):

"Suppose, for example, that a structure is formed of spheres, each sphere being in the centre of the tetrahedron formed by its four nearest neighbours. Let each sphere be joined to these four neighbours by rigid bars, which have spherical caps at their ends so as to slide freely on the spheres. Such a structure would, for small deformations, behave like an incompressible perfect fluid. Now attach to each bar a pair of gyroscopically-mounted flywheels, rotating with equal and opposite angular velocities, and having their axes in the line of the bar: a bar thus equipped will require a couple to hold it at rest in any position inclined to its original position, and the structure as a whole will possess that kind of quasi-elasticity which was first imagined by MacCullagh.

"This particular representation is not perfect, since a system of forces would be required to hold the model in equilibrium if it were rotationally distorted. Lord Kelvin subsequently invented another structure free from this defect."

There is the ether atom, complete in all details except for the nuts and bolts that hold it together and perhaps the manner in which its flywheels are lubricated. The novelty of the conjecture relieved to some extent the dissatisfaction over the state of aggregation of the ether atoms; for Kelvin's atoms formed a unique substance about which the question of fluidity or solidity need not be asked. Yet the scientific mind was not at ease: even though a theory was now available that could explain in lumbering fashion the observed facts of light propagation, its features violated all the canons of simplicity and economy of thought by which theories are judged. The question, therefore, arose whether nature could possibly be as complicated as the only acceptable ether hypothesis required, whether in trying to save the material ether, the physicist had not encumbered his explanation with completely unnecessary and wholly grotesque devices. Perhaps the use of Ockam's razor was called for here. Inquiry into the workings of nature had run into a serious impasse, and it occurred to some that a wholly new attack upon the problem might be needed. And soon a further, still more embarrassing difficulty made its appearance.

Setting aside the question of the internal structure of the ether, a new line of inquiry was begun. Scientists said: Suppose the ether does exist. It ought then to be detectable

111

in some way other than by the phenomenon which it was designed to explain, namely the propagation of light. Let us concentrate our attention upon the *state of motion* of the ether substance itself.

If the ether is a material medium and fills all space, it must be governed by one of two alternatives. It may be completely stagnant, filling the whole of space without any relative motion of its parts. In that case, astronomical objects like the earth move through this stationary ether, and as they do an observer on earth, for example, ought to experience what might be called an ether wind. Then there is another possibility. It might be that every heavenly body carries along its own part of this universal ether. In that instance, the earth, the sun, the moon, and all other celestial objects would entrain their own private atmospheres of ether.

The second of these hypotheses can be tested directly. If it is true then light, in passing from one stellar body to another, let us say from the sun to the earth, must traverse a tortuous path. It cannot move along a straight line because the ether is partly carried along by the sun, partly by the earth, and there must be streaming movements of the ether between them. Consequently, there will occur peculiar aberrations from straight-line paths in the light that comes from the sun and arrives at the earth. Computations show that these aberrations from straight-line motion of the light beam ought to be large enough to be measured, but investigations show them to be absent. All astronomical observations can be explained by supposing that light suffers no such aberrations,[4] and the assumption of a streaming ether

4. There is a certain regular kind of aberration (Bradley's) which does not depend on ether motions. This is not drawn in question here.

SUBLIMATION AND VANISHING OF ETHER

is ruled out. We are left, therefore, with the former alternative supposition, namely that the ether is stationary, that astronomical objects move through it without hindrance and without disturbing it.

Two physicists, Michelson and Morley, decided to put this hypothesis to experimental test. Michelson had invented and perfected his famous interferometer, an apparatus designed and able to measure very small differences in the time taken by light waves to traverse preassigned paths. With the use of such an interferometer, these men measured the velocity of light, once along the line of motion of the earth in its orbit about the sun, and then in a direction at right angles to this motion. In the first case the light ray, travelling in the direction opposite to the earth's motion, will benefit from the earth's proper motion and seem to go faster when judged by an observer on the earth. In the second case, when a light ray moves at right angles to the motion of the earth, it will have no such advantage and travel with its own proper speed; i.e., somewhat more slowly than in the first instance. The difference in speed can be calculated, and it turns out that it should be easily measurable. In actual fact the experiment was not quite as simple as this. The light ray must be made to return, and it loses on returning the advantage of speed which it gained in going out in the direction of the earth's motion. But when the calculation is made for its going and its coming, it is found to be moving with a slightly greater overall speed than a light ray which has gone the same distance to and fro at right angles to the earth's motion.

The experiment was carried out with great ingenuity and care and would have yielded a discernible difference in the speed of light, had such existed. But the answer was completely negative. It represents one of the most significant

113

"no" results of modern science. Its very failure gave birth and vitality to the new idea that perhaps the ether does not exist as a material entity at all.

Logically, the material-ether hypothesis had now been reduced to an absurdity. The ether did not conform with either of two mutually exclusive and exhaustive alternatives; it was neither stagnant nor was it moving through space. At that point Einstein appeared on the scene and proposed that the ether hypothesis be abandoned in toto. He developed the theory of relativity, which explains the null result of the Michelson-Morley experiment and at the same time all other known features of light propagation without any reference to an ether. Indeed, as we have seen in the previous chapter, it does far more than this. It represents the confluence of two great movements in physical science. One is the esthetic quest, the search for invariance of scientific principles previously described. The other is the tendency outlined in this chapter, the emancipation from the restraints imposed by materialistic explanation. And when the merging of these two streams results in a great river of scientific inquiry which uncovers and washes ashore new and unexpected facts, facts as astonishing as the consequences of the Lorentz transformations, then all reserves of doubt collapse. In this way a freer spirit arose at the beginning of our century, and the theory of relativity was its usher.

That theory gave a correct account of the propagation of light waves, of the behavior of clocks and yardsticks and of actual bodies in motion. It had the added virtue of logical simplicity, and its specific competence in all domains of modern physics established its essential correctness beyond reasonable doubt. Since this theory needs no luminiferous ether, modern physics has abandoned it and has come to

114

recognize the reality of empty space, and along with it the possibility of an influence pervading space, an influence which is not material. This shift in scientific attitude has given the doctrine of materialism its first serious blow.

The development was accompanied by a change in the physicist's conception of the nature of forces. The homely contact forces of an earlier day were conceived to be only one special kind, but not the only kind that could occur in nature. Physics had to acknowledge the possibility of "actions at a distance." One body can act upon another body through empty space; matter is not required to transmit force. An influence may still be invoked, either for necessity or convenience, to envision or describe the transmission of forces in a vacuum. Such an influence is often called a field. Few scientists today, however, regard every field as a material entity.

2. *From Atoms to Elementary Particles to Singularities in Space*

Having traced the fate which befell continuous matter during the development of modern physics, let us now see what happened to the atom—that discrete bit of substance which entered the stage of science in ancient Greece and in India and persisted in occupying the attention of physicists until today. The atom, the fundamental building block of matter, was conceived as something spherical and compact, as a globular bit of stuff. It was impenetrable. Two atoms could not occupy the same space, but they could combine to form molecules and larger aggregates. Invisible as individuals, many atoms together could rise above the threshold of human vision. According to the Vedas three double atoms form the smallest visible complex: they are the mote one sees in a sunbeam. Just what it is that composes an atom was

115

not carefully specified; in antiquity stuff was held to be in-
definable, being the primordial stratum of physical reality.
Later it was identified with electricity, but the latter term
was left undefined as to its essence.

The atom then passed through a stage of dissolution, its
decomposition into elementary particles, which occurred
in the first decade of the 20th century. To be explicit, reference will be made to the early Bohr theory, which assigns
to the atom a very small central core called its nucleus, and
this nucleus is surrounded by light floating objects called
electrons. The latter are conceived as moving about the
nucleus in orbits, some of which are circular, some elliptical.
When an electron "jumps" from one orbit to another, the
atom either emits or absorbs light. The entire structure is
similar to that of a planetary system, the sun being replaced
by the nucleus, the planets by the electrons. An important
difference between the two lies in the fact that while each
constituent of the planetary system is electrically neutral,
the nucleus and the electron are individually charged. The
charge on the nucleus is positive, that on the electron negative, and they are of equal amounts. A single quantum of
positive charge (proton) and a single electron make up a
hydrogen atom, a double positive charge and two electrons,
a helium atom, etc. The heaviest natural element, uranium, has a nucleus carrying 92 positive charges, which is
surrounded by 92 circulating electrons. I recall these well-
known facts with apologies to the knowledgeable reader.

To gain a visual conception of the magnitudes involved,
let us magnify the entire hydrogen atom by the enormous
factor 10^{13}, that is to say, a one with thirteen zeros. At this
magnification the nucleus, i.e., the proton, would appear
to have the size of a marble, something like half an inch
in diameter; the electron would be as large as an ordinary

116

house, and the distance between the two would be about one mile. The electron is large, but light and fluffy, it revolves at an enormous speed about the marble. There is also the anomaly that the marble, the proton, is nearly 2000 times as heavy as the cloud, the electron. The strangest thing about this picture, however, is that it represents the atom as being made up almost entirely of empty space. The vastness of the magnification, incidentally, can best be grasped by noting that if a man's size were magnified by 10^{13}, his head would be in the neighborhood of the star Sirius.

Bohr's theory is called a quantum theory chiefly because it restricts the motion of the electron to certain orbits, periodic and separated in space, somewhat like the orbits of the planets about the sun. But unlike the planetary orbits, the electron is able to move only on paths for which the "year" is one unit, or two units, or in general n, an integral number of units. Only a "year" here means not a period of time but something rather similar to time called action, and the unit is Planck's famous constant, h. Quantization refers to the fact that the increase in action on every permitted orbit is an integral number of units per revolution: we say that action is quantized. As to the shape of these orbits, they are always elliptical as in the case of the planets. (A circle is, of course, a special form of an ellipse and therefore a possible orbit.) On each ellipse the electron has a certain (constant) energy, and this amount of energy in general differs from orbit to orbit. If the Bohr theory were taken literally, an electron could not change its energy since it is trapped in a given orbit because of the quantization rule. For if it were to pass from one orbit to another, it would have to go through the forbidden states of motion in which action is not exactly nh. In the face of this difficulty the theory relaxes its rigor and permits the electron to alter its state occasionally, allowing it to "jump" from one quantized orbit to another. Strictly speaking, it returns to the electron a privilege it had previously taken away, but it does it grudgingly, admitting that a jump is a sort of miracle for which the theory makes no provision. And a miracle indeed it is, for when the jump occurs another entity is born or dies: a photon is created if the electron loses energy during its jump, absorbed, i.e., killed, when it gains energy.

There was a time when physicists regarded protons and electrons as particles, photons as waves. As we shall see later, this distinction can no longer be maintained. They are still often called "elementary particles," but as we shall also learn neither the word "elementary" nor the word "particle" fits the case. Let me name them simply *onta* (singular: *on*) after the Greek word for being (ὄν, plural ὄντα). We may then say that, as an electron jumps, i.e., as it violates the quantum conditions, another *on* is created or destroyed. More will be said about creation and destruction of *onta* in due course.

We now turn to heavier and larger atoms. It is customary to label atoms by reference to the place they occupy in the periodic table and to assign to them an atomic number, Z. This number goes from 1 for hydrogen to 92 for uranium, the last of the natural elements. Man-made elements range at present from Neptunium ($Z = 93$) to Mendelevium ($Z = 101$), doubtless with others to follow. An atom of atomic number Z has a nucleus consisting of Z units of positive charge with Z electrons in quantized orbits about it. The electronic charge is denoted by $-e$; hence the nucleus carries a charge of $+Ze$, which is neutralized by the charge $-Ze$ on all the electrons. Figure 10 is a pictorial representation of the electron orbits in the radium atom, published by Bohr in 1923.

In that picture the nucleus appears as a tiny dot. Its actual size is about 10^{-12} cm, that is, less than one-million-millionth of an inch. Despite its smallness it has a structure

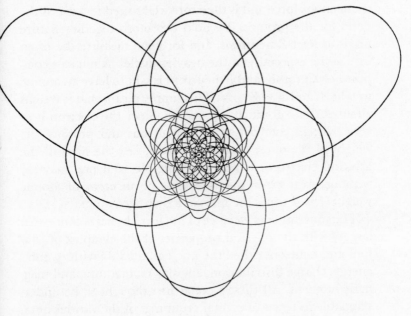

Fig. 10

which is almost as well known as that of the external parts of the atom, in as far as it can be described by the simple ideas of the Bohr corpuscular model. As already mentioned, the nucleus of an atom of atomic number Z carries Z units of positive charge, and these charges reside primarily on protons. But Z protons would never stick together; when compressed into the small space of a nucleus, the repelling

119

charges would force them apart explosively. Hence a sort of cement is needed to make them cohere, and the cement is provided by other onta named neutrons.

A neutron has about the same size as a proton and also about the same mass. But it carries no charge; hence its name. Yet it attracts a proton and another neutron with a tremendous force and is therefore well suited to serve as the bond for the protons. To hold Z protons together nature needs at least Z neutrons, and for good measure she often uses more, especially in the heavier nuclei. A nucleus composed of Z protons and N neutrons is said to have an atomic weight A, and $A = Z + N$. This simply means that it weighs about A times as much as a proton. Since the electron is so very light in comparison with neutrons and protons, the weight of the outer shell of an atom, i.e., the mass of the orbiting electrons, is almost negligible, and one may say without great error that the mass of an *atom* of atomic weight A is A times the mass of a hydrogen atom.

The contemporary science of nuclear physics is concerned largely with the physical properties of the complex of protons and neutrons called the nucleus, notably with its total energy, charge distribution, angular momentum, and magnetic moment. All these were at first thought to be understandable in terms of orbital groupings of the various onta, but no very successful visual picture has so far emerged. Many specific models have been tried, models with names like α-particle model, liquid drop model, independent-particle model, and cloudy-crystal-ball model. None of these claims ultimate significance, but their number suggests the intensity and the frustration of groping now going on among searchers for an explanation of nuclear structure. The root of the difficulties seems to lie in the nature of the onta which is gradually unfolding and, while their proper-

120

ties are being studied, belying their earlier name, elementary particles. Let me review their history.

3. *"Elementary Particles"*

In 1930 two basic particles of matter were known to physics: the negatively charged electron of small mass and the (1840 times as heavy) positive proton. The word "elementary" in those days still retained its dictionary meaning; it was a synonym for simple, unmixed, primary, radical, irreducible. Properly speaking, a third kind of particle, the photon, should be added to the two because it had already been recognized as having many corpuscular properties. But it was not a constituent of matter in the strictest sense (although it was known to possess mass) for it showed an idiosyncrasy which seemed to bar it from the class of respectable elementary particles: it could be created (emitted) and destroyed (absorbed). Moreover, men had for too long a time thought of it as a wave to welcome it readily into the society of the electron and the proton. Now, in retrospect, this gesture appears ungenerous, for the photon is certainly as elementary as other particles whose basic character has been attested to by Nobel prizes.

The year 1932 saw the discovery of the two new "particles": the neutron, which is the neutral representative of the heavyweights, and the positron, the counterpart of the light electron. Then, beginning in 1935, a whole set of new entities of medium weight (some 200 electron masses) came to be known, some carrying positive, some negative charge. Their baptism has not been completed, but as a class they are now known as mesons. Two types certainly exist: the π-meson (Fermi's pion) which has a mass 270 times as great as an electron's, and the slightly lighter μ-meson (Fermi's muon), weighing 207 electron units. Both occur with either

121

a positive or a negative charge, the charge being always equal in value to that of the electron. Indeed it is strange but true that charge is the only physical observable which has thus far proved invariable in amount when found on elementary particles. The pion occurs also in a neutral variety.

The π-meson was hailed as the last important member of an expected list of elementary particles when it was discovered in 1947, for it had been predicted by Yukawa and proceeded to occupy an already established theoretical niche. Unfortunately, however, it brought in a lot of unwanted relatives for which no niches were ready and which did not fit into any theoretical scheme. They were the "strange particles," the K-mesons (thetons and tauons) and the hyperons. The former have masses about 1000 times greater than an electron, the latter are heavier even than a proton. Hyperons are thus far designated by the three Greek symbols Λ, Σ and Ξ.

There is good reason for the belated discovery of neutrons, positrons, mesons, and hyperons, for they are unstable and do not present themselves long enough for leisurely experimentation. But spontaneous decay, while interesting in itself, is at once indicative of the existence of further entities that do not enter the scene of observation directly; it thus suggests new entities to the theorist. And some of these have actually been identified from the decay processes prior to their experimental discovery; their existence was established before they were "seen."

The propriety of such acts of theoretical fiat is often doubted by the uninitiated, but with no justification. If an elementary particle suddenly lost its charge, would it not be proper to suppose that the charge had gone off somewhere, and would we not give that disembodied charge a name? If the particle suddenly stopped, would it not be correct to assume that it collided with something, and to give that something a name? It is through reasoning of this very sort that the physicist has been forced to postulate *new* particles to account for the ones he sees. Some of these are the neutrino (neutral, having very small mass if any), the antiproton, the antielectron (positron), the antineutron, and the antineutrino. The last four have the same mass as the ones which they seem to oppose, but the charge, if any, is opposite. Neutron and antineutron differ observably; neutrino and antineutrino may possibly be the same in all respects. All these were first "predicted" on indirect and sometimes on purely speculative grounds, and all of them have now been experimentally established.

Here are some of the tricks played by these evanescent particles. A positron can unite with an electron and give rise to a pair of photons. A neutron may disintegrate into a proton, an electron, and a neutrino (beta decay). It can also transform itself into a negative pion and a proton temporarily, capturing the pion again before it gets away, and thus restore its neutron status. A pion will decay naturally into a muon and a neutrino, and the muon itself finally disintegrates into an electron and two neutrinos.

A tauon transforms itself into 3, a theton into 2 pions. Or either may go into a muon, a pion, and a neutrino. Hyperons transform into one another plus mesons and photons, protons and pions, neutrons and pions. It seems as though we were beginning to learn a whole new chemistry of strange onta. Our account of typical transformations is very sketchy indeed but is perhaps sufficient to indicate the complexity of the interrelations between nature's ultimate constituents.

Ultimate? This word hardly occurs in the physicist's dictionary. Indeed the simple meaning of "elementary" is gone; its use betrays an uneasy conscience. We often find it more convenient to retain a word and change its meaning than to retain meanings but change the words. Hence "elementary" has now come to denote the equivalent of cryptic, arcane, perplexing, enigmatic, inscrutable.

The reader who is interested in further details concerning the presently basic onta may study Table 1, which is prepared from an article by M. Ross[5] and summarizes knowledge available in September 1963. For each of the onta listed, with the exception of the photon, a so-called "antiparticle" is now known. The antiparticle for the photon is the photon itself.

The discovery of antiparticles has led to very interesting speculations about the occurrence of antimatter. Our atoms, as we have seen, are built of positive protons, neutrons, and external negative electrons. All these have antiparticles, and it is reasonably certain that atoms can be built from nuclei of negative protons and antineutrons, surrounded by positive electrons. Many overall properties of such atoms would be identical with ours, but if they ever collided with regular atoms, they would set off an annihilation process much more violent than fission or fusion. The very symmetry of nature which expresses itself in the existence of "particles" and "antiparticles" makes it seem most strange that antimatter does not exist.

Harmony could be restored, however, by the following consideration. We know that gravitational forces between particles of regular matter are attractive. This in itself represents an element of asymmetry that is unpleasant, for why should there not be two kinds of matter as there are two kinds of electrical charge, and therefore two kinds of inter-

5. M. Ross, *Rev. Mod. Phys., 35,* 314 (1963).

Table 1: THE "PARTICLES" OF PHYSICS

Mass in Units of 9.1085×10^{-28} g.	Generic Name	Name	Symbol	Charge in Units of 4.80×10^{-10} esu	Spin	Lifetime in Free Space (sec.)	Decay Scheme	Energy Release Mev
0	Leptons	Photon	γ	0	1	stable	—	—
0		e-Neutrino	ν_e	0	½	stable?	—	—
0		μ-Neutrino	ν_μ	0	½	stable?	—	—
1		Electron	e^+	-1	½	stable	—	—
206.9	L-Mesons	Muon	μ^-	-1	½	2.15×10^{-6}	$e + \nu + \nu^-$	105.2
264.5		Neutral pion	π°	0	0	5×10^{-15}	2γ or $\gamma + e^+ + e^-$	135.1
273.3		Negative pion	π^-	-1	0		$\mu^- + \gamma$	33.9
974	K-Mesons	Neutral Kaon	K°	0	0	9×10^{-11}	$\pi^+ + \pi^-$	214
966		Positive Kaon	K^+	1	0	1.2×10^{-8}	complex	
1835	Nucleons	Proton	p	$+1$	½	stable	—	—
1837		Neutron	n	0	½	10^{20}	$p + e + \nu$	0.78
2181	Hyperons	Lambda Zero	Λ°	0	½	2.6×10^{-10}	$p + \pi^-$ or $n + \pi^\circ$	40
2340		Sigma Minus	Σ^-	-1	½	1.6×10^{-10}	$n + \pi^-$	111
2331		Sigma Zero	Σ°	0	½	?	$\Lambda + \gamma$	
2327		Sigma Plus	Σ^+	1	½	8×10^{-11}	$p + \pi^\circ$ or $n + \pi^+$	111
2583		Xi Minus	Ξ^-	-1	½	1.4×10^{-10}	$\Lambda + \pi^-$	67
2573		Xi Zero	Ξ°	0	½	3.9×10^{-10}	$\Lambda + \pi^\circ$	

action: attraction and repulsion? Gravitation is the force whose origin is least understood by science, and our ignorance easily tolerates the assumption that matter and antimatter repel each other. This would restore symmetry and explain at the same time why we have not made the acquaintance of antimatter. For if it is repelled by the atoms making up out part of the world, it may well be present in galaxies far from ours—indeed the presence of antimatter could be responsible for the well-known expansion of the astronomical universe. This, however, is sheer conjecture.

Nowhere in our account has there been a suggestion of a physical picture of an individual on. To tell the truth, none is available. Surely it is not a globular bit of solid stuff. The main tendency today is to represent onta, mathematically at least, as points in space which may or may not be localized precisely. Einstein and many others sought to picture them as point singularities in some continuous mathematical field whose behavior controls their motion. This program has not succeeded, but a variant of it has yielded one impressive accomplishment, an understanding of nuclear forces. Perhaps the greatest mystery of nuclear physics is the strength and the origin of the forces which join the nucleons, i.e., protons and neutrons. Field theory is making rapid strides to resolve the mystery, somewhat in the following fashion. If the photons are assumed to form a field whose elements can be absorbed or emitted by electrons, in other words, if electrons create a photon field, the originators of the field, i.e., the electrons, must experience forces. These turn out to be the Coulomb forces, long known to exist. By looking through the mathematics one sees that the notoriously long range of these forces is occasioned by the absence of mass on the part of the photons.

Let us now assume that neutrons and protons create a

field in the very same manner, though not a field of photons. In order to account for nuclear forces and their very *small* range of action, it is necessary to endow the onta (elementary particles) constituting the field with mass, and the mass must be that of a pion! Yukawa, who proposed this explanation in its original form, had thus converted the meson from a useless adjunct to the family of nuclear constituents into the much-needed agent for the creation of nuclear forces. According to this picture, the neutron is a proton surrounded by a statistical distribution of negative pions. These pions are continually emitted and reabsorbed. If they were massless photons they would fly away, with little chance for reabsorption. Being massive, however, they get out only to a certain distance by the time absorption takes place. This distance happens to be the range of the nuclear forces; for if another proton comes within range, this proton can absorb the pions from the neutron's atmosphere and thereby undergo a strong attraction. Presumably, then, a nucleus is held together by the propensity of nucleons for stealing each other's pions.

To make such kleptomania more respectable and more reasonable, I quote Fermi, who adds a detail of interest to physicists. "The force field of a nucleon," he says, "extends as far as the pions, which it continuously emits and reabsorbs, are able to reach. When a pion is emitted the system 'borrows' an energy of order mc^2. This loan, according to the time-energy complementarity, cannot last a longer time than about $h/2\pi mc^2$. In this time the pion, even if it travels with the velocity of light, cannot move farther than $h/2\pi mc$. This is, therefore, the order of magnitude of the range."

We have become rather technical in our answer to the question that launched this chapter: is everything that exists material? A simple but perfectly proper answer would be:

matter is no longer material, in spite of the literal contradiction in terms. But since the ultimate constituents of
matter have resolved themselves pretty much into mathematical singularities haunting space, materialism is no
longer the comfortable doctrine it used to be, and one may
dismiss it as having lost its major point.

The next chapter will present further damaging indict-
ments of this simple view, by showing that the onta haunt
space not in the manner of old familiar objects with predictable trajectories, but with some at least of the material-
izing and vanishing habits often imputed to ghosts.

Chapter VI

THE FADE-OUT OF CONCRETE MODELS

1. *Classical Mechanics*

Laotse wrote in Taoteking: "He who penetrates all being with visual clarity may well remain without knowledge."

Since the days of Descartes, clarity (clarté Cartésienne) was taken to mean portrayal of observable facts in the visual symbols of three-dimensional mechanisms. Explanations involved bodies moving in space and time, miniature clockworks which despite their infinitesimal size are nevertheless governed by the laws of the macrocosm. The preceding chapter showed how the progress of science thinned out the *material content* of these models; in the present I endeavor to indicate how the *laws* governing them took on an increasing measure of strangeness which finally drew the significance, indeed the attainability of visual clarity, into serious question. While striving for it physics "remained without further knowledge" of a fundamental sort, even though it learned many new facts.

We sketch first a few of the details of this abortive program. One of the most precise statements of it is again found in the famous lecture on the principle of conservation of energy given by Helmholtz in 1847 before the Berlin Academy of Science. He says: "Finally we discover the problem of physical science to be to refer natural phenomena back to unchangeable attractive and repulsive forces whose intensity depends wholly upon distance. The solubility of this problem is the condition of the complete comprehensibility of nature." To be sure, this setting was too narrow even for the science of the last century, but the major insistence on forces acting between bodies to cause accelerations and continuous motions remained until the quantum theory demonstrated its inadequacy.

Objects moving under forces are subject to Newton's laws of particle dynamics. They are embodied in the canon of postulates which students learn in their early physics courses, i.e., in the branch of physics called classical mechanics. Their venerable age and their successes have made them part and parcel of the thinking that bears the label common sense. We do not require here a technical mastery of these laws and therefore limit our discussion to their general features. In the first place, we note that they are cast in the form of differential equations. This requires that their solutions, the functions which describe the positions of a material object as it moves in time, are *continuous* functions, defined for every, or nearly every, instant of time as was already seen in Chapter v. In the second place, they make reference to specific *points* of space, points occupied by matter, and forces are supposed to act at such specific points. The laws do not require matter to be bulky; they hold in principle even for the singularities to which the particles have been reduced. Hence the conclusion that the laws are wrong, if established, will deal a further, independent blow to the traditional concept of matter.

Newton's method implies that there are intuitable objects capable of motion. Each object has a position x at every instant of time t, and x is a continuous function of t as we have seen. The size of the object does not matter; it may be as large as a star or as small as an atom, and it may be intricately connected with other objects forming a complex mechanism or it may have an isolated path.

Two features of this picture have succumbed to scientific repudiation: (1) continuity of motion and (2) identifiability of material points. Hence I shall now review classical mechanics in a more general and qualitative way but with these two aspects held in view.

Classical physics is a lineal descendant of astronomy and has inherited the grandeur as well as the inexorability of that ancient branch of science. Kant, whose philosophy was the metaphysical distillate of Newtonian mechanics, classed the starry heavens with the human conscience as the two deepest sources of our knowledge and our attitudes.

The motion of the stars is impressively continuous. They occupy every point of their path. The apparent slowness of their motion accentuates its continuity. Clouds often obscure the stars, thus seeming to destroy their steady course, yet this very obliteration by other equally steady motions makes the fact of continuity all the more sure and convincing.

Once the pattern is set, the scientist experiences little difficulty in recognizing continuity in the more ordinary motions of his daily life. Here, to be sure, perceptory evidence is not unequivocal, for we do see lightning flashes, hear shots, and receive sudden blows. But a little analysis, a little reliance on the essential simplicity and perfection of the world, restores harmony with the astronomical universe and reestablishes continuity as a ruling principle of science.

But continuity of motion is only one facet of a more general principle which is espoused in its totality by classical mechanics. The stars have attributes besides position and speed of motion; they exhibit brightness and color as well.

131

Continuity is assigned to all of these, and the whole complex of phenomena called a star is expected to behave in a manner we might call *consistent*. On the lower plane of everyday experiences, consistency comes to mean continuity of an ever widening set of properties, such as size, color, shape, temperature, and indeed all the refined attributes which physical science attributes to its objects. And beyond this, consistency requires an interrelation between all of these. Things that are consistent and orderly seem somehow predestined and predictable; thus the inexorability which the human interpreter sees in the stars is also implanted into lesser nature as determinism or causality.

Another aspect has been borrowed from astronomy and invested in classical mechanics generally. It is the aloofness of the stars, their inaccessibility to designed experimentation. Human actions have no effect on them, their fate is independent of man's. This absolute kind of independence, to be sure, cannot be carried into objects which the experimenter can manipulate, for he is clearly able to make them do some things they would not do without him. The classical physicist therefore lessens the rigor of celestial motions by advancing the notion of *interaction*. He supposes that object A, e.g., the human observer, can influence object B in a precise and determinable way, precise in the sense that he is always able to specify which is object A, which is object B, and which is the influence. In this way, while he admits of interaction between the observer and the object of observation, he nevertheless retains the essential features of the conviction that "here am I," and "over there is the universe." These two are separate entities both participating in the universal process, which presents itself under the forms of a spectator and a spectacle. This spectator-spectacle distinction, generated by the early contemplation of the heavens, has continued to be a hallmark of classical mechanics and characterized all thinking up to the year 1925. Its renunciation, which is forced upon us by modern physics as we shall see, is sometimes regarded as destructive to science and to the acquisition of any secure kind of knowledge. The reason for this reaction is a belief that the spectatorial doctrine is the only one which achieves objectivity and insures reliability. We now know from von Neumann's analysis of Heisenberg's uncertainty principle that there are other ways of representing our experience, not involving this traditional form of the spectator-spectacle distinction, which achieve these desiderata.

It is perhaps well to pause here and see more concretely what these vaguely worded conceptual presuppositions of classical physics are. For contrast, then, I shall describe the kind of experience that would falsify these premises and then raise questions that would be natural if such experiences were encountered. Imagine that a star, while being observed, behaves very much as it does in our world, remaining stationary or slowly moving so long as our eye or the telescope is trained on it. But assume in defiance of our experience that when we turn away and then look again, the star has altered its position, only to behave regularly again while under observation. Certainly, although this does not happen among the stars in our world, it is conceivable and not contrary to any laws of thought. If it did happen, would we still say without qualification "the star has position," "its motion is continuous," "the fate of the star is independent of the observer," and would we still maintain the spectatorial doctrine?

Or suppose an object had the ability to outdo a chameleon and change its color erratically on different occasions of observation. Would we then still assign a color to the object? If our super-chameleon displayed a different color every time we looked but retained it while our gaze is fixed upon it, would we regard ourselves as mere spectators, or would we feel in some way *responsible* for the phenomena observed? Again, the physicist is ordinarily not confronted with this situation and is prone perhaps to smile at the naïveté of such questions.

But there are fields of experience in which very similar questions do make sense and are perplexing. This occurs where observation is very indirect, and where the attribute observed is of an abstract character, as in psychology. A young lady observed by an attractive young man is very likely to exhibit even a visual appearance which depends on the fact that she is being observed. But when her mental state, her composure, her thoughts, are probed by questions, the form of the question or its intent may strongly condition the answer or indeed engender a state of mind not present before the question was asked. And let us recall that there exists a vast area of human experience in which the asking of questions, i.e., personal inquiry, is the only method of "observation"; inquiry here takes the place of physical measurement. All social sciences belong in this area.

Here, the simple look-and-see quality of an observation is destroyed by the very nature of the knowledge sought, since that knowledge is not directly accessible. This happens partly because of the possibility of deliberate lying, but also when no conscious dissimulation is involved. The young lady may have been entirely honest in all her reactions and still they depended upon the circumstances in which the questions were asked. Her father or her employer might honestly have received quite different answers. If I ask a friend whom I meet, "how are you?", the response may be pleasant and unconcerned; if his doctor asks him the same question in the doctor's office, the same friend will become pensive and may even become aware of a pain. All this is commonplace but important, for the success of certain scientists, for instance psychiatrists, depends upon a clear understanding of the interplay, the correlation or, to use a fashionable phrase, of the feedback between an observation and the response to it.

To focus our thought I shall select from the vast class of sociological and psychological qualities which are subject to indirect observation a rather uninteresting but simple one, a person's anger. To be sure, anger can be openly exhibited, but it may not be; in the latter case its presence must be ascertained by indirect means, let us say by verbal inquiry. This may result in what we normally call a true report; or, the subject may from real embarrassment disclaim his state of anger; he may lie about it; indeed anger may actually rise in him because of an infelicitous wording of the question. The results of such inquiries at different times are quite likely to be erratic and unpredictable, and it is certainly not a foregone conclusion that the subject's states of mind are independent of the fact that the inquiry has been conducted. The important fact illustrated by this and all the other examples is that the spectator-spectacle view can become very artificial. When it is maintained in the biological and social sciences, an appeal is often made to classical physics, in the pious hope that the stars provide a model for man. This hope is not fulfilled.

If we take the facts of our simple observations on a person's anger without embellishment, we find, in the first place, that he is sometimes angry and sometimes not. We would therefore not speak of anger as a property which a man always possesses, but one which he *may* at times exhibit. In the physical world, objects have certain properties, like position and size, in fact all the normal attributes of visible things, at all times. They may be considered to be continually possessed by the objects to which they are assigned. Locke and Galileo spoke of them as primary qualities and distinguished them from secondary qualities which arise in the act of perception (e.g., taste and color). Nowadays this distinction is difficult to maintain, chiefly because it is impossible in many instances to prove that a quality owes its occurrence to the perceptory process. Still, there is a difference between the anger of a man which is merely a *latent* or *possible* attribute, and the position of a physical object which is assumed to be inalienably possessed though its value may change. Thus, for the sake of fixing attention, let us speak of *possessed* properties when referring to such determinate and intuitively objective qualities as the position of a tree, the mass of a stone, the velocity of an automobile; of *latent* properties when referring to such undependable qualities as the anger of a person, his feeling of pain, the affection of a woman, and the value of a commodity.

In this language, classical mechanics may be characterized by saying that it regards all properties which it uses in the description of experience primarily as *possessed* by objects. What was called continuity, consistency, independence is seen to be included in this generalization, and the spectator-spectacle distinction is a part of it. Sensory experience, as it explores our far and near surroundings in the macrocosm, justifies the point of view of classical mechanics.

2. *The Microcosm*

Reasoning based on classical mechanics has largely come to be identified with common sense. As we transport ourselves to the world of atomic magnitudes, which we now

136

propose to do, we shall be violating common sense. Hence there is need to indicate at once on what grounds we are entitled to abandon this time-tested criterion of truth. And here, as in our previous consideration of the relativity problem, it may be a shock to the reader to be told that so-called common sense has never had a shred of validity in the face of new and revolutionary theories of nature. The latter have ever had to assert themselves in the face of reactionary beliefs parading under that guise, and when these new theories succeeded, common sense readily adjusted itself to include them, as it should; for this overrated principle of truth is nothing more than the popular residue of accepted scientific theories and embodies their familiar features. It never leads, it always follows scientific discovery.

To survey the facts of the microcosm, i.e., the observations which have led to the construction of the quantum theories in their present form, we assume our sense organs to be replaced by more sensitive devices, by detectors which the electronics expert can actually build, and which allow us to discriminate very small distances, very short intervals of time, and extremely light objects. While somewhat idealized, this assumption is not pure fiction; nor are the deliverances of these devices fanciful dreams. The fact that apparatus of the kind here invoked have actually been built and used saves our story from being imaginary and makes it empirically relevant.

In this atomic world we perceive no coherent objects. Our "eyes" are now sensitive to the single darts of light (photons) cast off by single luminous atoms. Hence our microcosm is not uniformly illuminated and filled with moving things; it presents a speckled kind of vision with bright patches emerging here and there from utter darkness, different patches having different durations. Distant objects of large

137

size and mass exhibit a kind of uniform glow and suggest some cohesion in this chaotic scheme of things, but the smaller dots nearby give very little indication of uniformity or pattern.

An unimaginative observer restricted to this world would hardly postulate permanent bodies present at all times; he might indeed doubt the existence of entities except at the moment of vision. He would not find it plausible to speak of the flow of time; he might regard "emergence of sensed intervals" as a more satisfactory phrase. To him, continuous space might seem a far-fetched abstraction, and if he were to postulate the presence of objects he would hardly suppose them to have definite positions at all instants of time. Certainly, he would have little occasion to invent the differential calculus.

On closer examination the microcosm reveals some degree of coordination. Patches of light are not completely random but appear in more or less ordered sequences. There are times when nothing can be seen, and then again the visual field is dotted with perceptions. Furthermore, these perceptions often indicate a preferred location in space—though they rarely mark a point. The physicist who knows about the microcosm, when noting this modicum of regularity, will of course take it as the occasion for postulating the existence of objects, vaguely localizable in space and somehow progressing from one place to another; his instinct for causation and determination is thus satisfied. But if he had never seen a perfectly continuous path he would hardly regard them as moving in our sense—position and velocity would doubtless be what I have previously called *latent properties* of an object, like anger in a man. He would encounter as much difficulty in the idea of *continu-*

ous motion as we ordinarily do in the suggestion of *discontinuous emergence* in our familiar world.

Properties of atomic objects are like anger of a person in another respect. Our microcosmic observer will see things under two conditions only: either he illuminates them by means of an external light source, or he waits for them to emit photons. In either case their manifestations will be random (to be sure, there are possibilities for "tying down" an atom by forcing it to move in a very small enclosure in a most erratic manner and with great speed—but such cases are the exception and not the rule). The macroscopic physicist feels uneasy about this, and he advances the conjecture that he himself, or incidental circumstances, are to be blamed for the randomness. When things are illuminated, he reasons, they are being bombarded by photons, and their impacts are the random causes of lawless appearance; when atoms are self-luminous, recoils from ejected photons propel the emittors in unpredictable fashion. But how is he going to tell? No observation is possible without the agencies of external or of self-illumination; a control experiment is out of the question. The psychologist can at least ask his subject "Are you angry *because* I am asking you this question?" The physicist can ask his atom only the equivalent of "Are you angry?" Despite all this, it does no harm if the physicist tries to explain the erratic behavior of the atomic world by a reference to causative agencies; it affords him comfort and makes the microcosm seem less strange. The fact is, however, that he is then indulging in a bit of metaphysical speculation, and he ought to be aware of it.

Closer study of phenomena discloses a certain degree of order imposed on randomness even in the Lilliputian world.

139

The *mean* position of what was construed as objects seems to obey definite laws. That is to say, if a list were made of the appearances in space of a group of luminous dots and their mean position were computed at every instant in the manner by which one obtains the point called the center of a population, this center would move more or less in accordance with macroscopic laws. In fact, nature often relieves us of the need for this computation by performing it herself. We have already said that the more distant objects of the microcosm show coherence and a measure of consistency. This is because they are made up of many atoms and large masses of which we can observe only the mean positions; the erratic behavior of individuals is thus obscured and we confront relative certainties.

It is a long journey from the atomic to the celestial sphere, from apparent caprice to the majestic imperturbability of the stars. And yet one can pass from one to the other without changing one's philosophical equipment. The *statistical* regularity, which we noted in the microcosm and which is entirely compatible with individual randomness, can condense itself to practical lawfulness in the domain of large and heavy objects, just as a probability can tend to the limiting value one. This is indeed what happens: Newtonian (classical) mechanics can be shown to be the limiting form of the new branch of physics called quantum mechanics. The universe is therefore still of one piece. Note, however, that the story is not reasonable when told the other way around. Quantum theory is not a limiting form of classical physics, for it cannot be readily conceived how mechanical lawfulness could degenerate into statistical behavior unless the latter had been embryonically present at the start: Statistical regularity is the more general concept and must be regarded as primary. This confers upon the quantum theory the status of logical priority over classical mechanics and over common sense.

Summarizing, we may say that sensory experience in the microcosm lays bare the precariousness of assuming physical properties, like positions and velocities, to be necessarily and at all times possessed by physical systems. They may become latent observables.[1] In particular, continuity and consistency are not always suitable attributes of individual atomic behavior.

The departure from familiar thinking I am suggesting here is so great, the new attitude is so unconventional that consideration of further examples may be desirable to show cause why it should be adopted. Let us therefore study once more the idea of continuous motion in a familiar setting and consider the flight of a firefly in a dark summer night. To the eye, the motion of this insect is not continuous; what it presents is a succession of bright spots or streaks at different places in the observer's field of view. The judgment that this phenomenon represents the uninterrupted passage of an object from one point of space to another is based, strictly speaking, on an interpolation between the bursts of luminosity that are actually perceived. Yet common sense, and indeed scientific description, regard themselves fully justified in performing that ideal supplementation of immediate perception which the interpretation of these sporadic darts as continuous motion demands. The chief reasons for this attitude are the following.

First, the hypothesis of continuous motion is testable through other experience. It is possible to watch the firefly in the daytime, when its progression from point to point

1. The term observable, introduced by Dirac, has come to mean any property of a physical system which can be observed directly or indirectly.

becomes visible. This settles the issue in large part, although it may not convince the inveterate skeptic who feels that, when unilluminated, the firefly behaves like the angels to whom St. Thomas attributed the ability of emerging at separate points without having to traverse the intervening distance. To answer the skeptic, we must demonstrate the simplicity and convenience of the continuity hypothesis. Thus we add, to the fact of partial testability, a second item of evidence of a more rational sort, namely the simplicity of the geometric curve on which the luminous dots are situated. If the interpolated path were very irregular, showed unlikely curvatures and strange convolutions, doubts as to continuity might remain; the smoothness of the plotted trajectory goes a long way toward removing them.

The validity of every scientific theory, even the simplest, rests ultimately on two kinds of evidence: (1) empirical verifiability of some of its consequences, and (2) rational coherence, economy of thought, or simplicity conveyed by the ideas composing the theory. The latter were called metaphysical principles in Chapter I.

Atomic entities, like electrons, present phenomena which, on the purely empirical side, are not unlike the sporadic emergences of a lightning bug at night. To be sure, the electron in an atom cannot be seen. Nevertheless if the results of experiments and observations using the refined techniques of modern physics can be trusted, an electron in what is called a Bohr orbit reveals its position as a random set of points located throughout a region of space in the neighborhood of the classical orbit. More precisely, if a series of position measurements were made while the electron is in the unvarying state known as the ground state of the hydrogen atom, the results would form a probability aggregate of known spatial distribution; the individual positions thus established would dot this region in a curious manner, offering no immediate suggestion as to continuity of motion. Such measurements can actually be made; they involve bombardment of the atom by X-ray photons, and the reflected photons are scattered in the way described.

Thus the question naturally arises: can we regularize those emergences by the same principles which we employed in concluding that the path of the lightning bug was continuous? Or do we confront here a situation calling for entirely different treatment?

Unfortunately, the road leading to empirical verification of the continuity hypothesis is blocked, not merely by incidental obstacles arising from imperfections of measurement or observation, but by infelicities of a fundamental kind. The electron is *intrinsically* too small to be seen; the act of vision, even if it were possible, requires a time too long for a clear ascertainment of instantaneous positions; last but not least important is the fact that elementary particles are promiscuous and indistinguishable entities with a perversity which prevents us from ever being sure that we see the same individual in different observations. If these difficulties seem inessential, if hope still remains that they may be overcome in the future, then we need to remember that their denial contradicts the basic tenets of the quantum theory, the only theory capable of explaining what can in fact be observed about electrons. The conclusion is inescapable; there is no daytime in which the electron's path could be watched.

Let us therefore examine the continuity interpretation from the point of view of simplicity or economy of thought. Here we encounter another failure. A curve drawn through the measured points becomes complicated and aimless, wandering in erratic fashion, with no preference for connecting neighbors, a curve intertwining and crossing itself in obvious labor to accommodate the recorded positions of the particle. Certainly, nothing is gained in ease of conception, in plausibility, or in power of prediction by this familiar artifact.

Thus it is seen that the physical microcosm, the atomic realm, confronts the physicist with a novel kind of problem in interpretation, with a challenge to simplify or rationalize perhaps in ways to which he is not accustomed. And nature is not very generous in providing hints for the solution of this methodological puzzle; the difficulties of direct verification we have already noted are so great that theories cannot be readily exposed to test. The sphinx is non-committal. The physicist has an embarrassing amount of freedom in making his interpretations.

In the end, as we shall see, he was forced to relinquish classical physics and accept description of a more abstract sort, relying on what we have called latent observables, foregoing the facility of visual models and of continuity of motion. But he did this reluctantly. Indeed, he first tried a compromise which still dominates the teaching of quantum mechanics in our elementary courses; he seized upon the proposition that onta are not unique in their physical nature, that they are sometimes one physical entity (particle) and sometimes another (wave). Thus began the belief in the dualism of the nature of elementary particles; it will form the substance of the next section.

3. *The Dualism in the Nature of Onta*

Under certain conditions the points of luminosity visible to our microcosmic observer form a wavelike ensemble; it is therefore not surprising to find physicists supposing in the early stages of the quantum theory that onta are in fact waves, not particles, or that at any rate their motion is somehow guided by waves. This is so important a phase of physical thought that I do not wish to content myself with mere allegorical allusions; let me therefore present some of the specific evidence for the supposition that onta are waves, and contrast it with the evidence suggesting that they are particles.

The two basic entities (onta) which have the longest scientific history are the photon and the electron. One was known as light, the other presented itself in various states of electrification, in lightning discharges, St. Elmo's fires, and so on. We now know that both light and electricity are quantized; the quantum of light was a subject of speculation in Newton's time and became clearly recognized in this century. The quantum of electricity, the electron, was discovered as such by Thomson in 1897. In all preceding centuries light was thought to be a wave; the reasons for this belief will now be summarized.

In the first place, the very mode of propagation of light, its advance along a broad front or in an expanding sphere, recalls the movement of water waves, of ripples in a pond or sound waves in air. This simple analogy is greatly strengthened by mathematical analysis, for there exists a principle discovered by Huygens which explains almost every detail of light propagation in terms of the basic conception that light is a wave. Whether the wave travels in a material medium like the erstwhile ether, or whether it is a less concrete undulation of some sort of field in empty space, is not suggested by this mathematical theory. It requires only the fluctuating amplitudes present in any wave and does not ask what it is that fluctuates; for this reason Huygens' principle, and the theory that light is a wave, was able to survive a great variety of different assumptions as to the substance in which the waves were thought to occur.

When two waves of light coming from the same source are made to travel different paths but are then brought to the same focus again, interference takes place. If a screen or the eye or an optical instrument is placed in the area where the two waves are recombined, dark and bright bands can be observed. The dark bands are explained as places where a trough of the light wave coincides with a crest, so that there is no resultant disturbance; bright bands are loci of constructive interference, where a crest falls on a crest or a trough on a trough and the luminosity is therefore enhanced. Only waves have crests and troughs, hence the occurrence of interference is strong evidence for the wave nature of light.

Light can be polarized, that is, it may be made to take on different properties in different directions transverse to the line of propagation. The substance called polaroid absorbs light vibrations in a certain transverse direction, transmitting with undiminished intensity only a ray of light which has its vibrations in one specific plane. The properties of such polarized light can be investigated in many ways, and the nature of polarization, that is to say, the presence of vibrations in only one plane transverse to the direction of propagation, can be clearly demonstrated. Water waves, too, are transverse, and the similarity in behavior again suggests that light partakes of the properties of transverse waves. *Particles* with different properties in different directions are more difficult to conceive.

If light were a material particle, it ought to have a mass even when the light particle is at rest. Physicists speak of this mass as intrinsic mass or rest mass. We know from

Chapter IV that particles, when moving, do have an increased mass, to be sure, but when a particle is stopped its mass does not become zero. Light shows an altogether different behavior. It too has mass when moving; when a light wave is stopped, however, it ceases to exist, hence its mass becomes zero. Now the only physical entity known to classical physics which has a zero rest mass is a wave, and we reach again the apparently inescapable conclusion that light is a wave.

Particles can be accelerated by forces and sent through a medium with any speed (except for the relativity restriction which limits them to velocities smaller than the velocity of light). This is not true for the waves we encounter in nature. The ripples on the surface of a pond, provided they have a certain wavelength, go with a velocity which is entirely determined by the properties of water; sound waves in air travel with a definite speed which depends on the density and the pressure of the air. In other words, a wave cannot move in a given medium with an arbitrary velocity, its velocity is unique, fixed by the properties of the substance through which it passes. This is precisely what one finds for light. In a given medium, such as vacuum, or air or water, light of a single wavelength travels with a single speed, and no one has ever succeeded in accelerating or retarding it by forces. Hence again the conclusion that light must be undulatory.

Our story is almost convincing. It is disturbing, therefore, to learn that a contradictory proposition, namely that light consists of particles, can be supported by equally strong experimental evidence. We review some of this evidence below, mentioning at once that at a time when less was known about the properties of light than is available today, the term "photon" was coined to emphasize its corpuscular

147

properties. A photon is held to be a single "particle" of light, insofar as light can be said to consist of particles. Some writers ascribe the photon hypothesis to Newton. Historically this can hardly be justified, for in the Queries at the end of his book on "Opticks" Newton states clearly that he conceived of light as a hybrid having both particle and wave-like qualities. According to his view, light particles proceeding through the ether set up waves in it; these waves cause interference and determine by their reaction upon the particles what he calls their periodic moods of easy transmission and easy reflection. This complicated picture has now been abandoned completely; it has no relevance for contemporary quantum theory.

When a black solid body is heated to incandescence, it emits light of many frequencies. Sent through a spectroscope, this light produces a "black body spectrum," in which different frequencies are present with different characteristic intensities. Very low and very high frequencies are weak; maximum intensity occurs at intermediate frequencies, for instance in the blue-green part of the spectrum for light coming from the sun (which in the technical sense is very nearly a black body). The distribution of frequencies can be analyzed in accordance with the laws of classical mechanics and electrodynamics, but the result expected on the basis of that analysis is not in fact observed. A great deal of effort was therefore spent upon this problem in the early years of the present century, all without avail. In 1906 Max Planck took a radical departure from classical reasoning. He investigated, first in rather tentative fashion, the theoretical consequences of the assumption that light is emitted by the molecules composing the incandescent black body, not in the manner of a continuous wave, but as if it were sent off in darts or bundles, each containing a definite amount of energy. Surprisingly, he thus obtained the actual frequency distribution in the black body spectrum. Exact numerical agreement resulted if the energy within a quantum, i.e., a photon, is taken to be proportional to the frequency of the photon itself, say ν, the constant of proportionality being a number which in c.g.s. units has the value 6.62×10^{-27}. It is denoted by h and called Planck's constant. In symbols, then, the energy of a photon is

$$E = h\nu$$

Accordingly, the energy resident within a light wave is not distributed continuously through space but is concentrated in small bundles or packages, each of which contains an amount of energy proportional to the frequency of the light, the universal constant of proportionality being Planck's constant h. This state of affairs is often described by saying that light is quantized.

Further evidence for the correctness of this picture is supplied by an examination of the photoelectric effect, as Einstein was the first to discover. When light falls upon a metal surface, electrons are emitted by the surface. These electrons, which normally reside within the metal, obtain energy from the impinging light as it is absorbed by the metal, and when each electron has accumulated sufficient energy it is able to tear itself loose from its metallic confinement. One can measure the amount of energy needed for the electron to free itself from the metal by methods well-known to the electronic physicist, and it is possible to compute the time in which a light wave of known intensity conveys the needed energy to an electron.

If the illumination of the metal surface is very feeble, then it might be that the time required for an electron to accumulate enough energy to leave the metal is as long as

149

one minute. Assuming that light is a wave and that the electron withdraws energy from it in continuous fashion, one concludes that the light must shine upon the metal surface for at least one minute before electrons can make their photoelectric leap. After this period of one minute, electrons should all swarm out of the metal in one great volley. This, however, is not observed. On the contrary, a few electrons come forth almost at once without waiting the period of one minute; these show no regard for conservation of energy, and they are followed by others in random sequence, many of them emerging a long time after the minute is up.

All this could be understood quite easily if light consisted of darts in photon fashion, and if these darts were distributed at random through the region of what we normally call the light wave. For suppose that these photons strike the electrons of the metal as rain strikes pebbles. During each impact the electron then gets the full amount of energy of the photon, or at least a large fraction of it, and may thus be enabled at once to jump out of the metal. This qualitative idea takes on precision and compelling force when it is coupled with Planck's discovery, that is, when an energy equal in amount to $h\nu$ is attributed to every photon of frequency of ν. Einstein showed that all the features of the photoelectric ejection of electrons from metals by light waves are satisfactorily accounted for by this corpuscular model of photons.

X-rays are light waves of very small wavelengths emitted by a metal when its surface is struck by electrons. In a sense, therefore, the production of X-rays is precisely the reverse of the photoelectric effect. It is interesting to note that the production of X-rays can be explained in precisely the same way as the photoelectric effect. Agreement with experience

150

results if it is supposed that an electron, having an energy $h\nu$, converts it into photon energy according to the Planck formula, $E = h\nu$. If this explanation is true, high energy electrons impinging upon the metal should release X-rays of great frequency, and this is indeed observed with quantitative precision.

Most striking evidence in favor of the corpuscular hypothesis comes from the Compton effect, which involves the scattering of light by individual particles such as electrons. If we picture the electron as a corpuscle, and imagine a wave to be incident upon it, the corpuscle will reflect and scatter the wave without changing its frequency. The frequency is the most indestructible characteristic of a wave; when a wave has once been produced its wavelength can be changed; its speed may alter when it passes into another medium; its intensity can diminish. But its frequency is indelibly marked upon it and survives all these vicissitudes. It is an innate characteristic which the wave retains throughout its life.

Hence it is remarkable to observe, as Arthur Compton did, that in the act of being reflected by an electron, light does change its frequency. This grotesque violation of the principle of wave motion finds a simple explanation when the act of reflection is viewed as an interaction of two corpuscles. For if one calculates what happens when a corpuscle of energy $h\nu$ (the photon) collides with a particle of mass m (the electron) it turns out that $h\nu$ after the collision will be a little smaller than it was before. Since h is a universal constant, this implies that ν has changed. The amount of change is completely in accord with the results of this simple collision problem. It is now known that the Doppler effect, originally explained by the wave model, can also be understood in corpuscular terms.

151

Finally, let us recall that light waves can trip Geiger counters. These are closed cylinders in which a gas at low pressures is maintained under a high electric potential difference. If the potential were raised very slightly, an electrical discharge in the form of a spark would pass. A charged particle entering the vessel will cause a sufficient electrical disturbance to raise the potential and force a current to flow. It is therefore easy to see that a cosmic ray or a fast moving ion when entering the counter will activate it and produce a discharge. But it is difficult to understand how a wave can do this, how it can have the sharp directional qualities, the dartlike character, which makes it go through one counter and not through another which is placed nearby. Yet this is what happens, and it bespeaks again the photon nature of light.

To summarize, light manifests itself as a wave in one set of experiments or observations, as a corpuscle or a particle in other. Is it proper to say that it has a dual nature, that it changes its properties as we pass from one class of observations to the other? The question is a weighty one, for the dualism affects not only the nature of light but also the nature of the electron as the following considerations show.

The electron was originally regarded as a particle; hence we present first the evidence in favor of that hypothesis. Electrons were discovered in an electrical discharge, in an evacuated glass vessel containing two electrodes. When a high potential difference is applied to these electrodes a discharge takes place, and at sufficiently low pressures of the gas a luminous bundle of rays is seen to be emitted at right angles to the cathode. These are called cathode rays, and they represent the first historical instance of a ray of pure electrons. If the rays are allowed to pass between charged condenser plates, one above and one below the discharge tube, they are bent away from the negative and toward the positive plate. This behavior demonstrates two things: first, that the constituents of the beam carry negative charges, for they are attracted by the positive and repelled by the negative plate; second, that the constituents have masses, for the beam is not sharply bent upwards to the positive plate but continues with a slight upward curvature showing that the electrons have inertia and, therefore, mass. It is inconceivable that a wave could carry mass or charge; hence these observations are clear evidence for the corpuscular nature of electrons. They can be varied and made more precise. For instance, by passing the cathode rays through a magnetic field, there results a curvature of the beam which leads directly to a determination of the charge-to-mass ratio of the electrons. Millikan's celebrated oil drop experiment, in which he was able to arrest the fall of an oil drop bearing an electron by electrostatic attraction, gave a very accurate measure of its charge. These experiments jointly therefore allow the calculation of charge and mass of an electron separately, thus providing strongest confirmation of the proposition that electrons are corpuscles.

There are ways in which the velocities of these electrons can be measured, and these velocities are not unique. They depend on the acceleration which the electrons have undergone and range all the way from zero to the velocity of light. Hence they violate the principle we found true for waves, namely, that they can travel with only one velocity determined by the nature of the medium through which they pass.

If a weak beam of electrons is allowed to impinge upon the surface of a zinc sulphide screen, the individual impacts cause visible scintillations. Nothing but a corpuscular hypothesis can account for this appearance. Equally dramatic and equally indicative of particle behavior is the shot noise heard when a microphone is inserted in an amplifier circuit. The noise results from the fluctuations in the plate current of the vacuum tube, whose origin is in the fact that discrete amounts of charge are transferred by individual electrons.

Like the photon, the electron also presents itself in the guise of a wave. This wholly unexpected character was proposed for the first time in 1924 by Louis DeBroglie and on the basis of purely theoretical arguments. DeBroglie wrote an epoch-making doctor's dissertation in which he investigated the formal consequences of combining the theory of relativity with Planck's quantum hypothesis. He concluded by showing that the electron, and along with the electron all so-called material particles, must have wavelike properties, in particular, a particle of mass m must have a wavelength in accordance with the now famous formula $\lambda = h/mv$. Here h is again Planck's constant, m the mass of the moving particle and v its velocity. The greater the mass and the velocity of the moving entity, the smaller its wavelength. DeBroglie's theory is based on nothing more than a postulate of mathematical consistency between the relativity principle of Einstein and the quantum hypothesis of Planck, and it does not specify any medium in which these waves occur.

Quite naturally this theory met with a good deal of skepticism because of the strangeness of its conclusions and its wholly formal contentions. The sensation was great therefore when in 1927 Davisson and Germer of the Bell Telephone Company discovered by accident that an electron beam, reflected from a nickel crystal, showed a diffraction pattern very much like that produced by X-rays which are known to be waves. The wavelength of the electrons could

154

be computed from the diffraction pattern, and lo and behold, it agreed very nearly with DeBroglie's formula.

One year later G. P. Thomson, the son of J. J. Thomson, who first established the corpuscular nature of electrons, sent electrons through metal foils and observed the formation of diffraction rings very much like those produced when X-rays pass through crystalline powders. From these observations he was able to calculate the wavelength causing the interference pattern, and it turned out to be in complete accord with DeBroglie's formula.

Another year later German scientists succeeded in diffracting electrons by means of ruled gratings, that is to say, by the use of the very same device which spreads light waves into a spectrum of colors. The observed spectral lines again yielded to the DeBroglie formula. At this stage, the undulatory nature of electrons was established beyond doubt, and physicists began to use their new knowledge in the successful design of electron microscopes. All experiments which previously were thought to speak so definitely for the wave nature of light had now been performed for electrons as well.

Light, we saw, was a transverse wave and therefore capable of polarization. Even this last attribute, polarization, was shared by the electron, for it turned out that the electron "spin," well-known from previous experiments, and ordinarily regarded as a rotation of the particle about its axis, could be interpreted as the direction of polarization of the electron waves.

At this point a person accustomed to thinking classically about photons and electrons will see before him two alternatives. The first, and by far the easier to accept, is to regard each entity as having the properties of *both,* particle and wave. It might be supposed, for example, that the electron

155

is actually a particle but that in its motion it sets up a wave which guides its course. This idea, it will be recalled, originated with Newton who applied it to his light corpuscles; it has been revived in several forms to explain De-Broglie's discovery but has never been found to do justice to the experimental facts. A particle plus a guiding wave is not a satisfactory solution of the dualistic dilemma.

The second alternative supposes that electrons and photons are either *one* or *the other* on different occasions, and suggests that there are some experiments in which they have to be treated as waves, others in which they appear as particles. Admittedly, this view does violence to one's monistic intuition, but in an age of positivism one may have to assuage one's metaphysical conscience by relying on facts and logic alone, yielding the natural desire for unity of explanation, the philosophic instinct which abhors a fundamental ambiguity in the realm of nature's ultimate constituents. Men have tried to live with this solution, they have coined words like "wavicle" to hide their embarrassment, or to make it endurable, for when a word is coined the validity of what it implies is more easily accepted. A "wavicle" was alleged to be an entity which is sometimes a wave and sometimes a particle.

It affords relief to be able to report that neither the name nor the concept survives. Among the reasons for its rejection is the recognition of a fact, already implicit in the foregoing accounts, which even the dualistic hypothesis of different natures on different occasions cannot readily comprehend. For it happens that *both* natures may be needed to explain what happens on a *single* occasion, in a single experiment. The dualistic hypothesis attempted to make an *on* into a chameleon; it then found that its chameleon had to be red and green at the same time. This is best understood, perhaps, in connection with an experiment in which an electron *must* be conceived as a particle in some phases and as a wave in others, all during a single transit across a physical apparatus. To round out our argument I anticipate the lesson we shall learn and give away the clue to the resolution of the dualistic dilemma at once: it is impossible to assign a unique position to an electron at every instant of time; position is a *latent* observable in the previously established meaning, as are other qualities like velocity and energy. This, in a certain sense, permits the retention of an integral, even though abstract, identity of onta.

Our experiment involves an electron gun and two screens, S_1 and S_2, placed in vertical positions, S_2 some distance behind S_1. At the center of S_1 there is a small circular hole; the electron gun is pointed at the hole and sends electrons through it. These electrons impinge on screen S_2 and form an impact pattern. The electron gun is a cylindrical tube which carries at the end away from the screen an incandescent filament emitting electrons. These electrons pass through diaphragms placed across the axis of the cylinder and carrying suitable potentials, so that as they go through the exit end of the gun they are accelerated to speeds which can be adjusted by the experimenter. Electrons fall upon S_1, some of them going through the hole and impinging upon S_2. The resulting impact pattern is a series of concentric rings as depicted in Figure 11.

This figure is characteristic of a diffraction pattern made

Fig. 11

by light waves passing through a similar circular hole. Hence it is natural to believe that the electrons are indeed waves as they pass through the hole in S_1. But they are certainly not waves when they are moving through the electron gun, for only particles carrying charges can be accelerated by an electric field. They must likewise be regarded as particles when they impinge on S_2, for it is possible to see scintillations, i.e., individual impacts of point-like entities, upon the surface of the screen. Are we then to suppose that an electron in this experiment begins its career as a particle, transforms itself into a wave, and ends up as a particle again all in less than the wink of an eye? Even if we are willing to accept this interpretation as a theoretical possibility, it could easily be proved wrong by one added feature in our experiment. If we close the hole in S_1 and observe the impacts on this screen, again by watching for scintillations, they will be seen to occur. In this case, we are apparently forced to conclude, the electron, knowing that there was no hole, did not bother to alter its nature from particle to wave.

Clearly such reasoning is absurd. Let us therefore see what happens when we maintain consistently the identity of our electrons. It will hardly do to regard a single electron as a wave throughout its course, since at both ends of our experiment, that is to say wherever it was directly observed, it appeared like a corpuscle. In a sense its wave nature is only an inferred item of knowledge, something which we conclude must be present in the neighborhood of the hole in order that the observed phenomena shall make sense. We shall therefore speak of it in the sequel as a particle passing through holes and impinging on a screen.

To make things interesting let us introduce *two* circular holes in S_1, one slightly above the other. Now the impact pattern on S_2 has the appearance of Figure 12. Note that it is not a superposition of two patterns, each arising from a single hole, but a completely different arrangement of destructive and constructive interferences. If we close one hole the pattern immediately reverts from that of Figure 12

Fig. 12

to that of Figure 11, all in accordance with the expected behavior of waves. But as we have seen, a reference to waves is no longer legitimate, and we are attempting to explain happenings in terms of corpuscles. An electron going through the upper hole must clearly have modified its behavior because of the presence of the lower hole. Is there then some interaction between the electron in one hole and the other hole through which it did not pass? Are there forces, called into play by the supernumerary hole, which affect the path of a given electron? Consideration of these straightforward possibilities in terms of known interactions rules them out.

Remember now that each electron when it arrives at S_2 makes but a single hit, and that the total pattern is the result of many successive impacts. Its overall regularity results from collaboration of, at least some sort of correlation between, the various electrons passing through the holes. But correlation or collaboration between different electrons responsible for the pattern can reasonably be ascribed to the individuals only as long as they have a chance to collaborate, that is, so long as they approach the holes together in a swarm of limited size, or in sufficiently rapid succession to have an opportunity for conniving.

This point can be tested by making the stream of electrons very feeble, by accelerating single electrons at widely separated instants of time. This experiment was actually performed by the Russian investigators, Biberman, Sushkin, and Fabrikant. The fate of each electronic bullet can now be safely assumed to be independent of the others, and one might expect to obtain on S_2 a distribution showing none of the regular features of Figure 12, but exhibiting merely a random Gaussian arrangement of impacts. Such, however, is far from true; as the observer waits he will witness the gradual evolution of a pattern just like Figure 12. One now wants to ask with pardonable anthropomorphic bias: if each electron had its own behavior determined by the hole through which it passed, how did it know through which hole its predecessor had gone and its successors were to go? How did it achieve correlation with the action of its precursors and successors which is so manifest in the regular pattern on S_2? Short of assuming some mysterious sort of influence pervading through time and relating the electrons in this very attenuated beam to one another, there seems to be no reasonable answer to these questions—unless we are willing to strike out the implicit premise that at every instant of time the electron had a definite position. Denying this, we can admit that an individual electron, rather than passing through a single hole, passed through both holes at once, and in this way we avoid speaking of an influence between an electron and the hole through which it did not pass, or a strange force acting through time. Or conversely, to admit that an electron passes through two holes at once is to grant that during this accomplishment, it did not have a determinate position in space. The electron can be in states in which a determinate position cannot be assigned to it.

Alfred North Whitehead spoke of the fallacy of simple location. He meant to warn his readers that there are things, among them the most fundamental things in the universe, which may be quite real and yet not permit description in terms of definite locations. Human thoughts and emotions, abstract qualities like love and friendship evidently fall into this class, but the physicist has not been willing, and many scientists are not willing even today, to acknowledge that the onta of inanimate nature share some of the qualities of this realm.

In retrospect, then, we reach the following conclusion. We have considered two alternatives: (1) That an electron is *both* a particle *and* a wave; (2) it is *either* one *or* the other, more particularly it is sometimes one and sometimes the other. Both alternatives were found unsatisfactory. There remains a third possibility, namely that the electron be *neither* one *nor* the other. Its correctness is strongly supported by the inference we were forced to draw with respect to its position. The electron cannot be said to have a determinate position at every instant of time; hence it must be something more abstract than the concrete thing we took it to be. It is something we can no longer picture in terms of visual models. Perhaps Laotse was right; insistence on visual clarity can forestall understanding. Henceforth, then, we shall feel free to inquire into modes of description of onta which do not burden them from the beginning with the paraphernalia of mechanisms and with the features of common sense. Even if the electron cannot be pictured in such terms, its nature, though abstract, may nonetheless

161

be perfectly self-consistent, unique and manageable by competent theory.

The dualism, widely espoused by scientists in the earlier decades of this century, has now been sublimated into the current concept of complementarity. This term was introduced by Niels Bohr; its use animates his writings, for he regards complementarity, the need for dual types of description of human experience, as inevitable, as grounded in the nature of things and in the limitations of man's understanding. The appeal is to the deeper concerns of our being, somewhat reminiscent of a modern trend in theology which suggests that the knowledge of divinity is possible only through myths, allegories, and paradoxes.

Eloquent accounts of the complementarity principle are found in the lectures and publications of Robert J. Oppenheimer.[2] He sees examples of complementary reasoning in the following pairs of theories, each of which is devoted to the understanding of a specific realm of problems: the kinetic theory of gases and the dynamics of molecular motions; the biological theory of life and the physico-chemical description of life; introspective analysis of consciousness and its behavioristic description.

The philosophic status of complementarity as a basic principle of explanation requires very careful appraisal. I shall not undertake it in this book but leave it as a challenge and hope to return to it in a later publication.

4. *Waves of Probability*

If solid matter, mechanism, continuous motion fade away, does science likewise disintegrate? The answer is an unqualified no. Profound changes in philosophic concep-

2. Notably in *Science and the Common Understanding*, R. J. Oppenheimer, Simon and Schuster, New York (1954).

tion are necessary, but the quintessence of scientific method remains. The required changes culminate in the final realization that events, point-like essences, and particles are not the last things that matter; nor can they, as the preceding examples indicate, be caught individually in the net of scientific determination. The scientist must renounce *in principle* his attempts to predict individual occurrences— even though in many instances he can still do this sufficiently well for practical purposes; he must confer his attention upon statistical aggregates of happenings, on ensembles of essences, on probabilities. These probabilities are at present his last concerns; they are the physical quantities that figure in his theories—they are, strange to conceive, the medium in which his waves exist! I hasten to fill this seemingly absurd discussion with more meaningful content.

If Bohr's picture of the hydrogen atom were correct, the electron, in its lowest energy state, ought to move exactly on a circle with a perfectly definite speed. Yet it is possible to ascertain the position of the electron, albeit somewhat indirectly. When a series of position measurements (scattering of X-rays) is made and interpreted, they distribute themselves in random fashion about the Bohr circle, much as indicated in Figure 13. The electron is found a greater

Fig. 13

number of times in the neighborhood of the circle than in any other equally large domain. But we recall from the example of the firefly that these positions are not taken on progressively as one goes around the circle: emergences on the left of the figure alternate erratically with appearances on the right, and with those on the bottom and on the top. There is no rhyme or reason in the interpretation of this pattern as *motion;* what makes sense is the concentration of points in any given area, their statistical density or, still more technically, the probability of finding the electron in a given small area dA of the figure.

Now let us reflect upon probabilities. A die is a physical object whose properties can be described in many ways. Normally one would characterize it by its visual appearance (it is a regular cube with the numbers from 1 to 6 on its faces), but one could also employ the structure of the material of which it is made, its reaction to X-rays or to infrared radiation. None of these modes of description excludes the others; custom and familiarity recommend description in terms of visual appearance. Yet it is reasonable to designate this particular physical object by means of the events that happen when it is used in certain ways, e.g., one might say it is something which can be thrown and yields the numbers from 1 to 6, without making reference to its geometric appearance. One might add that the numbers from 1 to 6 appear with equal probability, namely 1/6, which means that in 120 tosses there will be an approximately equal number of ones, twos, etc., each occurring approximately 20 times. Assignment of probabilities means in some respects a great deal more than visual appearance, for it allows the inference that the die is unloaded, that its center of gravity is at its geometric center. In a sense, this description is complementary to the others, and it may remain meaningful when others fail.

If we couple the description in terms of visual appearances with the latter probability description, we obtain a theory which may serve as an explanation of the probability description, since this coupling allows deduction of the probabilities from the visual picture. Understanding the fact that the die has 6 faces with one number on each, and invoking the laws of mechanics, one can infer the probabilities. But this does not indicate that there is a unique correspondence between the visual states and the probable events. The latter fall into 6 categories, the appearance of a 1, 2, . . . 6. The former are exceedingly numerous, since the die can exhibit an infinite variety of positions relative to the observer. A person accustomed to the probability description will ascribe to the die 6 properties and assign a probability to each. But these properties or observables from the point of view of the die thrower, i.e., the appearance of a number on the top face of the die, resting on a table, do not exhaust all visual states and may be of little interest to the physicist. If we ask, what property in the sense just defined is present when the die is held in someone's hand, or while it falls, the answer is: none. The die is in a state in which the probability observables in question are not "enacted." In the same way it may be said that the position of the electron was not enacted when it approached the two holes in the screen S_2, discussed in our earlier example (p. 159).

The visual description of the die is compatible with its probability description and may, as we have seen, be regarded as its explanation (cf. Chapter III). Let the former be denoted by A, the latter by B. The relation between the two may then be stated in the form: if A then B. But it has also been shown that this relation is not reversible, that B may well be true or meaningful without A. As a matter of fact A is in a sense like classical physics, B like quantum mechanics, and A has consequences besides B which are unacceptable.

As a description of quantum mechanical reasoning, the example of the die is not satisfactory, for it still allows us to visualize the condition of the die when it does not exhibit the observables under consideration. Let us then imagine a closed box equipped with a screen. Whenever we shake the box a number from 1 to 6 appears on the screen, and the relative frequency of these numbers is 1/6. Doubtless we would wonder whether perhaps the box contained a die or some similar mechanical device subjected to random tosses, together with some electrical and optical equipment flashing the result on the screen. We now open the box and discover, much to our amazement, that there is no die, nor any other obvious random device responsible for the probability distribution of the numbers appearing on the screen.

Next, we might surmise a subtler design, perhaps a combination of electrical circuits with random properties, hidden somewhere in the box and producing the statistical results. But a search for them yields nothing; the most painstaking investigation both empirical and theoretical, complete decomposition of the box so far as present techniques permit it, reveals no mechanism of the sort expected: the box is simply of a nature that, when you shake it, numbers appear, and these numbers display a definite probability distribution. According to the most widely accepted (Copenhagen) interpretation of quantum mechanics, that box is like an electron (or a photon, or any on), and we have to learn to live with it. Position, velocity, and many

166

other observables are like the numbers that appear haphazardly but with statistical consistency. Einstein wondered, when thinking about this state of affairs, whether God played dice, and he rejected that hypothesis. Strictly, we must say—whether there be a God or not—there are no dice; things just happen that way.

Many threads of evidence, less allegorical than the ones here presented and carefully examined with experimental and theoretical rigor, are woven together into the fabric of the quantum theory, a highly mathematical science. Its main feature, however, is not difficult to grasp: this new discipline has ceased to speak of visual states, of electrons and photons moving in space and time, of miniature clockworks inside atoms; it has relinquished its reference to individual, single events. These are important only as instances in a probability aggregate. When quantum mechanics describes the hydrogen atom, it employs variables which yield at once the pattern of Figure 12 but not one of its dots; it permits the inference of a similar probability distribution for the electron's velocity, energy, angular momentum, but not point values for any of these observables.

If mathematics is the queen of the sciences, presumably because of the cogency and precision of its predictions and its supremacy over chance, then physics in its own estimation was certainly the queen's consort because it, too, prided itself upon possessing these very talents in its description of the inanimate world. Such claims have now been abandoned; statistical reasoning, long regarded as appropriate and necessary in the social sciences, has now been recognized as the last resort for physics as well.

In saying this we are speaking about fundamental matters of principle. Practically very little has been changed in the visible world around us. For it happens that the probabilities of quantum mechanics, when calculated for the large and heavy objects of our common experience, congeal to certainties, much as they would for a die so biased that it must always fall one way. In more technical language, the principles of quantum mechanics reduce to the laws of classical mechanics in the limit of large and massive bodies, yielding probabilities for the outcome of observations upon them which are not 1/2 or 0.76, as they would be for the observables of electrons and photons, but something like 0.99999. . . . Hence there is no contradiction between Newton and Heisenberg or Schrödinger; the arena is peaceful, and we understand in retrospect why classical mechanics could be as successful as it was despite its shortcomings.

Quantum mechanics is sometimes called wave mechanics. Aside from its historical origin (DeBroglie gave a first though fragmentary account of the new science in terms of waves), this phrase has adequate justification. For it turns out that an elementary "particle," if contained in a box and left to its own devices, will develop a probability distribution with respect to position which has nodes and loops conforming to the DeBroglie wavelength. At the nodes, the probability is zero, i.e., the particle will never be encountered at the nodes, it will be found most frequently at the loops. The waves are, in a strange but perfectly simple sense, waves of probability. A free particle in a box is the elementary example through which most students are introduced to the new subject, hence the favorite name, wave mechanics.

In general, however, the probabilities are not satisfactorily described as waves. Nor are they constant in time, as previous examples suggest. A probability may be a function of space—different points of space presenting different occasions for the emergence of observables—and they may in addition be functions of the time. Again, while unfamiliar, this situation is by no means incomprehensible. Countries tolerating slot machines occasionally change their regulations regarding them, forcing owners to alter the odds of their machines by mechanical adjustments. This makes probabilities functions of the time. Travellers on MATS, who tend to be grounded in the Azores on transatlantic flights and there associate with one-armed bandits, report such periodic variations.

Chapter VII

REALITY, DETERMINISM, AND
HUMAN FREEDOM

1. *Scientific Law in a Random Universe**

Before drawing philosophic consequences from the new aspects of our atomic world, let us stay in it one further moment and see what has happened to the concept of a scientific law. Is it lost altogether, or is there still a residue of regularity significant enough to be called a law? Galileo would have found it difficult to demonstrate to the inhabitants of the atomic world the validity of the laws of free fall. Were we to transfer his experiments to the microcosm, we should have to take note of the fact that there are no continuously visible small bodies. Furthermore, remembering the fact that a body consists of many loosely coherent molecules, we consider it wise to deal at once with a large collection of objects. Hence we do what, macroscopically speaking, would be called gathering a handful of stones. True, this figure of speech is hardly descriptive of our exact procedures. For the stones are but intermittent patches of luminosity, and to confine them to the space of our hand is a difficult task. When transferred to the hand they are

---

*This section, which treats finer, somewhat controversial points of atomic theory, may be omitted by the general reader without detriment to the continuity of our main arguments.

171

not densely packed nor do they stay at rest; all indications are that they jostle and bounce about, and there seems to be no way of quieting them down.

This unruly collection of bodies is dropped from a place high above ground, perhaps from some microcosmic leaning tower, and their progress is carefully recorded. It is impossible, as we have seen, to trace a single stone, our record being a multiplicity of individual light emissions or reflections. Yet there is some semblance of coherence, especially to an observer far away who is unable to distinguish the light flashes coming from individual stones. To him the falling group has the appearance of a swarm of fireflies which is clustered fairly tightly at the beginning but diffuses into a larger and larger assemblage of luminous dots as it approaches the ground. When all the facts are assembled our observer reports: (1) He was unable to trace unambiguously the path of any individual stone. (2) The center of the swarm seemed to move with an acceleration of 32.2 ft/sec², i.e., in perfect accord with the macroscopic law of falling bodies. (3) The swarm grew larger and thinned out as time went on.

At this point we, who are accustomed to the regular behavior of falling things, are strongly tempted to read their regularity into the microcosm. Every stone, we are prone to say, obeyed exactly the laws of motion as it fell. The reasons why we failed to observe it are not hard to see. First, we only caught glimpses of an individual stone and did not trouble to reconstruct its complete path. Second, it was admitted that the stones were not at rest in the beginning. Hence the initial conditions of motion were different for different individuals and their spreading during the fall should have been expected. And so we go on to assert with apparent safety: *If* we had known the velocity and the position of every particle at the moment of its release we could have calculated its path, and the whole firefly phenomenon could have been predicted.

The argument just stated attempts a *mechanistic denial of atomic uncertainties*. It considers motions as essentially continuous, unique, and determinate, and it blames other physical agencies for the vagaries manifest in observations. Before turning to specific forms of the argument, I wish to examine it on general philosophic grounds and appraise its value as a methodological directive.

The argument is an extrapolation of ordinary experience with things of normal size. It is highly questionable, however, whether an observer familiar with the ways of the microcosm would have need for an hypothesis of detailed predictability and consequently whether an investigator who regards the atomic world as primary should properly be disposed to make it. Perhaps these are matters of methodological preference. Let us therefore see what the argument nets us in the way of advantages, or of simplicity of description.

Practical advantages, aside from a certain satisfaction of our intuition, do not result from the hypothesis that atomic uncertainties are due to mechanical agencies. No theory has yet been proposed to render the vagaries understandable in detail, none is able to predict them. Indeed Heisenberg's principle, when disengaged from the "explanations" with which physicists so liberally suffuse it, says precisely that such predictions are impossible.

With respect to simplicity, the case against the mechanistic argument is even stronger. There is a parallel to it in the theory of the ether, which we examined in Chapter v. This theory made, in effect, two assertions. One was that space is a medium capable of transmitting electrical and gravitational influences; the second was more particular and insisted in assigning the familiar properties of *material* media to the ether field. The hypothesis was finally discarded because the models invented to account for the behavior of the medium violated every canon of conceptual simplicity. Quite analogously, the facts of the microcosm are being explained, first by the postulate that *there are, indeed, permanent entities called electrons, protons, and so forth;* to this, the scientist who argues for the reduction of atomic uncertainties in terms involving insufficient knowledge, unforeseen interactions, and the like, adds the further thesis that the *postulated entities have the familiar mechanistic properties* of our more primitive experience. This latter thesis complicates matters needlessly; unless it is eliminated we may waste time in wrestling with problems whose very artificiality, like the structure of an ether molecule, denies their importance.

Neither of the last two italicized propositions is obvious. The imputation of permanent existence to an atomic stone that reveals its presence only in the manner of a firefly, indeed with lesser consistency than a firefly, is already a posit not wholly required by the observations. This assumption, however, has proved helpful and is incorporated in most valid theories of nature. There are those who doubt it, among them so distinguished a person as Erwin Schrödinger, whose work created the quantum theory. If I interpret his view, kindly communicated to me in correspondence, correctly he holds that even the existence of onta is a latent quality. I shrink at the moment from taking this radical step and retain the notion of permanent existence. Assignment of *exact position at all times,* however, which is demanded by the mechanist, is another, in fact a more risky, hypothesis, as is shown by the circumstance that no

174

theory embracing it seems to have as yet fully succeeded. This latter hypothesis should therefore be abandoned.

A particularized version of the mechanistic argument we are criticizing is the following. Granted that the luminous spots accompanying what is called the motion of a microcosmic stone (e.g., an atom) do not mark a simple continuous path. The reason—says the argument—is to be seen in the unavoidable recoil momentum imparted to the stone by the photon it emits. This causes it to zigzag in a peculiar manner, the corners of its path being made luminous by emissions. If the explanation stops at this point it is innocuous, for it adds nothing of scientific or cognitive value to the patent unpredictability of the stone's behavior. If the argument goes on to give directions for computing the trajectory, it fails.

The idle theory which endeavors to restore continuity by cryptic supplementation of observable facts can take other forms. For instance, if the stone is not self-luminous but perceived by reflected light, the theory can say that the reflected photon disturbed its motion unpredictably; if the stone manifests its presence by collision with another object, the latter can be blamed. Nature's perversity seems forever to prevent the argument from becoming specific or, as I should prefer to put it, seems always to grant mechanism a hiding place. In sum: Man's inability to trace the path of atomic objects is grounded in something far more serious than ignorance; its roots lie in actual indetermination of perceptions. And finally, it should be pointed out that the argument, even when accepted, will in our example not account correctly for the spreading of the swarm of stones at it "falls." This involves what physicists call "diffusion of a wave packet" and has no macrocosmic counterpart. It is thus necessary to take the lawlessness of the microcosm as it affects individual objects at its face value, to desist from trying to embellish it.

But it is quite essential that we recognize the regularity-in-the-mean exhibited by the center of the swarm of stones as it fell. How are these facts to be reconciled? What is it in the individual particle that makes it obey laws of the aggregate? Does it know what the other particles are doing and behave in relative conformity with them? Is an attracting force holding all particles together while some sort of individualistic repulsion keeps them apart? Physics holds neither of these specific suppositions to be adequate. It proceeds on the most neutral plane that will join regularity-in-the-mean with individual caprice; it assigns neither purposes nor forces, but colorless *probabilities* as innate qualities to the microcosmic stones. This is clearly the least committal and the most efficacious course in such circumstances.

The lessons drawn from the falling swarm of stones, which concern the laws of mechanics, might have been derived from any other branch of atomic physics. For example, the laws of *optics* in the microcosm—to take one final example—are equally as peculiar as those of mechanics. On heating a large body it is found to glow, not with uniform incandescence, but with pointlike luminous spurts of different colors. As the temperature is raised, the bluer ones begin to predominate at the expense of the redder scintillations. No law suggests what color will appear at a given point at any specified time, but in the aggregate the color distribution agrees with Planck's law at every instant. A small object (a single atom), too, may be subjected to heat treatment and become self-luminous. But the light it emits is not continuous; it reminds us even more strongly of a firefly in the dark, except that now the emissions are in different colors. No rule governs the details of the color sequence, yet in the long run the frequency of the individual color obeys the laws of quantum theory. It may surprise us, however, that every elementary kind of body has its own assortment of colors by which it can be identified, the irregularity of sequence notwithstanding.

These examples may be regarded as fairly typical of the microcosm. They defy lawful description when attention is focussed on emergent, incidental, perceptual detail, yielding orderly pattern only when treated en masse.

Regularity attaches to *probabilities*. Indeed what was mistaken for the fundamental lawfulness of individual events in older science stands revealed as the conformity of probabilities having values near one. To disregard these laws would be to abandon the whole of classical physics. Their significance remains; but the philosopher must recognize that basically these laws no longer speak of events but of the probabilities of events.

2. *Reality in the Microcosm*

Our bewildering experience may be summed up in a simple question not often faced candidly by physicists: *What things are real in the atomic world?* On the ordinary scale of magnitudes a similar reflection hardly arose. What we saw was describable by continuous processes and by accurate laws relating to individual events. Perception was predictable, the emergent and the incidental were surprising but normal features of the one regular face of nature. Atomic nature presents two faces and therewith a dilemma.

Or is there no dilemma? Suppose you heard an airplane in the sky and located it straight overhead. You look away, and after a moment you observe it again, noting to your astonishment that it is at an entirely different point in the sky. After a while you observe it once more overhead. Would you not conclude that you were mistaken at least once about the location of the plane? Nevertheless, as sense impressions, all three observations were real enough; so real that each might have been the occasion for a definite course of action under critical circumstances. If you discredit any of them it is not because it is less real as an observation, but because it is incompatible with the detailed lawfulness of nature, which does not allow a plane to jump from one place to another spontaneously. In the microcosm there is no such lawfulness in detail, and the criterion for rejecting an individual observation as incompatible with others does not exist. Hence again the question: What is real, the individual darts of the microcosmic fireflies, or is it whatever inheres in them to make the aggregate of darts conform with laws?

Perhaps both are real. Admitting this without qualification, however, is fatal to the proper understanding of large branches of modern physics, and it obscures whatever significance already formulated deductive science may have for other disciplines. In short, failure to make a distinction is an invitation to ignore a problem. Nor has the problem in fact been overlooked by theoretical physicists. Their voices, however, are discordant, often reflecting deep esthetic convictions, sometimes philosophic preconceptions, and occasionally disregard of basic philosophic issues. Three different responses are on record: the answer of the *rationalist* who favors the coherent aspects of our experience and regards them as primarily accented with reality; the plea of the *positivist* who recognizes the schism but limits his reality to observations, relegating to theory a secondary importance commensurate with its auxiliary function as handmaid to fact; finally, there is the counsel of the *skeptic* who, acknowledging the schism, sees in it an indication of error in our fundamental theories of nature. Representatives of the last-mentioned attitude are at present in the minority. Clearly, we cannot deal with their position very well because it will not grant the validity of modern science, which we are accepting.

True, we cannot rule out the possibility that, as science advances, it will repudiate the irreducibility of chance. To me this seems extremely unlikely because of the vastness of the advantages and the unifying qualities which the new view offers. This, however, is a matter of conjecture. At any rate I deem it proper to base a philosophy of science upon the best that science now presents, thus ruling out the compromise which suggests that science may be in error.

The other two answers bear responsible messages; partial, to be sure, but complementary. We wish to analyze them against the background of procedures actually used in science. This is best done, perhaps, by considering specific examples.

Every observation, every measurement, indeed every perception, introduces errors. A measurement without error is an absurdity. Let the measurement (and measurement is after all only refined perception) be of a star's position in the sky, of the length of this table, of an automobile's speed, or of an electrical current; its outcome is never to be believed exactly. This is apparent in the circumstance that the same number will not ordinarily result when the measurement is repeated, regardless of the care taken in performing it. Characteristically, only the careless experimenter and the ignorant observer believe raw nature to be unambiguous. To be sure, the different numbers found by the astronomer for the latitude (and longitude) of a star in successive observations lie within a reasonable interval, and this convinces him that he is somewhere near a "true" value of the quantity he seeks, that nature is not fooling him with hallucinations. Yet in a very fundamental sense he is witnessing a behavior not unlike the lawless emissions of the microcosmic firefly; we thus see that even the macrocosm is not wholly without its vagaries, but that it confines them sufficiently so that the observer with some credulity can feign their absence: he can blame himself for nature's equivocality and call the departures from a true value "errors."

But what is the *true* value? Let us look into scientific practice. If ten measurements of a physical quantity yield ten slightly different values, not one of them is necessarily regarded as true. Their *arithmetic mean* is singled out for this distinction, even though it may not have occurred among the measurements. The justice of this choice is not provided by the ten measurements, nor by any finite number of observations; it comes from a belief in, or rather the postulation of, a certain uniformity of nature. Thus the very determination of a true value, and in the end the selection of whatever is believed to be true perceptory fact, involves a reference to law and order not immediately presented in the sensory structure of that fact. Here we find the clearest expression of the attitude which has led to the development of deductive science: it relies upon rational elements to straighten out erratic data. It does not ignore the latter's presence, nor does it accept them unrefined. It distills from them an essence and *calls* it *true*. But the nature of the essence is partly determined by the process of distillation.

Now it is this true value which science takes to be characteristic of its reality. If an electron be real, its charge and mass are assumed to be true values in the outlined sense, whether or not they have occurred with the precision assigned to them in any measurement.

The real iceberg is not the exposed portion which the sailor sees; it is a largely unseen object compounded of the essences extracted from former observations and joined by postulations. The farther something is removed from immediate perception, as in the case of atomic entities or the facts of ancient history, the more dependent is its real character upon the lawfulness of the context in which it appears; it is real if that context is true. And here again "true" does not necessarily mean "observed," any more than it does in the process of measurement. It means "inferred from observations," and the nature of an inference, a word too often carelessly used, far transcends observations. What is physically real is rather close to the ideal.

Truth does not imply finality. The term is not to be taken in an extravagant metaphysical sense but signifies simply the best available. Truth may change. The scientist readily admits that he never knows a true value with infinite precision. This right to maneuver gives him the advantage he needs in rationalizing his observations, in making the best of an equivocal nature pitted against himself, an agent with rational propensities which force him to *construct* reality in accordance with rules.

A similar lesson can be drawn from many other instances. Real entities have often been inferred from lacunae in natural order before their existence could be certified by the standards of empirical science. Elements were predicted from gaps in the periodic table, planets because of irregular movements of known heavenly bodies; radio waves owed their conception as real constituents of nature to the simplicity of the equations of electromagnetism which implied their existence. The most significant advances of modern physics were motivated, or at least anticipated, by conjectures based upon the neatness of our universal laws; cases in point are the discoveries of the positive electron, the neutron, and many types of meson. The whole case of the neutrino rested for a considerable time upon the empirically slender premise of valid conservation laws; this particle simply *had* to exist if the principles of energy, momentum, and spin were to be retained. Yet it has never been seen even in the sense that other elementary particles have been observed. There is good evidence that it can never be seen, and even this consideration does not count against its admissibility as a component of real nature. How can such generosity be countenanced except by granting that the real draws its sustenance in large measure from a belief in the lawfulness of the cosmos?

The same sentiment finds its expression in the philosophic view which identifies the real with those elements of our experience that are causally connected in time and space. Current theories of physics, relativity, much of quantum mechanics, are reared upon this rationalistic credo. Hence it is fairly safe to say—and this is one of the theses supporting the remainder of the present discussion— that physical science would lose its hold on reality if an appeal to law and order were interdicted as a major claim.

We have seen, however, that lawfulness is at a premium in the perceptory realm of the microcosm. There, regularity is found primarily in aggregates, or, when assigned back to individual events, in the *probabilities* which inhere in these events. Laws govern these probabilities; they do not govern single occurrences. To be in harmony with the spirit of physical science we must therefore accept a conclusion unpalatable to many thinkers of the past, the conclusion that *probabilities are endowed with a measure of* *reality.* What this means in detail and what pitfalls must here be avoided will be analyzed in the following section.*

Now we do not claim that it is fair to put these arguments in reverse, i.e., to pronounce events resistant to lawful description, *unreal*. The perception of a single dart of light certainly happens, and the lawful multitude is made up of them. The fact of an hallucination is real and may be of great historical importance. Non-predictability hardly lessens the practical significance of certain unique occurrences both in the microcosm and the macrocosm. But the point is that they arrange themselves within the structure of our cognitive experience in a manner different from the simple order envisioned by traditional laws of nature.

To reconcile these disparities, and to accentuate their presence, I have advocated in *The Nature of Physical Reality* a distinction between *physical* and *historical* reality.[1] It seems to me that the need for this illuminating division is very great indeed, not only for the sake of terminology but also as a means for stating clearly what science can and what it cannot do. The data of immediate experience always belong to the latter sphere, the enduring entities of physics always to the former. But the spheres often overlap. In the macroscopic world they are nearly coincident, for the seen trajectory of a missile is also describable by the laws of mechanics (to take the simplest example). This accounts for the unimportance of this dis-

---

*Common sense seems to shrink from this assertion. The attitude of men creatively working in the field of probability is much more tolerant. W. Feller says, in his introduction to *Probability Theory* (New York: John Wiley, 1957), Vol. 1, "Probabilities play for us the same role as masses in mechanics." In this same spirit, I hold that probabilities are as real as masses.

1. *The Nature of Physical Reality*, McGraw-Hill, 1950.

tinction in classical physics. In the microscopic realm, however, the two spheres break apart and science becomes obscure unless this break is recognized.

3. *Probabilities, Continued**

Single events, as we have seen by studying the world of atoms, have in general only probabilities for occurring. In special cases, particularly in cases involving objects of ordinary size, these probabilities take on values very close to 1 and thus reduce to certainties. But let us consider an elementary particle for which experience indicates that the probability of its being in a given place cannot be 1 for any finite interval of time. Physical laws predict its *mean* position in a number of observations; for any given position they indicate a probability only.

Now suppose an observation is made and the particle is seen at a definite place. Must we not conclude that at the moment of observation the object was surely at the place where it was seen? And if we grant this much, are we not driven to admit certainty for its position at that instant? Expressing our suspicion more formally, we seem constrained to say: the act of observing the particle has caused the probability of its position, which was less than 1 prior to the observation, to jump suddenly to the value 1 during the act of observation.

This consequence expresses an orthodox view, widely accepted and emphasized in a number of textbooks on quantum mechanics. If correct, it raises difficulties with some of the remarks made in the earlier parts of the present chapter, and indeed with some of the basic axioms of quan-

*This section, which treats finer, somewhat controversial points of atomic theory, may be omitted by the general reader without detriment to the continuity of our main arguments.

tum theory. For instance, it would be preposterous on this view to subject probabilities to physical laws—the discontinuous change during observation being precisely the feature that defies these laws. The advantage of using probabilities as regular, and as real, entities arose from their immunity to such erratic changes, and the result now tentatively reached once more injects lawlessness into them. The gain sought is thus destroyed.

This is not the only defect of the view under consideration. If it is valid, there is no sense in talking about probabilities at all. For it is then obvious that a single observation *can* determine a supposedly erratic property exactly. Hence the initial conditions in any problem of motion *are* ascertainable (remember the example of the falling particle!), and experiment will always prove our theory to be in error. Instead of providing a valid theory, the notion at issue can at best demonstrate that none is attainable.

It also implies that, whenever an observation is made, physical reality suddenly transforms itself into historical reality. There is no a priori reason why such a transformation should not occur; however, the mathematical features of this conversion are most perplexing and, we feel, objectionable. Suppose that we have given a charged particle an exact momentum by sending it through an accelerating chamber equipped with diaphragms. We then know precisely in what direction and with what speed it is going, but we cannot say at all where it *is* if quantum theory is to be believed. The probability of position for this particle has the same small value everywhere. Now let a measurement of the particle's position be made, perhaps by noting the point at which a silver bromide grain is blackened (after development) on a photographic plate. According to the thesis under criticism we must then say: the probability after

185

the measurement is zero everywhere except near the position of the blackened grain.

Thus the probability extended through all of space, like a continuous medium. It formed in fact a field. At the instant of observation this field proceeds to vanish everywhere in space and concentrates itself as historical reality upon a point, where it takes on an infinite density. And all this because some human being chose to make an observation! Aside from the miraculous features of this theory, one is inclined to wonder whether it aims to deal with the physics of particles or the psychology of perception.

The confusion and the welter of contradictions accompanying the thesis stated in the second paragraph of this section disappear when we avoid a simple error in our understanding of the term probability. To discover the error we consider a familiar example.

As we have seen in Chapter VI, the physical condition of a regular die may be specified in many ways, some more complete than others. The die might be described as having a certain mass, shape, and size. It might be said to have six equal black faces with white dots on them. Another perfectly good way is to assign the probabilities for the appearance of the numbers from 1 to 6 when the die is thrown at random. These are well known to have the value 1/6 each. We repeat, knowledge of these six equal numbers is just as significant with respect to the intrinsic nature of the physical object, the die, as the knowledge that it has six equal faces or that it has a certain mass and size. These parcels of information are not equivalent, to be sure; but each can serve as a basis for the prediction of certain physical occurrences. The psychological stigma of incomplete knowledge which we habitually attach to probabilities must be erased. Let us fix our attention on these probabilities.

Suppose the die is thrown and a five appears. According to the reasoning employed in the italicized paragraph above, the former probabilities (1/6, 1/6, ... 1/6), for the numbers 1, 2, ... 6 have now suddenly changed to (0, 0, 0, 0, 1, 0). Still, it is obvious that the physical characteristics of the die have not been altered by the incident of the throw, and the reader doubtless has an uneasy feeling that the meaning of the word probability has shifted during this discourse. Clearly, here is what happened. Initially we meant by probability the quality of the die by virtue of which the results of a long series of throws, say n in number, will contain $n/6$ ones, $n/6$ twos, and so forth. In the end we meant by probability the degree of certainty of *our knowledge* with respect to the outcome of a particular throw. These two are not the same logically, and the confusion incurred earlier was occasioned by our mistaking them to be identical. Their difference is well understood in the theory of probability, where the distinction between the frequency interpretation and its counterparts (Laplacian, a priori definition and others) is fully recognized. If we stick consistently to the frequency interpretation, a single throw, or any number of throws, alters nothing so long as the physical character of the die remains unchanged, and the conclusion reached above is fallacious. On the certainty-of-knowledge interpretation the conclusion follows.

Now the certainty-of-knowledge interpretation in the present form is not tenable because it is hopelessly indefinite. To be acceptable it requires a statement of the *evidence* to which the knowledge relates. Probability becomes a function of two variables: the event considered and the evidence available. If the evidence is confined to the normal properties of the die, the probability for throwing a five is 1/6; if it includes knowledge that the thrower habitually cheats and has a way of getting sixes, the probability is less than 1/6; if the throw has already occurred and has yielded a five, and if its outcome is included in the evidence, all other evidence becomes irrelevant and the probability is clearly 1. Strictly speaking, all these probabilities are different physical entities and must not be confused. Hence, if the degree-of-knowledge interpretation is to be employed the evidence variable must be held constant during its use; in our example, evidence must be restricted to knowledge of the normal properties of the die, nothing may be smuggled in en route. But then the two interpretations agree, the probability does not change when the die is thrown, and the dilemma is avoided. Henceforth, we shall employ the frequency definition of probability, as is customary in most scientific work. It will be called the *objective* interpretation.*

Description of physical states in terms of probabilities need not have the trivial character exhibited by the ordinary die, whose properties may be specified by writing: $P_1 = P_2 = \ldots = P_6 = 1/6$. Here the probabilities P_i for throwing the numbers i are constant in time. The die can, however, be imagined to have an internal structure which changes in time. Suppose for definiteness that it is hollow and contains a sprocket with a small weight at its end. The other end of the sprocket is fixed to an axle extending parallel to an edge through the center of the cube, and this axle is driven by a small clockwork. We now have a strangely loaded die, but one in which the load revolves when the motor goes. The probabilities P_i are functions of the time. If the mechanism is known these probabilities can be cal-

*The logical and mathematical implications of this view with regard to quantum mechanical measurements are discussed in a forthcoming publication by the author.

culated; the reverse, however, is not true. Quantum mechanics, as we have seen, asserts that there is no mechanism, that the probabilistic behavior is in the nature of the physical object and is ultimate.

Yielding nonetheless to our propensity for mechanical models we could invest our die with further appliances. Let us assume that the sprocket can be set in one definite position by some manipulation from the outside which does not interfere with its being thrown. The same operation also starts the clockwork. We shall speak of this operation as "activating the die." Normally the die is in a stationary state; its probabilities are constants in time. After activation they become functions of the time.

How can we determine the variable probabilities by measurement? If the die is known to be in a stationary state it may be thrown a sufficient number of times and the relative frequencies can be computed without any reference to time. Otherwise, more elaborate procedures are necessary. Merely repeating throws will not do when the die is activated, because different throws then catch it in different internal states, and a computation of relative frequencies is meaningless. Nevertheless, two correct methods for determining the probabilities in their time dependence are at hand. One is to activate the die, wait a time t and throw it; repeat this procedure many times, always allowing the interval t to elapse before a throw. The results can then be used to calculate $P_i(t)$. Another method is applicable when many dice with the same internal structure are available. It consists in activating all of them at once, waiting a time t, and then throwing them all.

Such are the typical features of the quantum theory of measurements. The die corresponds to an atomic system, e.g., a hydrogen atom. This can be in a stationary state, as it will be for example when it has been left alone for a sufficient period of time. In that condition we are unable to say where the electron is relative to its proton, but we can perform measurements (illumination by short X-rays) each of which will locate the electron at some point r, not of course at the same point. From a sufficient number of such measurements we construct P_r.

The situation is different when the atom is "activated." There are many forms of activation, called "preparation of state" in quantum theory. Perhaps the simplest is exposure to a light wave, which causes the atom to be in a time-dependent state. The probabilities are determined as in the case of the activated die: either by repeating many times the act of switching on the light, waiting a period t and making a measurement upon a single atom; or by exposing many atoms simultaneously to the light, waiting a time t and then measuring all of them at once. The result is found to be a P_r which is a function of t, the same for both methods. The latter method is the one which the physicist most frequently uses.

It is not our intention to discuss fully the quantum theory of measurements, which presents complexities for which the activated die provides no analogs. For instance, to make the story more realistic the die should often break after it falls, so that another one must be used when the throw is to be repeated. A fall can also change the setting of the sprocket and thus produce further difficulties which have here been ignored. The intent of our discussion was primarily to illustrate the sense in which time-dependent probabilities can be *objective* physical quantities. The mechanisms invoked are fictitious and should be discarded if a proper understanding of quantum theory is sought.

4. The "Bankruptcy" of Modern Physics

To the outsider, especially to the older humanistic scholar whose early training has prepared him to view science as explanation by reference to solid stuff, the conclusions reached by a modern physicist seem almost like a declaration of the bankruptcy of science. Everything palpable and stable, he must feel, has been dissolved in a mist of mathematical relations; what was given concretely by God or Nature has been reduced to shadows of human thought. And because of this very understandable attitude on the part of the liberal scholar, over against the stolid complacency of the working scientist who professes no interest in an integration of knowledge and of views, there has descended a silken curtain of incongruity, incompatibility, and even discord; the threat of a cleavage between the sciences and the arts appears again.

I shall set forth a few of the reasons why a scientist cannot accept this assessment of his present state of affairs. He would question the view that solid stuff is more reliable than mathematical relations, that reality is to be assigned only to concrete things. What makes old-style matter so eminently acceptable as a candidate for reality if not its permanence, its indestructibility, its impenetrability? The fleeting sensory effects of matter can all be produced by nonmaterial forms such as waves, shocks, and vortices, forms which are not held to be real in the sense of matter. But if permanence and qualities of that general character are the discriminating features of the real, then it is clear that reality depends on mathematical law, even in the classical scholar's view; for permanence, indestructibility, mean constancy with respect to time and similar mathematical relations.

191

Perhaps this reminder seems forced; let us therefore reflect upon mathematical law in another context: its occurrence in experience. It is all very well to say that we discover matter but invent relations and laws. Careful examination, I feel, will not substantiate such disparagement of ideal structures. There is something cogent, stable, and binding in correct ideas, mathematical or otherwise, which somehow defies the claim that they are mere inventions. Most theoretical physicists would affirm, I think, that good ideas, valid theories, are discovered much like new particles and elements, and the alleged distinction violates that fact. The search for reality in the material domain is not much different from search among ideals: in one realm science must separate actual bodies from illusions and hallucinations, in the other truth from error. If reality is that which needs to be discovered rather than invented, it may very well lie in the field of the abstract.

But there are better reasons than these. The controversy between the theoretical physicist and the humanistic scholar arises primarily from a difference in training and the resulting divergent habits of thought. We often confuse what is acceptable with what is familiar. Our understanding progresses in the narrow area of our specialties; here the fluidity of our thinking never allows crusts to form. But when questions turn to unfamiliar matters we have no better resources for judgment than the knowledge we have acquired in our youth, knowledge which has become stale without our being aware of it. The maladjustment between a specialist's view in his proper field and his opinions elsewhere, which is said to afflict the professor and more generally the scientist, has its origin largely in this anachronism insofar as it exists, but it impairs the judgment of the man of letters with respect to science as it does the scientist's judgment of human affairs. Young students who learn physics today, if they are properly introduced to the subject, think of psi-functions, probabilities, and Hamiltonians without a troublesome sense of mystery. They learn to handle them with phenomenal ease and often take them to be more natural than the older mechanical models when they have acquired sufficient familiarity with them. To tell the truth, our teaching methods are not as yet completely suited to bring this about, for they, too, are largely based on the physics of the last century.

We saw in Chapter III how the process of scientific explanation moves back through successive stages from the particular to the universal. A given fact, or set of facts, is first interpreted by means of a fairly simple model, usually of the mechanical kind. The first model, however, is likely to be limited in its range of application; it may be satisfactory in view of the concrete evidence at hand but not if wider evidence is considered. Science can then develop in two ways: it can employ other, different simple models for other parts of the evidence, resigning itself to the use of incompatible explanations for disparate experiences on the motto of different theories for different observations. The most thoughtful scientists, however, reject a multiplicity of models, one for each domain of science; they search for a system of concepts extensible to as large as possible a domain of facts. When this is done, theory invariably becomes abstract, models lose their mechanistic and indeed their intuitable features; in short, abstractness is the price science pays for embraciveness of conception. When this is seen in its full historical and methodological context, the feeling of strangeness and dissatisfaction at the lack of concreteness of recent science is perhaps relieved. What appeared as a declaration of bankruptcy may be seen as merely a disavowal of the gold standard when it became apparent that the gold of solid matter was less valuable in practice than it was reputed to be.

Finally it should be emphasized that for most transactions the gold standard still exists. We have seen that the psi-functions and probabilities of quantum mechanics, singularly important in the description of atomic behavior, reduce smoothly and naturally to the regularities visibly present in our everyday world. Abstract theory provides complete justification for our reasoning in terms of concrete models. The scientist, therefore, does not want to talk the humanist out of his customary thinking about the world; he tells him that it is quite all right, but with the modest caveat that man will run into trouble when he indiscriminately applies visual models to invisible things.

5. *Historical Reality*

The lawful world of physical existences contains all external objects, from stars down to our own bodies and to electrons. It contains the states in terms of which the objects are described, the fields they generate, the time and space in which they are embedded. Notably, too, it contains the causally evolving *probabilities*, the states of the quantum theory which modern physics has taught us to regard as functionally ultimate. Man has, of course, experience of this world, not experience in the narrow sense of empiricism but in the wider one of constructing concepts and of creating their correspondence with observational experience. This is the universe of strictly physical reality.

Over against it stands the multitude of immediacies over which, as we have seen, physical theory has lost its direct control. A sensation, a measurement, an observation, a will, an action, and certainly a psychological introspection, belong to this class. I do not argue that it is always possible to tell whether a given element of experience is to be assigned to this class with certainty—as in many other instances, here, also, experience shows no sharp boundaries. The failure of a sharp logical distinction is never serious when recognized. At any rate the items last enumerated, and others which partake similarly of the character of immediacy, spontaneity, and coerciveness in our experience will be said to compose *historical reality*.

Epistemologically, the two worlds are related by rules of correspondence (Chapter I). My sensation of an object is the historical component of the event in question; reification is the rule of correspondence; and the postulated external entity (desk, tree, lamp) is the physical component of the experience. The distinction made is admittedly useless and grotesque in ordinary instances of regular cognition, where lawfulness extends into the historical realm and thus annexes it to the domain of physical reality. Classical physics was the formalization of this all-pervasive causal doctrine. Recent discoveries, described in the earlier portions of this book, force the distinction upon us. The microcosm obviously fails to convey sense if its lawful and its historical phases are confused, and to what extent the distinction can be ignored in the large-scale world of action requires to be investigated, and we shall return to it later.

An electron, if it moves in accordance with classical laws of mechanics, describes a physical path, a trajectory; it has no history. The actual electron, subject to the laws of the quantum theory, appears unpredictably here or there; it has no path but a history. To be sure, it also has a determinate physical state associated with its "motion," a wave function in this case. This wave function, however, hovers abstractly over its history, guiding it by enforcing a sort of disposition

195

without concretely assigning its fate. Historicity involves knowing, it implies observation; it arises through a union of a knower and his object of knowledge.

The inveterate mechanist tries to explain historicity as an aberration from path-like behavior through an appeal to "unpredictable interactions," as we have seen. So long as this mode of reasoning is forced to fall back on "unpredictable" matters, it fails to achieve its mechanistic end and becomes what may be called an idle theory.

An equally idle, but no more idle, theory is one herewith proposed: the electron itself, as an individual, *decides* what value of a physical observable it will exhibit in the act of measurement. While nothing of scientific importance depends on whether we accept this dogma—and I believe the meaning of decision in this context is not very clear—physics cannot refute it any more than it can invalidate the mechanist's assertion. What is true is this: to account for experience in its fullness even in the atomic realm, physics calls for supplementation by aspects of actuality, incidence, decision—in short, historicity.

All that precedes seems to show that the accent on emergence is particularly strong in the atomic world, that the atom is the prime actor in the drama of history. When many atoms cooperate, when masses and distances become large, classical physics with its unhistorical lawfulness results. Quantum theory "reduces" to classical physics in the familiar world.

While this is generally true, there are important exceptions to the rule. Nature permits arrangements in which the randomizing effects of large numbers do not occur, instruments through which the caprice of the microcosm can be projected into the world of ordinary experience. Every amplifier is such a device. A Geiger counter amplifies the

196

passage of a single elementary particle by precipitating an avalanche of ions when a few are initially produced, and the current thus generated can be further increased by the use of electron tubes. As is well known, much of modern physical research employs such arrangements. Feedback mechanisms achieve the same purpose of amplification, and the biophysicist is apparently discovering their widespread occurrence in organized nature. There is indeed an increasing volume of evidence to indicate that the delicate balance of metabolism and self-maintenance called life depends for its establishment on precisely those mechanisms which are able to amplify a random atomic impulse into historically significant proportions.

An example often cited in this connection is the mutation of a gene. A single X-ray photon can bring this about. Suppose now that the frequency of this photon has been observed and is known. According to the uncertainty principle the position of the photon is then entirely random. Indulging in an anthropomorphism, we might say it is wholly "up to the photon" where it will interact with its surroundings. If it chooses to invade the neighborhood of a gene, the latter undergoes a change which may, under certain circumstances, spell the doom of an individual.

In the inorganic world similar processes of random triggering are easily found. A somewhat unrealistic but impressive one is the release of a uranium bomb by a single neutron. Place a sufficiently large block of U^{235} in a space free of neutrons, then allow a single neutron at some distance from the block to move toward it. Quantum mechanically, its wave function is known, and along with it we know the probability that it will impinge upon the bomb and cause disaster. The historic fact whether it will or not is left open by the physics of the situation.

These instances demonstrate the ingression of atomic historicity into the generally lawful macrocosm. The merger between physical and historical reality of which we spoke, and which takes place to some degree in the macrocosm, is therefore not complete. Our distinction carries its validity far beyond the atomic domain and must be reckoned with to some extent everywhere. Astronomy is about the only science which is relatively immune to it.

Yet all this, while true, seems to have very little bearing upon the problems of history as this subject is usually understood. History is the arena of *human action,* and action has not yet entered our discourse. What, then, is action? When analyzed, I believe it is seen to be a composite of arrangements and processes in accord with physical laws, *plus* here and there an element of voluntaristic *decision.* It is the decision which transfers action from the physical to the historical universe, or rather, makes it an inhabitant of both realms.

We used the word decision, albeit in a loose and tentative manner, when the discussion was about electrons in the act of manifesting their presence to the perceiver. There we were unable to invest the term with accurate meaning. In human action there is a similar element of decision, similar in the sense that it also transcends physical lawfulness (as did the manifestation of the electron's position); but in human action we can study it by introspection. And it is recognized as conscious, active, voluntaristic intervention, a true component of historicity.

The problem of human freedom enters here. Its traditional features, however, are peculiarly foreign to the present line of thought. What is obviously, introspectively true is the occurrence of voluntary decisions, the existence of what earlier philosophers called acts of the human will.

Physics has little to say about the freedom of that will, about its dependence on motivation, habit and so on. Still the actuality of *conscious decision* is clear for all to see, and the latitude needed for action consequent upon decision is guaranteed by the probabilistic features of physical reality. This is as far as we need to go at this point.

Indeed it is risky to go farther. The physicist who tries to prove freedom on the basis of quantum theory invariably meets misfortune, whether he recognizes it or not. For if he makes psi-functions govern human behavior he can prove *randomness* of action, but never freedom. He can show that man will act in accordance with ethical precepts a certain percentage of the time, that he will act immorally in another percentage of instances. On this theory man's behavior would be a set of random doings, some good, some bad, without a clue indicating which are good and which are bad. This is not the kind of thing philosophers call freedom. What the argument needs to make its case is again the element of choice above chance, of historicity. To this we shall return in a later section.

Since we left the atomic world our discourse has increasingly taken on the character of speculation, at least to the extent that conscious decision and action have assumed a dominant role. We now return to safer matters and show in what manner the *possibility* of action, regardless of its psychological essence, depends upon the modifications of physical lawfulness.

Consider again the neutron on its way to the uranium bomb. *If classical physics were true,* a single set of observations on the position and velocity of the neutron at a suitable time would decide whether an explosion occurs. It would leave room for action only to the very limited extent that, if the neutron is found headed for the bomb, we can

199

try to intercept and deflect it before the impact. Usually this is impossible because the speed even of a thermal neutron is greater than ours, and we are forced to resign ourselves to fate instead of being agents in the developing course of events.

Notice, too, that according to classical mechanics the very decision to intercept the neutron must be taken as a physiologically determined consequence of all-pervading physical reality, whose historicity can be but an illusion. Decision as such is an impossibility on the basis of classical mechanics.

The new physics, with its concession of autonomy to historical reality, leaves greater room for action and avoids this difficulty. Even if a set of observations reveals the neutron to be headed for the bomb we can still hope and act for our survival, because what is now dynamically determined is a probability of collision, not a necessity. There is less cause for fatalism, but accentuated need for action. This is true even if, classically speaking, the neutron is seemingly winning the race for collision with the bomb. In this instance, as in all others, the physical situation leaves alternatives which action can seize in numerous ways. Decision fits neatly into the spaces presented by the semi-deterministic honeycomb of historical reality. But we do not pretend to have shown that it actually resides there, nor why. That is an illuminating conjecture made reasonable by the probabilistic nature of physical reality.

To illustrate this point minutely, let us analyze a decision. The suggestion is always strong that we should reduce the psychological act of deciding to physiological bases. In other words, when explaining the outcome of a so-called choice we advert to physiological processes taking place in the brain, to reverberating neuron currents, firing synapses, and the like; and we assume, following traditional doctrine, that in the ultimate analysis molecular events determine the outcome of our choice. *This avenue is now blocked,* for clearly such a process of reduction will lead us into the realm of atomic uncertainties. There is no unique road from the event of voluntary decision to the laws of physical reality. Again, we are forced to take decision as an irreducible act, a component of historical reality which stands aloof from physical lawfulness.

Conclusions such as these take us back to the credo put forth in Chapter III and provide substance for earlier claims.

To summarize, nineteenth-century natural science conceived of man as a detached spectator of an objective universe. It held the spectator-spectacle polarity to be genuine and fundamental. During the present century, discoveries concerning the nature of atoms rendered this doctrine untenable. The nucleus of a new philosophy of nature emerged with Heisenberg's principle of uncertainty, whose basic meaning implies a partial fusion of the knower with the known. The theory led to a mathematical formalism which, in order to attain its purpose, namely lawful description of experience, has to speak of probabilities rather than unique events. Individual events are no longer related in causal fashion, as we shall see in the following section, although in the domain of probabilities causality still reigns. Thus has been introduced another, more significant principle of division than the old spectator-spectacle bifurcation: the distinction between physical and historical reality has appeared.

Along with these developments, man has been transformed from a spectator to an active participant in the drama of becoming. Room has been made for decision and choice, which had no place in the older scheme of things. What was formerly fate has become history.

One might here raise a thought or two for historians to ponder. Physical science has yielded autonomy to the historical process. The detachment of the latter from physical lawfulness is the more pronounced the greater the abundance of momentous, unique events having a potency to release an avalanche of history. We live in an era charged with such potencies. The distinction between physical and historical reality we have tried to describe may have a sinister chance of becoming fatal before it is universally recognized. Hence its grave importance.

The other thought concerns the possibility of a science of history. Let no one deny this possibility on the grounds that history has too many variables to be susceptible of scientific treatment, or that it deals with human situations in which inquiry has a profound effect upon what is sought to be known, or in which unpredictable decisions intervene. Natural science has solved these difficulties in its long course of evolution, the first by judiciously eliminating irrelevant variables and searching for significant ones, the others by injecting probabilities into the last constituents of its universe. It might be supposed, therefore, that history can take on the structure of science by adopting the pattern of physics. If this thesis were accepted it would follow that history, like physics, can predict only mass phenomena such as economic cycles, large-scale migrations, periods of cultural activity, and the like. But it will be unable to address itself to peak events, to the emergence of powerful personalities, which have so decisive an influence on the course of human affairs.

Such a "science of history" that wishes to bring these collective phenomena within its sphere of prediction must of course not follow slavishly the detailed pattern of physical science; it must doubtless strike out on its own along paths hitherto uncharted by existing disciplines, and operate with concepts quite different from those met in the sciences of nature. One would hardly expect that a mere transcription of the concepts of force, energy, mass, or indeed the more abstract ideas of thermodynamics can perform the vitalizing task of making history meaningful and predictive.

6. *Causality and Determinism*

In mechanistic science causality was a relatively simple relation, best illustrated perhaps in connection with Newton's laws of motion. One desires to describe the (continuous) motion of an ordinary object. At a given instant (at time t_1) it has a position x_1 and a velocity v_1; at a later time (t_2) it is at x_2 and moves with velocity v_2. The two observables, x and v, define the *state* of the moving object. If the state $S_1(x_1, v_1)$ is known, the state $S_2(x_2, v_2)$ at the later time t_2 can be calculated by solving the differential equation usually called Newton's second law of motion. In Fig. 14 we present the situation schematically:

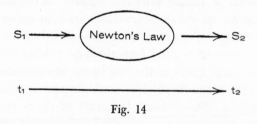

Fig. 14

The state of the system, S_1, is "fed" as an initial condition into a mathematical formalism called a law. Then, by formal procedures, one can predict a later state S_2, which is the solution of the "law" for the given initial condition, evaluated at time t_2. Expressed more simply: the state of a physical system is known at a certain time. Then, by means of some scientific law, the state at a later time can be computed and thus predicted. When this kind of analysis is possible, modern science calls the earlier state the *cause,* the later state the *effect,* and the law which mediates between them is spoken of as a causal law. Causality is the relation between the states; it is simply a methodological relation conferred upon a situation by virtue of the manner in which science is able to describe it.

To say that causality holds in nature is at best an elliptic way of claiming that science succeeds in understanding temporal changes in its physical systems as a sequential unfolding or propagation of states of the kind just outlined. The statement refers directly to a procedural element of science, and indirectly to nature in holding that the procedure is successful when applied to nature. For it is conceivable that our experience does not countenance the device portrayed in Fig. 14.

The details of that device, however, need inspection. Why do we choose as a state of the moving object the set of 2 variables, x and v? Why not include in the definition of its state all its other observables such as color, shape, chemical composition, etc.? The answer is that the former two suffice, that the causal formalism gets along with them in self-consistent fashion, the law being so constituted that x and v transform themselves without effects from other observables: a state defined in terms of them retains its causal integrity (under a specified, known set of forces, which is always assumed). If other variables were added to the set they would either remain constant during the motion or would vary in a manner wholly unregulated by Newton's law. Thus, x and v form a proper causal state with respect to *motion*. Other states are required to describe optical or chemical changes.

Now the x-v state has this significant peculiarity: it can be determined, naively speaking, by a pair of single observations. One measures x and v simultaneously and knows the state. I said, naïvely speaking; for, as we have seen, the incidence of inevitable errors requires in principle that even here a statistical aggregate of measurements should be performed. This circumstance, however, was conveniently forgotten in pre-quantum days, or it was deliberately ignored on the blissful assumption that error was a human importation into the physical world and therefore beneath scientific notice. A state, under this assumption, is conceived as a pair of individual events. Hence a cause is a set of individual events, and so is an effect. Both belong to the realm of historical reality. In classical physics this does not matter since historical and physical reality are thought to coincide.

The example of the moving object we have chosen is special but typical, and there is no difficulty in illustrating the formalism of Fig. 14, by innumerable instances from physics, astronomy, chemistry, economics, psychology, and the biological sciences. Usually, the states encountered involve the numerical values of a set, often more extensive than the two observables x and v, of eventlike variables subject to individual observation, and linked in time by some law. In the physical sciences this law is usually a differential equation, or a group of such equations, and the time is always among the independent variables.

It should be admitted that the preceding characterization of causality is not the only one employed in science, but it has the merit of greatest clarity, and enjoys the patronage of modern physics as well as the endorsement of philosophers responsible for the causal controversy (Kant, Laplace, Cassirer, Bohr, Heisenberg, Born). Other views, while interesting to naturalists, lawyers, and philosophers, must here be omitted from consideration for lack of space. I should point out, however, that the philosophic view which asserts the universality of the causal relation throughout nature and human experience, in the sense of causality as outlined here, is called *determinism*. It was in this vein that Laplace proclaimed the doctrine, maintaining that a powerful intellect, aware of the position and velocities of all the components of the universe at the present moment, could know the state of the universe at any later (or earlier) time. The determinist usually includes men and men's minds in the state of the universe.

It is clear, of course, from our earlier discourse that the causal relation as set forth will no longer do. If the object under study is an atomic particle, we must reckon with the impracticability of the experiences that go into the meaning of x and v, with the lawlessness attaching to individual events, with their control by chance. Fig. 14, in this new interpretation, tries to connect states belonging to the realm of historical reality with a law operating within physical reality. If causality is to be retained the meaning of S must be changed to something which does in fact relate to physical reality, something that partakes of the regularity and objectivity forming the quintessence of scientific law. The states can hardly be anything but the *probabilities* we have encountered: S in the case of the moving atomic object means the probability with which it will be found at different points of space. This S will change in time, and the change is regulated by a law (Schrödinger's), different from Newton's to be sure, but of similar form. With this reinterpretation of states and laws, the causal relation remains formally unchanged and continues to be correctly depicted by Fig. 14.

While the method has thus been only slightly altered, the philosophic effects of the new meaning of S are profound and arresting. A shift of terminology from dynamic causality to statistical causality, certainly called for and justly advocated by some authors, is hardly commensurate with the philosophic gulf that separates the new description from the old. I have tried to accentuate the change by saying that the causal relation has been pushed back into the domain of physical reality, having lost its hold upon historical reality. Others prefer to argue, misguidedly, I think, that causality has been abandoned, refusing to modify the Newtonian meaning of state. Their feeling arises from the conviction that probabilities are mere defects of knowledge, unworthy of recognition as components of reality. If the reasoning here presented is correct, this conviction is an illusion attributable to a subjective misrepresentation of probabilities. Probabilities must, it seems, be given the status of physical objectivity and accorded the rank of the former Newtonian states. Heisenberg[2] has expressed the profound change in the principle of causality in a most perceptive and striking way; reverting to Aristotelian language, he speaks of the new science as describing potentialities in contrast to the actualities existent and emerging in the world. These potentialities compose physical reality.

7. *Human Freedom*

Traditional decorum forbids the treatment of human freedom within the narrowing context of science; limitation of space counsels further against raising this problem here.

2. W. Heisenberg, *Physics and Philosophy*, Harper, 1958.

Its ramifications are indeed too vast for quick survey and ap-praisal—yet the modified sense of causality has so strong a bearing on some aspects of freedom that the temptation to deal with them is overwhelming. I shall do so in schematic fashion, merely sketching connections and calling attention to matters already resolved and to difficulties still remain-ing.

Figure 15 is a diagram of topics and relations; it will provide the (oversimplified) structure for the following discussion.

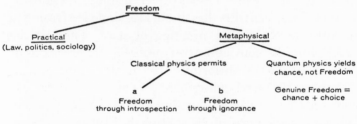

Fig. 15

Freedom, like causality, has many meanings. We shall at once eliminate a large class of them by making a distinction between practical and metaphysical freedom, retaining for analysis only the latter. Practical freedom is an amorphous idea, adverting largely to conditions in which man is not prevented by external constraints from carrying through a course of action leading to a goal already set. It does not refer to motives, nor to the philosophic question whether human actions are predetermined by physical or mental causes, nor to the freedom of the will. When man is forced to act under compulsion he lacks practical freedom, even though the will under which the prohibited act would have been performed might be regarded as free. Practical freedom is of utmost importance in sociology, jurisprudence, politics, and in non-axiological ethics, but it has almost no contact with epistemology and stands aloof from the bases of natural science, while depending on the results of science for its maintenance.

Metaphysical freedom is a deeply philosophic issue; it involves the question whether human actions or, in case the actions are premeditated, the motives and the will that precede them, are uniquely bound and determined by prior states in the sense of physical determinism, all external impediments notwithstanding. If such determination is present, there is evidently no clear place for personal moral responsibility. This latter kind of freedom is very closely tied to scientific methodology and will form the substance of the present section.

One further word concerning practical freedom. I have called it amorphous: the reason is close at hand, for whenever one searches for structure in this area of freedom one finds new features. Hence the current tendency of using the plural, freedoms. The reader may be sure that practical freedom is in reference whenever the plural is invoked. Whether this proliferation is helpful even in politics may be questionable, especially when one recalls that the philosophy of cause and effect reached its lowest point in the 17th century, when writers gloried in the discovery of 40 different kinds of causes. Other devices have been used to rationalize such confusion, notably Nietzsche's famous distinction between freedom from and freedom for. But I shall leave all these interesting matters aside and concentrate on metaphysical freedom.

This problem takes on different forms in the framework of classical and in that of quantum physics. Strictly speaking, it is solved in classical mechanics, but solved in a way which has seemed unsatisfactory to many thinkers. For that discipline, if assumed to be correct in its essence and also universal in its applicability—in which case mental processes must be regarded as physiological and ultimately as physical—confers determinism on all phenomena and therefore denies metaphysical freedom. In failing to recognize the irregularity of the historical, existential realm, classical science precludes the positive answer which moral philosophers are seeking.

However, during the centuries in which moralists were forced to live with the Newtonian doctrine various accommodations were found to alleviate the stringency of the deterministic impasse. The easiest *modus vivendi* was achieved by those who simply refused to believe that mechanism had anything to do with man, or at least with man's mind. This resolution proved mildly acceptable because the mind-body problem, suggesting an unmitigated dualism between two worlds, posed itself anyhow, and here was further confirmation of duality.

A more sophisticated version of metaphysical freedom which gets around the rather arbitrary act of curtailing the validity of mechanistic physics (though not around the mind-body dualism) makes freedom an invariable symptom of consciousness. Man's actions are bound, it holds, and an external observer would judge, in conformity with the Laplacian doctrine of determinism, that his behavior is minutely caused. Yet man himself, when becoming introspectively aware of his actions, necessarily deems himself free to perform them. Just as a curved object may be concave when viewed from the inside, convex from the outside, so may man's actions appear free from within consciousness, determined from without. Spinoza claimed that a stone in flight, if it were awakened to consciousness, would regard itself free to pursue the trajectory on which Newton's law forces it to move. Freedom through introspection, as indicated in Fig. 15, is indeed compatible with classical science, even though its plausibility is low.

A better formula for reconciling mechanistic determinism with metaphysical freedom involves the notion of ignorance. Laplace's supreme intelligence, this doctrine affirms, is not possessed by man, for even if he knew the world formula, he could never comprehend the full detail of any momentary state of himself, let alone the universe, which is required for prediction. Thus only God is bound, and man has freedom because he has ignorance—determination is the price God pays for his omniscience.

There is an interesting theological argument which illustrates this point. When a child has a choice between a piece of pie and a dish of spinach, the conscious certainty of freedom clearly attends his choice, even while he takes the pie. His parents, who know from experience that the child abhors spinach intensely, knew in advance what he would choose; their greater knowledge makes the child's behavior appear predetermined. This solution of the freedom paradox in classical physics is to me the most acceptable. Indeed it has features so satisfying and realistic that its validity carries over into quantum science, where in principle the need for reconciliation no longer exists. Ignorance, however, is always with us, and ignorance always increases facilities for freedom in a manner to be reckoned with. Man is less free, in a metaphysical sense, when he gains knowledge, experience, and wisdom. Perhaps this proves that an excess of virtue can become a fault. We shall have occasion to return to this tentative conclusion. At this point, let us acknowledge that an important theory of economics[3] rests upon the correspondence of freedom with ignorance.

We now turn to modern science, to quantum mechanics, with its recognition of historical randomness. Human acts, decisions, conations belong to the realm of historical reality, to Heisenberg's actual universe and are bound but loosely into the lawfulness of probability aggregates, of Heisenberg's potential. Therefore they are not causally determined in the mechanistic sense, and the strictly negative answer to the question of metaphysical freedom is wiped out. But it is not replaced by a positive one, because absence of determination is chance, and chance is not freedom.

This point hardly needs elaboration. Unfortunately, however, the scientific literature contains a few misleading claims which require correction, and I ask the reader's indulgence for undertaking that trivial job. As already recorded, some biophysicists have said that a living system is an amplifier, able to magnify atomic impulses into large-scale movements such as human actions. Our retina can register the incidence of very few photons and translate this stimulus into behavior. Since the incidence of an individual photon is not a predetermined event, the result of the translation which follows it shares the indeterminism of the atomic world. If this view is correct—and the scientific evidence clearly favors it—an organism can project atomic uncertainty into the macrocosm, thereby extending the domain of historical reality to human acts. However, a person behaving merely in response to random impulses performs actions in accordance with the laws of chance, some good, some bad, and their distribution is calculable

3. F. A. Hayek, *Individualism and the Economic Order,* University of Chicago Press, 1948.

by a formula similar to Poisson's. The claim that this spells freedom is not valid.

Again, it has been said that man's destiny lies outside the causal nexus of physical determination and is therefore not fate but freedom. The mutation of genes is called upon to substantiate this claim. A genetic carrier, a large molecule, is struck by an X-ray photon. If a certain zone within the gene is hit it will undergo mutation, which may be lethal or beneficent, the odds being in favor of the former alternative. Hence catastrophe attends the process of mutation which is uncaused in the classical sense of determinism. All this, of course, may be true, but lack of causation is chance, and chance, as we have said, is not freedom.

What, then, is the difference between freedom and chance? It is *choice*, choice supervening upon chance. There can be no choice in a world regulated by strict determinism of the classical mechanistic type; choice *is* possible in quantum physics, yet it transcends that science. I do not know how to define choice precisely despite the clarity and forcefulness with which it manifests itself in my decisions. Choice is a primitive in man's experience; it has not been caught up (as yet) in scientific theories and therefore defies analysis at present. It is like the example of subjective blue before man learned to describe it adequately, which is far from vague and ineffectual, and declares itself impressively in every subjective vision. In spite of this, I cannot regard choice beyond human, and therefore presumably scientific, understanding. That physics alone will achieve this understanding seems extremely doubtful; the task may require the joining of hands between natural science and psychology, between science and philosophy. Moreover, it seems most likely that in this process the principles of science, as

213

so often in its history, will be further extended and further humanized.

Our failure to understand choice completely does not deprive us of an important advantage in treating the problem of freedom vs. ignorance. Mere chance, as conceived and formalized in quantum mechanics, *is* sufficient to resolve it. For it leaves us the possibility of freedom even in the presence of perfect knowledge. Laplace's intelligence, knowing every aspect of historical reality, i.e., every event at the present time, could still not predict the future. Ideal knowledge, complete absence of ignorance, remains compatible with freedom. But the point still stands that less than ideal knowledge offers chance an even wider range.

Considerations such as the foregoing, including the need for understanding choice, were in the author's mind when, at the end of Chapter II he claimed that modern science has transformed freedom, which was a paradox in mechanistic physics, into a challenging problem to be solved.

In closing this chapter, I can hardly do better than to quote one of the most appropriate and suggestive descriptions, short of understanding, pertaining to the meaning of choice. St. Augustine, wishing to contrast the blissful coercion under which an angel can do only good with man's freedom, wrote "angelus non potest peccare; homo potest non peccare." Man has chance, to be sure, but also choice.

Chapter VIII

OPEN VISTAS

1. *Looking Outward: Cosmology*

Man's anxiety and man's reverence are aroused strongly by
the occurrence of two kinds of unlimited perspective in his
experience: looking outward he perceives a series of marvels that propel his conception toward infinities of space
and time; looking inward he becomes aware of even deeper
mysteries of individual existence. Kant put it well when he
said, toward the end of his *Critique of Practical Reason,*
"Two things fill the mind with ever new and increasing
admiration and awe, the oftener and more steadily they are
reflected on: the starry heavens above me, and the moral
law within me." In this last chapter we give thought to the
two mysteries encountered at opposite ends of the range of
scientific inquiry, the far reaches of space and time at one
and intimate religious experience at the other.

This present section might be entitled cosmology, the
descriptive and speculative study of the cosmos. It will also
deal with cosmogony, with matters concerning the origin
of the universe. Eschatology, the science of last things, will
be excluded because there is almost no scientific evidence
that bears on it, even though writers at one time were fond
of extrapolating the second law of thermodynamics to project the gloomy picture of a heat death as the ultimate state
of existence, a state in which all organized motion and all
life have ceased. No careful scientist can do this today, and
if the reader is concerned about the situation of the world

ten billion years from now he may take comfort in knowing that according to all present indications, the world will still be there, life will still exist not only in its present but probably in many richer forms. But such indications are vague, unreliable, lacking the fine texture of proved scientific theories.

Cosmology, too, is speculative, because the facts upon which it is based are to a large extent uncertain; astronomy has only recently become a truly experimental science. Mindful of these uncertainties and of the speculative character of the subject under discussion, I shall not pretend to reason in closely disciplined fashion but present the accepted facts in succinct and somewhat arbitrary manner using the vehicle of Pythagorean philosophy or, if you please, numerology. The ideas involved come mostly from P.A.M. Dirac and Pascual Jordan, the method of presentation follows the latter author.[1]

According to Pythagoras, the realities in the world are simple numbers; beauty consists in harmonic ratios, in the numerical simplicity of equilateral polygons and regular solids. Small integers and geometrical constants like π have an almost mystical significance. Modern science disparages mysticism, yet it stands in unreasoning awe before simple numbers. Physics revels in the fact that atomic masses are nearly integral multiples of a fundamental mass, that electrical charges are multiples of the electron charge, that spins are simply quantized. And conversely, when a numerical constant like the fine-structure constant occurring in atomic theory, turns out to have a value very close to 0.00730, one feels ill at ease until an Eddington arises and valiantly defends the view that this is exactly 1/137, and ought to be,

1. Pascual Jordan, *Die Herkunft der Sterne*, Wissenschaftliche Verlagsgesellschaft, Stuttgart, 1947.

in view of certain quasi-Pythagorean arguments he has proposed and which physics has not fully comprehended. In
some respects the scientist, though disclaiming the significance of simple numbers, continues to be fascinated by
them, and this fascination extends into man's thoughts
about his universe.

Table 2 below contains the most important constants
which enter into cosmological theories. The values given
are only approximate, even in cases like the velocity of
light where they are known with great accuracy; the units
are in the centimeter-gram-second system throughout.

Table 2

$c =$ Velocity of Light $\approx 10^{10}$ cm/sec
$K =$ Gravitational Constant $= 8\pi G/c^2 \approx 10^{-27}$ cm/gm
$t =$ Age of Universe $\approx 6 \times 10^9$ years $\approx 10^{17}$ seconds
$\rho =$ Mean Density of Matter $\approx 10^{-29}$ gm/cm^3
$R =$ Radius of Universe $\approx 10^{27}$ cm
$\alpha =$ Rate of Recession of Nebulae $= c\Delta\lambda/r\lambda \approx 10^{-17}$ sec^{-1}

As to the meaning of the symbols, c is the velocity of
light, 186,000 miles per second, obtained by timing light
rays.

K is the gravitational constant, written in a form convenient in the theory of relativity, $K = 8\pi G/c^2$. The value
G, sometimes called the Cavendish constant after the physicist who first measured it accurately, is the quantity which
appears in the elementary formula for the gravitational
force between two small bodies of masses, m_1 and m_2, a distance r apart:

$$F = G\frac{m_1 m_2}{r^2} \tag{1}$$

(G has the value 6.67×10^{-8} dynes/cm^{2}gm^2.)

The letter t stands for the age of the universe, and a brief explanation of its meaning and the method of its determination seems in order. It is hardly news any longer that the old view of an infinite age of matter has become questionable. On the other hand, it is difficult to say what happened when our universe, and matter as we know it, were born. Whether all "onta" sprang into being at once, whether they were already present and merely condensed into atoms we do not know. Significant, however, is the fact that at a certain time, about 5 billion years ago, a series of events took place which separated the present stage of the universe from another, perhaps from a stage in which no matter existed at all. It may even be that in the earlier stage there was no time inasmuch as no changes whatever occurred in the entities then present, so that the event or events in question marked the beginning of time. What evidence, then, is at hand for so strange an hypothesis?

The principal fact is that we have learned to "date," i.e., to determine the age of, rocks. The method is based upon the radioactivity of certain natural elements, which by emission of alpha particles or electrons, often accompanied by gamma rays, spontaneously transform themselves into different elements. Among these elements are some which change extremely slowly. Uranium of atomic weight 238, for instance, is known to have a "half-life" of 4.5 billion years, and this means that 100 atoms of U^{238} will have been reduced to 50 atoms after this tremendous period of time. To determine it is a relatively simple matter, for it is possible to count the particles emitted when the U^{238} atoms undergo transformations, and the rate just mentioned implies that many billions of atoms (which form a very small sample of uranium) will emit enough alpha particles to be counted within a reasonable time. Hence the half-life can be measured.

The product ultimately formed from the decay of U^{238} is a certain species of radio-lead, Pb^{206}. There are numerous intermediate elements between U^{238} and Pb^{206}, but all these have short lives in comparison with the 4.5 billion year span and can therefore be ignored. Besides U^{238} there is another interesting isotope of uranium, U^{235}, which ultimately decays into another form of lead, Pb^{207}. The alpha particles emitted during these transformations, being helium nuclei, finally turn into helium atoms by appropriating the requisite number of electrons. The important facts are summarized below:

Original Species	Half-Life	Final Product
U^{238}	4.5×10^9 years	$Pb^{206} + He$
U^{235}	0.7×10^9 years	$Pb^{207} + He$

When certain naturally occurring rocks are examined, they are found to contain atoms of U^{238}, U^{235}, Pb^{206}, Pb^{207}, and He in certain measurable ratios. We know of no process whereby heavy atoms like uranium and lead are formed naturally today, and it is therefore reasonable to assume that at the time when heavy elements were formed the abundances of Pb^{207} and of Pb^{206} were about equal, and also equal to the abundance of ordinary (primeval) lead whose atomic weight is 204. On the other hand, Pb^{204} is not the decay product of any radioactive process; whatever there is of it was formed in the very beginning and can be used as an index of the initial abundance of Pb^{206} and Pb^{207}. It is clear, then, that a calculable fraction of the radio-lead contained in a specimen of rock at the present time must be the decay product of the uranium it held originally, and the ratios of the number of uranium atoms to lead atoms are a measure of the age of a rock specimen.

There are, in fact, four independent ways of computing its age from atom ratios, namely, by measuring (1) Pb^{206}/U^{238}, (2) Pb^{207}/U^{235}, (3) Pb^{206}/Pb^{207}, (4) He/U. The last of these serves only as a check; it leads to an estimate of the lower limit of the age of a rock because some of the helium may have escaped its entrapment. It is found to be true that the age computed by the fourth method is generally smaller than the other values, as expected.

The results obtained for the ages of various minerals fall between 3 and 6 billion years. This would indicate when the earth was formed. But there is further evidence for meteorites whose ages, determined by isotopic analysis, turn out to be approximately the same as those of terrestrial rocks. Since meteors are in all probability members of the solar system, its age, too, is seen to be about 5 billion years.

By methods similar to these it is even possible to obtain an estimate of the age of the elements themselves and hence of the universe as a whole. Suppose that when the universe was created, the two isotopes of iodine, iodine 127 which is *not* radioactive, and iodine 129 which *is* radioactive and has a half-life of 17 million years, were created in equal abundance. The question is whether any iodine 129 was still in existence when the meteorites were formed, that is to say, when the solar system was created. If so, and if the ratio of its abundance to that of non-radioactive iodine could be determined, the age of these elements at the birth time of the solar system could be computed, for iodine 129 decays into the element xenon. Hence we ask: do meteorites contain xenon which may be regarded as the end product of the original iodine 129? The experimental answer at present appears to be that there is none or very little. Thus iodine 129 had already completely disappeared at the time at which the solar system was formed, and from this one may draw the conclusion that a time of several hundred million years had already elapsed. The inference is, therefore, that the elements are at least 100 million years older than the solar system itself. Very recent evidence suggests a period of 400 million years for the time between the formation of the elements and the birth of the solar system.

On the other hand, astronomers who have begun to understand the physical processes going on in stars, can now calculate how long the present rate of energy dissipation in the oldest stars is possible before all initial energy is consumed, and this leads to an estimate of perhaps 10 billion years. Table 3, taken from Unsöld,[2] shows the times of development of different types of stars revealed by such calculations. For all these reasons the figure for t here adopted is not likely to be far from correct.

Table 3

Spectral Type of Star	Time of Development in Years
O7	2×10^6
B0	1×10^7
B5	6×10^7
A0	3×10^8
F0	1.5×10^9
G0	6×10^9
K0	12×10^9

The fourth constant in Table 2, ρ, represents the cosmic density of matter. It is estimated from an actual count of stars and nebulae in the region accessible to telescopes, coupled with a knowledge of their average chemical composition and the assumption that universal matter consists approximately one-half of stars and one-half of dust. The

2. A. Unsöld, *Naturwissenschaften, 44,* 145 (1957).

value of ρ is highly uncertain; its smallness is impressive if we remember that the density of water in these units is 1, or indeed that it implies an average occupation of space by an atom or two per cubic yard.

Much could be said about the next entry in the table, the radius of the universe, R. To claim that the universe is finite is not equivalent to saying that beyond a certain distance, as ordinarily conceived, there is no space, or that an obstacle like an impenetrable wall is encountered at some place far away. A finite R can in fact have many meanings. I have outlined one in simple terms elsewhere[3] and will not repeat it here. Another has to do with the course of light: a ray, propagated along a certain direction into space, will return to its starting point after travelling a distance approximately equal to $2\pi R$. This is a simple but not a practical definition; the value quoted in the table is not determined from its use because even light would require many billions of years to traverse its cyclic course. The value stated is derived in very indirect fashion from certain theories of general relativity, which predict a change in the size of the volume element as the distance from our galaxy increases, and by fitting observations on the number of stars per unit of volume to this predicted change it is possible to determine R. The value thus found is extremely uncertain, but we shall see below that it accords well with another consideration based upon the expansion of the universe. That the universe occupied by stars must be finite is fairly clear, for as astronomers have long known (Olber's paradox) the night sky should appear as a uniform bright sheet if stars in every direction extended to infinity.

The last quantity, α, is known as the Hubble constant;

3. *The Nature of Physical Reality,* pp. 163–4.

it measures the rate of recession of the nebulae. Suppose a nebula is a distance r from us and sends us light which we recognize as coming from a familiar element and which, as we know it in the laboratory, has a wavelength λ. Invariably, the wavelength of a distant nebula is greater than λ by an amount $\Delta\lambda$ which is proportional to the distance of the emitting nebula from us. The accepted interpretation of this wavelength shift involves an appeal to the Doppler effect: just as sound travelling away from us has its wavelength increased by virtue of the motion of its source, so the light coming from distant stars suffers a wavelength change $\Delta\lambda$, and from Doppler's theory the ratio $\Delta\lambda/\lambda$ is proportional to the speed of recession v. Now, according to Hubble's observations, $\Delta\lambda/\lambda$ is greater the greater the distance r; hence the conclusion that the universe expands, the distant portions travelling away from us with greater speeds. The quantity α is a measure of this expansion, for it is defined as

$$\alpha = \frac{c}{r}\frac{\Delta\lambda}{\lambda} \qquad (2)$$

The values of the six constants in our table, though awesome to the casual observer because of their extreme range of variation from 10^{-28} to 10^{27}, are uninteresting, for their values depend on the units in which they are expressed. Only pure numbers, i.e., numbers without units, evoke Pythagorean fascination. One might therefore ask: what *numerical* constants can be constructed by multiplication and division from the list, and what are their values? The answer is pleasingly simple; there are just three (aside from powers and combinations between them), viz. R/ct, αt, and $\rho Kc^2 t^2$, as is apparent from an examination of units. And here we witness a numerological miracle, for the value of these three product-quotients is nearly 1. The pleasure one feels at this contingency is followed by a shock, however, for these combinations, which have the value 1, contain t, the age of the universe. This clearly changes as time goes on, and hence the combinations change their value as the universe grows older. One might conclude, therefore, that we live at the unique epoch in the history of the cosmos in which all three numerical constants happen to be unity.

Most of us, however, would not wish to add to the numerous homocentric errors of previous science a chronological anthropomorphism of this kind, and would rather suppose that 1 is the natural, perennial value of the combinations cited. But if this is true, then the other "constants" involved in the three combinations must change in a manner counteracting the change in t, that is to say, they cannot be true constants in time. Henceforth, I shall assume this to be the case and investigate the consequences.

The equation $R/ct \approx 1$ has an easy and a most acceptable interpretation. It means simply that the universe expands, provided we take c to be a reliable true constant, which shall henceforth be supposed. In this form the relation also affirms that the present radius of the universe R equals the distance a light ray would have travelled had it started when the universe was born. Hence we may think of the expansion as a race among material objects occurring since the birth of the cosmos, the fastest among them going with the constant velocity c, and these now occupy the frontier of space, a distance R from the common origin. Even though the value of R, determined as was suggested, is highly uncertain, its equality with ct confirms one's belief in its essential correctness.

To find that $\alpha t \approx 1$ occasions no very great surprise

224

either. For if that relation is written in the form ct/r $\Delta\lambda/\lambda \approx 1$ it merely means $\Delta\lambda/\lambda \approx r/R$; the relative Doppler shift equals the distance of the star in units of R, and consequently the light from a star at the "edge" of the universe will be completely wiped out by the expansion. The best telescopes now permit a view to about $\frac{1}{3} R$, and observations make this conclusion quite reasonable.

The third equation, $\rho K c^2 t^2 \approx 1$, presents a more difficult problem of interpretation since we cannot tell from available evidence which of the two quantities, ρ and K, compensates for the variation of t^2. Since c has been assumed constant, we can only conclude that ρK is proportional to $1/t^2$, in symbols, $\rho K \propto t^{-2}$. To carry the story beyond this point, it becomes necessary to bring further "constants" into our discussion.

Eddington, trying to establish the largest integer with direct empirical significance, seized upon the number of elementary particles in the universe and calculated it to be about 10^{80}. While his reasoning still overtaxes the ingenuity of most physicists, his result is roughly confirmed by empirical evidence, especially by the celebrated observations of Harlow Shapley and others who have counted stars and galaxies and divided their total mass by the mass of a representative elementary particle, such as a meson. This number, N, stands in solitary glory, the largest integer in the cosmos, unapproached by other meaningful numbers.

But an isolated mystery is annoying, while a connected set of them somehow pleases the mind. Let us therefore look for other large numbers to put beside Eddington's, perhaps as dwarfs flanking a giant. Clearly the simplest recipe for generating a large pure number with empirical meaning is to divide the size of the biggest thing by that of the smallest.

The biggest thing is the universe itself, the smallest probably the neutron, which has a radius $r_n \approx 10^{-13}$ cm. We thus obtain the number

$$n = R/r_n \approx 10^{40} \qquad (3)$$

Interestingly perhaps, it happens that

$$N = n^2 \qquad (4)$$

This may be of no significance whatever, for there clearly exists an arithmetical relation between every two numbers.

A number of the order 10^{40} can be generated in another way. Though physicists prefer not to be reminded of the fact, there is a skeleton that has rattled in their closet for a long time, and they are loath to speak of it. For consider two onta, elementary particles such as a proton, and a negative electron. When they are a distance r apart, they attract each other electrically with a force c_e/r^2; gravitationally, they attract in accordance with an inverse-square law also, but with a wholly different constant, the gravitational force being c_g/r^2. The creator, one might think, should have made our universe perfect in the sense of arranging for interactions following the same law to occur also with equal strength—instead of this, we find that $c_e/c_g \approx 10^{40}$. In more familiar notation, we see from eq. (1) that $c_g = Gm_em_p$, while $c_e = e^2$, e being the charge on an electron. Hence $c_e/c_g = e^2/Gm_em_p$. Let us call this number q. In sum, then,

$$q \approx n \approx 10^{40}; \qquad N \approx n^2 \approx q^2 \qquad (5)$$

Do these numbers also change in time? The clue to an answer lies in the definition of n, eq. (3). It is known that R changes with t, but in the absence of information a guess is required as to the temporal behavior of r_n. At this point, therefore, speculation may go in different directions and

226

lead to different cosmological conclusions. The most attractive hypothesis appears to demand that the properties of our onta (elementary particles) of all things, should remain truly invariable, and this would require us to fix r_n. Following this lead, we infer that

$$n \propto t \qquad (6)$$

and furthermore, since $q \approx n$, that

$$q \propto t$$

But q is again a combination of constants descriptive of onta which we agreed to hold invariant, and of the gravitational "constant" G; hence the last relation implies

$$G \propto t^{-1} \qquad (7)$$

Strangely, according to these conjectures, the "constant" of gravitation, and hence the force of gravitation, decreases in time, relaxes its hold as the universe grows older. Perhaps there is a connection between the progressive fatigue of universal gravitation and the expansion of the universe—but I know of no quantitative verification of this hypothesis. An amazing discovery is made, however, when we ask: *When* was q or n equal to 1, when were gravitational and electric forces between the constituents of an atom exactly equal? The answer is, 10^{-40} times the present age of the universe, that is to say, when the universe was 10^{-23} seconds old. But 10^{-23} seconds is the quantum of time, the notorious chronon.

From the time of the Vedas to the present era men have wondered about the smallest distance and the smallest interval of time, the *hodon* and the *chronon*. The idea of ultimate, unrestricted continuity of time and space has rarely been held and rests on uneasy foundations even today. Theories of the nucleons have a way of failing when they are applied to domains of space smaller than about 10^{-13} cm; characteristically, this is also the measurable size of the smallest onta. The suggestion is therefore strong that the smallest length, or the quantum of length, the hodon, be given this magnitude. One is then tempted to define the smallest time interval, the chronon, as the time which elapses when the fastest signal, light, traverses the hodon, and this is about 10^{-13} cm/10^{10} cm/sec $= 10^{-23}$ sec. The same approximate value is obtained by calculating the period during which the radiation created by the annihilation of the heaviest on—one of the hyperons—performs one oscillation, this being h/Mc^2. Perhaps this, too, is not mere coincidence.

One may therefore affirm, in a condonable effort to exonerate the creator, that the universe *was* perfect at the moment of its creation, which must have occurred at the universal age of one chronon since there is no lesser time; for at that instant the two types of force within an atom were equal.

Lest this discussion degenerate into a theodicy, we return to our numbers and see what else they disclose. Thus we encounter the suggestion of *continued creation* of matter. Combining equations (5) and (6) leads to

$$N \propto t^2 \tag{8}$$

The number of onta increases in proportion to the square of the age of the universe. This means that onta, and hence matter, must spring into being as time goes on; creation is a perennial contemporary affair which might perhaps be witnessed by man. But alas, a simple computation shows that the rate of creation is below presently attainable precision; indeed eq. (8) entails the birth of one elementary particle in a large laboratory per century. Nor does theory suggest in what form matter is generated, whether as elementary particles or as atoms or as full-fledged stellar masses.

The last mentioned possibility has a certain intellectual charm because it allows the retention of all verified conservation laws. It is often believed that creation of matter violates the principle of energy conservation. This is a popular error, as the following crude and elementary analysis will show. Compare, for example, the energy of dark space with the energy of a spherical cluster of mass particles of radius r and total mass M. The former is evidently zero; the latter is made up of several contributions. Chief among them is the relativistic rest energy of all constituent particles, the energy present if all these particles were infinitely dispersed. Its value is Mc^2. The other important contribution is the gravitational energy which arises from the work done when the particles are brought together under the action of gravitational forces; it is negative because the forces do the work, and it has the value $- kG\,M^2/r$, k being a geometrical constant which depends on the precise way in which the matter is distributed within r, but is not very different from 1. The energy of the cluster (which may well be a star) is the same as that of the space in which it was formed if its total energy equals zero, that is if, approximately,

$$Mc^2 - kG\frac{M^2}{r} = 0 \qquad (9)$$

This is true if $GM/rc^2 \approx 1$

Since neither M nor r is given, that relation can easily be satisfied; in fact it can be satisfied in an infinite number of ways.

As a mere conjecture let us suppose, following one theory in favor among a few astronomers, that the initial state of the new-born star has maximum possible density, i.e., consists of closely packed neutrons. The ratio of M/r^3 is then fixed, and we can determine M and r separately from eq. (9). The mass obtained in this way is about 50 times the mass of our sun, a fair average for stellar masses. The radius of the nascent cluster is about 60 miles.

If matter were created in the form of single elementary particles or atoms and not as stars, it would be more difficult to satisfy the conservation laws, although this might still be possible in the face of our ignorance respecting the physics of elementary particles. As summarized by Jordan, acceptance of the preceding considerations would lead to a cosmogony with stages such as these.

At the beginning of time, when the universe was one chronon old, there was but a single elementary particle or— theory permits this slight concession to biology—two parental onta, 10^{-13} cm in size. When the cosmos was 10 seconds old, its radius was about 1000 miles, it contained 10^{49} onta. Stars born at that time had sizes of about $\frac{1}{20}$ of an inch. The force of gravitation had decayed to 10^{-24} of its original strength, and it has become weaker ever since.

One final thought about creation and physical science.[4] Equation (9) which is the condition of zero energy for a mass M of radius r, is nearly satisfied for the entire cosmos, whose mass is about 10^{55} gm, while $G/c^2 \approx 10^{-28}$ cm gm^{-1} and R, from Table 2, is 10^{27} cm. Moreover, this equation remains satisfied because, as we have seen, $G \propto t^{-1}$, $M \propto t^2$, and $R \propto t$, c being constant, so that GM/Rc^2 is invariant. The whole universe could therefore have been created *ex*

4. For further comments, see the author's Aquinas Lecture, "St. Thomas and the Physics of 1958," Marquette University Press, 1958.

nihilo at any time without violence to the laws of physics as we know them. The same relations will also show that the third form of unity we encountered, $\rho K c^2 t^2$, is a stable one.

In closing this section, I desire to make a frank confession. I should be highly astonished if the conjectures here proposed were fully confirmed by observations. They do not compose what I should call a theory; rather, they form a set of suggestive hypotheses, a speculative matrix of ideas from which acceptable theories sometimes arise. Speculation is often the forerunner of fact and hence it is part of the business of science.

Such are the things we see as we look outward.

2. *Looking Inward: The Common Denominator of Science, Ethics, and Religion*

Reflection upon the human atom in its relation to the world about it, in its state of being "bound" through pleasure and pain to similar atoms, leads at once to the field of inquiry properly called *religio*.

Religion and science are said to be in conflict. The strife between them has sweeping consequences in human action, in the moral field, consequences which cannot be ignored. For religion, particularly in our Western sphere, has two aspects, one cosmological and one moral. Cosmological religion with its ancient, prescientific speculations about the universe covers in part the field of natural science, attempts to deal in its own way with problems of the type considered in section 1 of this chapter. In its moral phase, religion develops a code of human conduct and tries to commit men to it by an appeal to faith. Now, if science can show that the cosmological claims of religion are wrong, religion's case in the moral field is greatly weakened. This is precisely what has happened in our time. Men believe that science has overpowered religion in the natural realm, and they look to *science* for guidance in the sphere of human action and in the spiritual sphere. The unhappy and possibly tragic feature of this attitude is that it rejects a spiritual gift religion bears because man feels doubtful about the scientific pretensions it carries along with the gift.

I do not believe that the contest between religion and science has been decided in the cosmological field; nor that it ever will be decided. This belief is based, first of all, upon a simple fact of history. Science is not an unchanging, static set of propositions, not a permanent body of approved facts. Quite obviously it changes, and the changes are not merely additions of knowledge. Revision of basic tenets, overthrow of assumptions that proved erroneous are the marching orders of science, and the dynamism of this human enterprise is a result of the liberality of its method. Religion, too, is in a state of progress in spite of the reactionary insistence on codified eternal truth by so-called fundamentalists and others who refuse to enlarge their horizons. The evident fact is that both science and religion are involved in a process of growth, and if one were pitted against the other and were said to be the winner, who could guarantee the finality of that victory? Thus, if an adroit answer were sought to questions concerning the veracity of certain sacred accounts of creation, miracles and so forth, the attitude should not be one of rejection or acceptance. Rather, one must look upon them as partial not final revelations in an ever-unfolding historical process of human understanding.

There is in fact a need for continual reappraisal of the relation between religion and science, and never was this need greater than it is today, for science has recently undergone a revolution of its fundamental concepts that is unique in history. The complete refutation of old-style materialism in modern physics, the sublimation of mechanics, the reliance placed on abstract ideas, all these are sweeping in their philosophical consequences and many things that used to be said about the conflict in question are simply no longer true.

These are generalities; let us now face specific aspects of our theme. To me, it has always been a curious and yet significant fact that at the very beginning of the document which many regard as divinely inspired, religion is said to grant a charter to science, with an implication that the two shall live in peace. First, you recall, there was chaos, terminated by a divine act of creation. Then followed a period of lawlessness and confusion that ended in the great flood. One interpretation of the turbulent days prior to Noah's Ark, which is elaborated in the Jewish Talmud, emphasizes that during this period nature, and nature's God, did not act in accordance with consistent principles; that there were no natural laws and, hence, no possibility for natural science. Lawfulness, behavior in conformity with reasonable principles, causality, were God's gift to Noah, made in the beautiful covenant of the rainbow.

"Jehovah smelled the sweet savor; and Jehovah said in his heart, 'I will not again curse the ground any more for man's sake, for that the imagination of man's heart is evil from his youth; neither will I again smite any more everything living, as I have done. While the earth remaineth, seed-time and harvest, and cold and heat, and summer and winter, and day and night shall not cease.' And God said, 'This is the token of the covenant which I make between Me and you, for perpetual generations, I do set my bow in the cloud, and it shall be for a token of a covenant between Me and the earth. And it shall come to pass, when I bring a

233

cloud over the earth, that the bow shall be seen in the cloud, and I will remember my covenant, which is between Me and you and every living creature of all flesh.' "

If I understand this passage correctly, it means to say that the order of the universe is a divine gift. In a sense Judaeo-Christian religion here acknowledges the legitimacy of science. Perhaps it still remains for science to make an equally generous reciprocal acknowledgment to religion.

The symbolism of this covenant has remained alive as a vague religious motive in the work of most scientists. The very word "cosmos," meaning ornament or beauty, along with the Greek myth of the harmony of the spheres, discloses a remnant of elemental religion. Expressions of reverent amazement at the regularity of physical nature, at the simplicity of natural laws, at the sweep of the human intellect in its control of nature have sounded through the ages as religious overtones of science. It is heard in the utterances of modern scientists as clearly as it speaks from the eloquent writings of the theologian, Schleiermacher, who paid tribute to the one miracle before which all others lose their meaning, that miracle being the absence of breaches in the lawfulness of nature, the absence of miracles in the pedantic sense. But the lawfulness of nature, while big with religious implications, is hardly a sufficient basis for claiming general compatibility between religion and science.

Let me indicate some other areas of contact. To see them clearly, we must first remove a few very common prejudices that falsify the meaning of science, errors which have been popularized and are especially harmful today. The points to be made are mere recapitulations of our conclusions in preceding chapters, set out for their relevance in the present context.

It is widely believed that science deals exclusively with

facts and since facts stand supposedly in contrast with *values,* the latter are wholly immune to scientific treatment.

This view with all its harmful and divisive implications dominates American thinking so completely that it forms a major hindrance, not only to the perception of the correct state of affairs, but even to the establishment of a harmonious *modus vivendi,* a coexistence between the humanist and the scientist. Let us, therefore, examine the relation between facts and values, a relation which, as we shall see, remains incomplete unless it includes two further referents: theories and norms.

Facts clamor to be explained; they do not carry within themselves the elements of order which reason desires to bestow upon experience. Hence *theories* are constructed as correlates to facts; they point to facts but contain logical features, constructs, not encountered in the factual domain, and by virtue of these features they are rationally significant and logically manipulable. A dot, a line, a symbol on a blackboard, when regarded as existent facts are hardly of interest. But the symbol's constructional meaning which arises through rational context, the geometric properties of point and line which are reflected in theorems and axioms, these are the characteristics that make them memorable and noteworthy. This relation between P-plane facts and rational constructs, the way in which empirical confirmation converts constructs into verifacts, has been more fully studied in Chapter I.

As we have seen in Chapter III, explanation means the process through which facts are seen as particular consequences of more embracive propositions. To explain the motion of an object is to combine, theoretically, a set of concepts like mass, acceleration, and force in the manner of a syllogism entailing the facts observed. The facts alone are

235

meaningless. Only when they appear at the end of a deductive chain do they take on richness, perspective, and significance. The deductive chain is called an explanation; its links, together with other concepts, form a theory. One cannot ask the meaning of a fact, or the explanation of a fact, unless one is prepared to accept theory for an answer. Let us now turn to values, confining our attention mainly to ethics for the sake of definiteness.

Among those who study values we again find a group of isolationists who insist that values are self-sufficient and separately meaningful, that they belong to certain exclusive domains called ethics or aesthetics, the humanities or the liberal arts.

This academic view tries to maintain and defend itself despite the telling circumstance that no historical successful system of morals has ever been launched through a proclamation of values: men like Hammurabi, Moses, Christ, St. Francis, gave the world a *set of rules* and *precepts* but no values, and the moral sterility of our college courses in ethics, which largely shun precepts but harp on values, take them to be primary and then worry endlessly about their genesis, is another case in point.

Values in isolation are like facts in isolation; they are meaningless. Take the example "Honesty is a value." As it stands, this statement is either circular or false. To destroy its circularity one must either profess that honesty is a permanent ideal set into the sky as a guide for human action, demonstrable through inquiry and reflection; or else one must hold that honesty is preferred by people. The former has proved a useless and an unconvincing view; the latter is patently false. These two extreme interpretations, values as ideals unrelated to human behavior and values as *de facto* preferences observed in human behavior, are fruitless because they leave out of account the relation of values to the logical background which gives them meaning. What is that logical background?

Honesty does not stand as a value by itself. It is the agreement of people upon a *rule* or a *precept* that makes it a value. The precept is an exhortation or a command: thou shalt not steal; thou shalt not lie; and only if that precept is assumed valid will honesty be a value. There have been societies in which stealing from and lying to enemies is permitted; in these, honesty was patently not an unqualified value. In general, whether a pattern of behavior is a value can only be determined by an appeal to something logically prior to value, namely to the acceptance of a normative proposititon acting like a command. Such normative propositions I wish to call precepts or norms. The sense is now clear in which values take their meanings from precepts, in which precepts constitute and stabilize values: they are the medium in which values are supported and prevented from collapsing into insignificance, just as theory supports meaningful facts.

And where do we get these precepts? In our culture, they clearly come from the decalogue, the golden rule, and the sermon on the mount. In other words, they appear to come to us for the most part through religion. The existence of non-religious historical forms of ethics, however, together with the numerous philosophic attempts to establish norms (usually under the guise of values) independently of religious considerations rule out the claim that religion is the sole generator of ethical norms. In another volume I hope to show how the method of science, which succeeds in converting factual statements into universal propositions, when properly understood, can probably be relied upon to transform certain *de facto* preferences of concrete people into normative precepts with the discriminative power of an ought. The success or failure of that attempt, however, does not affect the present argument.

Here, then, is the situation with respect to the fact-value controversy:

As Fig. 16 indicates, there exists a parallel relation of en-

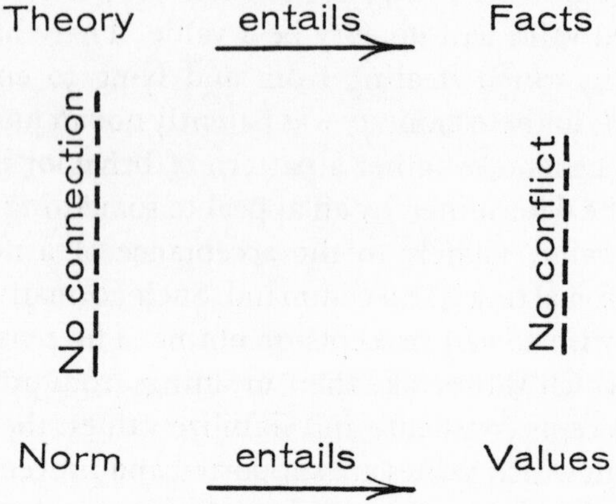

Theory   <u>entails</u>   Facts

No connection   No conflict

Norm   <u>entails</u>   Values

Fig. 16

tailment between theory and facts and between norms and values. Theories and norms are primary, their origins lie in acts of genius, perhaps divine inspiration; at any rate they are axiomatic in the logical sense and invite commitment. There is no connection between them because of their postulational character, just as there is no connection (at present) between the postulate of Einstein's metric and Maxwell's equation. If there were, one would lose its postulational character. Similarly, there is no connection, but also no conflict, between facts and values, for both belong to the realm of immediate experience and are thus related only existentially.

In most Western cultures the postulational elements of

LOOKING INWARD

ethics, the norms, are provided by religion. This is clearly one of its functions. But it is not the only, nor even the most important one; for religion also serves to order and regularize in an epistemological sense certain delicate, perhaps non-cognitive aspects of human experience which science ordinarily leaves aside. Before considering this role, however, let me insert a brief aside and recall the dynamism inherent in the scientific enterprise.

As we have seen, the judgment of science is never final. Science recognizes eternal *problems* but no eternal *truths*. It learns, it progresses; yet its job is never done. Nevertheless, science has its share of dogmatism. There are those who regard the present stage of scientific knowledge as ultimate and refuse to consider phenomena or experiences outside its momentary competence. They make a distinction between what science is now able to explain and what escapes its grasp; the former they call natural, the latter supernatural, and they believe this partition to remain meaningful. According to this unreasonable notion, radio and television were supernatural phenomena until the twentieth century, during which they were demoted, or, if you please, regularized to the status of natural. Yes, dogmatism in science arises from the mistaken belief that its present principles of explanation are forever valid and forever sufficient to embrace all experience.

And dogmatism in religion, equally indefensible and equally mistaken, rears itself upon the arrogant conviction that religious truth is laid down once and for all in a static pattern, rigid, lifeless, and inexorable, incapable of progress and improvement. These bone-dry dogmatisms always clash and clatter, and the noise they make through the centuries is usually taken as the sign of conflict between science and religion.

I now turn to the epistemological role of religion. What science does in this respect is well exhibited by Kant and most modern philosophers of science, who draw attention to the features of incoherence and irrelevance in our immediate experience, which exhibits a lack of order that reason alone can fill.

Kant says sense data are unordered, capricious, requiring to be regularized by the categories of reason which bring them under *concepts*. He speaks of the rhapsody of perceptions which is converted by principles of understanding into organized knowledge.

"Concepts without factual content are empty; sense data without concepts are blind. Therefore it is equally necessary to make our concepts sensuous; i.e., to add to them their object in intuition, as it is to make our intuitions intelligible; i.e., to bring them under concepts. These two powers or faculties cannot exchange their functions. The understanding cannot see. By their union only can science (knowledge) be produced."

What science actually achieves is a correlation of facts with ideas. It needs facts as our body needs food; but within the organism of science facts are processed, combined, organized, and connected by a texture of reason, and it is the whole of the organism, including that texture of reason, of ideas and conjectures, which is science. In a very deep sense, science has its origin in the circumstance that in the deliverances of our senses, the facts are not sufficiently well ordered to satisfy our desire for simplicity and consistence. Science is an elaborate answer to the paradox of the bruteness of our experience. To summarize: incoherent facts are unified by science into a consistent whole with the use of reason.

It seems to me that there is also an incoherent rhapsody of unique and troubling religious data which human under-

240

standing is called upon to organize into an orderly and satisfying pattern. What are the brute facts of religion?

For my part, I see them residing in those experiences most men acknowledge to be peculiarly religious, in the spontaneous feeling of gratitude that wells up in a man's heart on a joyous day, the feeling of awe in the face of overwhelming beauty, the contrition that follows a sinful experience, the experience of misery and abandon at the insufficiency of human power before fate, in our longing for grace and redemption. Just like the facts of science, they are unconnected, orderless and insufficient in themselves, requiring a texture of rational organization. And this, I take it, is what formalized religion or theology aims to provide—that its theory is replete with intangible ideas, that in the terminology of its detractors it bristles with the "technicalities of salvation" is small wonder to one who is familiar with the intangibles of science. Their presence in itself is no objection. The success of religion is measured by the degree of rational coherence which it bestows upon these singular religious experiences that assail the sensitive mortal.

Christian doctrine symbolizes the unrelieved and unembellished rawness of our natural reactions to the universality of sin, evil, and misery by its thesis of *original sin*. Guilt and terror strike the soul of man, and he feels unworthy of redemption. Indeed, if one analyzes the oppressive, brute facts of religion, one finds them reflecting, I think, very largely the message Genesis 3 speaks to Adam, "cursed is the ground for thy sake; in toil shalt thou eat of it all the days of thy life; thorns also and thistles shall it bring forth to thee; and thou shalt eat the herb of the field, in the sweat of thy face shalt thou eat bread, till thou return unto the ground."

Now pass from there to the words of Jesus in Matthew 11: "Come to me all ye that labor and are heavy laden, and I will give you peace." Here is a religious theme of supreme satisfaction, an organizing idea of power and simplicity in terms of which many crude experiences make beautiful sense.

To bridge this gap between Genesis 3 and Matthew 11 by a texture of rational connections is one of the important tasks of professional religion. And it is a task very similar to that performed by science when it converts "the rhapsody of sensations" into orderly rational knowledge.

BIBLIOGRAPHY

Chapter II:

P. SOROKIN has recognized and forcefully argued the importance of the relation between science, philosophy, and sociological structures in *Social and Cultural Dynamics,* American Book Company (1937); *Society, Culture, and Personality: Their Structure and Dynamics,* Harper's, New York (1947). The fallacies of relying on the merely factual are strikingly revealed in his *Facts and Foibles in Modern Sociology,* Henry Regnery Company, Chicago (1956).

The effects of science on philosophy and culture are eloquently discussed in F. S. C. NORTHROP's *Meeting of East and West,* MacMillan, New York (1946), and in his *Complexity of Legal and Ethical Experience,* Little Brown and Company, Boston (1959). See further *Ideological Differences and World Order,* ed. F.S.C. Northrop, Yale University Press (1949).

For the rise of the concepts of thermodynamics, briefly mentioned in section 3, see J. B. CONANT, Harvard Case Histories in Experimental Science, Vol. 1, cases 3 and 4.

Illuminating comments on the "visionary side" of science (our obscure movement) and the historical connection between philosophy and economics are found in A. H. TAYLOR, "Philosophies and Economic Theories in Modern Occidental Culture," Chapter VII in *Ideological Differences and World Order,* ed. F.S.C. Northrop, Yale University Press (1949).

Important treatises by physicists are: E. SCHRÖDINGER, *Science, Theory, and Man,* Dover Publications, New York (1957); ROBERT J. OPPENHEIMER, *Science and the Common Understanding,* Simon and Schuster, New York (1954); E. WIGNER, ed. *Physical Science and Human Values,* Princeton University Press (1947).

Chapter III:

ST. AUGUSTINE, *De libero arbitrio:* "Nisi credideritis, non intelligitis." Further limitations attending the use of formal logic, the construction of purely deductive systems, may be found in S. C. KLEENE,

243

Introduction to Meta-Mathematics, Amsterdam (1952). Kleene shows that a metatheory is required to complete every deductive system, and this metatheory always contains informal, intuitive elements and relations. Both A. TARSKI, "The Semantic Conception of Truth and the Foundation of Semantics," *Phil. and Phenomenological Research,* 4, 341 (1944) and K. GÖDEL, *Monatshefte d. Math Physik,* 38, 173 (1931) have given impressive and justly celebrated proofs of the insufficiency of formal reasoning within any given language, proofs which imply the need of a measure of faith in the sense of the present chapter. An excellent review of the problems connected with the process of empirical verification is given by C. HEMPEL, *Foundations of Concept Formation in Empirical Science,* University of Chicago Press (1952). M. POLANYI discusses the problems of logic from the point of view of commitment in his *Personal Knowledge,* University of Chicago Press (1958).

See further: PHILIPP G. FRANK, *The Validation of Scientific Theories,* The Beacon Press, Boston (1954) and *Philosophy of Science,* Prentice-Hall, Inc. (1957). Authoritative comments on the empiricist criterion of meaning are found in H. FEIGL, "Confirmability and Confirmation," reprinted in *Readings in Philosophy of Science,* ed. P. WIENER, Scribner's (1953).

Chapter IV:

This chapter has illustrated in one instance the influence of esthetic principles on science; the reverse effect, that of Greek science upon Western art, is beautifully demonstrated by MATILA GHYKA in Chapter V of *Ideological Differences and World Order,* ed. F.S.C. Northrop, Yale University Press, New Haven (1949). Readers with a taste for rigorous mathematics will enjoy the classic treatise by HERMANN WEYL, *Symmetry,* Princeton University Press (1952).

Matters dealing with the theory of relativity are discussed in PHILIPP G. FRANK, *Philosophical Interpretations and Misinterpretations of the Theory of Relativity,* Hermann Cie., Paris (1938); A. GRÜNBAUM, "Logical and Philosophical Foundations of the Special Theory of Relativity," *Am. J. of Physics,* 23, 450 (1955); H. MARGENAU and R. MOULD, *Phil. of Sci.,* 24, 297 (1957). Good expositions of the relativistic twin "paradox" are found in A. GRÜNBAUM, *Phil. of Sci.,* 21, 249 (1954), and G. BUILDER, *Phil. of Sci.,* 26, 135 (1959). P. ROSEN, *Phil.*

of Sci., *26*, 2, 145 (1959), draws attention to the possibility that aging of an organism may be subject to different laws than physical time.

The fundamental physical concepts of relativity are discussed in R. B. LINDSAY and H. MARGENAU, *Foundations of Physics*, Dover Press (1955). An excellent textbook on relativity is P. G. BERGMANN, *Introduction to the Theory of Relativity*, Prentice-Hall, Inc. (1955).

Chapter V:

In connection with the reality of a vacuum, see the discussion of the controversy between the Vacuists and the Plenists in J. B. CONANT, Harvard Case Histories in Experimental Science, Harvard University Press, vol. 1, pp. 25 ff. (1957).

The interesting notion of "an infinite chain of worlds within worlds," rejected by modern physics, was eloquently championed by B. PASCAL in his *Pensées,* translated by W. F. Trotter, Dutton, New York (1931).

Modern treatises presenting the details underlying this chapter in a thorough scientific manner are:

E. Fermi, *Elementary Particles,* Yale University Press (1951).

W. Finkelnburg, *Atomic Physics,* McGraw-Hill Book Company, Inc. (1955).

R. B. Leighton, *Principles of Modern Physics,* McGraw-Hill Book Company, Inc. (1959).

A. M. Thorndyke, *Mesons, A Summary of Experimental Facts,* McGraw-Hill Book Company, Inc. (1952).

R. F. Humphreys and R. Beringer, *First Principles of Atomic Physics,* Harper's (1950).

G. Holton, *Introduction to Concepts and Theories in Physical Science,* Addison-Wesley, Cambridge (1953).

C. V. Raman, *The New Physics,* Philosophical Library, New York (1951).

W. Heisenberg, *Nuclear Physics,* Philosophical Library, New York (1953).

Our treatment in Chapter V omits the details, but reflects the spirit of the more recent and complicated developments of qantum mechanics. To the mathematical reader and to the connoisseur of the elementary phases of this discipline I recommend that excellent text on modern quantum theory: *Mesons and Fields,* vol. 1, by S. S. Schroeber, H. A. Bethe, and F. de Hoffmann; Row, Peterson (1955).

Chapter VI:

A review of the earlier scientific events leading to the abandonment of classical mechanics may be found in A. D'ABRO, *The Decline of Mechanism,* Van Nostrand, New York (1939).

L. DEBROGLIE's book, *Physics and Microphysics,* Pantheon, New York (1955), translated by M. Davidson, casts many interesting sidelights on the developments of the present chapter. Among other matters, DeBroglie attempts to draw parallels between Bergson's theory of duration and the quantum theory.

The interested reader will not want to miss E. SCHRÖDINGER's exquisite discussion of quantum phenomena in his "Are there Quantum Jumps?" *Brit. J. Phil. of Sci., 3,* 10 (1952). This and other remarkable semi-popular publications are collected in E. Schrödinger, *What is Life and Other Scientific Essays,* Doubleday Anchor Co., Garden City, N.Y. (1956).

MAX BORN, another of the founders of quantum mechanics, gives an enjoyable survey of quantum theory in his *Physics in My Generation,* Pergamon Press, London (1956).

For a treatment of complementarity we refer to NIELS BOHR, *Atomic Physics and Human Knowledge,* John Wiley and Sons, New York (1958) and ROBERT J. OPPENHEIMER, *Science and the Common Understanding,* Simon and Schuster, New York (1954).

Theological use is made of the principle of complementarity in *Chance and Providence* by W. G. POLLARD, Scribner's (1958).

Further relevant philosophical considerations are found in the following books and articles:

A. Landé, "Non-Quantal Foundations of Quantum Theory," *Phil. of Sci., 24,* 309 (1957).

John L. McKnight, "The Quantum Theoretical Concept of Measurement," *Phil. of Sci., 24,* 321 (1957).

John L. McKnight, "An Extended Latency Interpretation of Quantum Mechanical Measurement," *Phil. of Sci., 25,* 209 (1958).

Peter Caws, "The Functions of Definition in Science," *Phil. of Sci., 26,* 201 (1959).

Virgil Hinshaw, Jr., "Determinism Versus Continuity," *Phil. of Sci., 26,* 310 (1959).

R. J. Seeger, "On the Teaching of Philosophy of Physics," *Am. J. Physics, 28,* 384 (1960).

It is interesting to record that the philosophy presented in this chapter and in most of the cited references is entirely in accord with important Russian views on the meaning of quantum mechanics. See, for instance, V. Fock's article "Über die Deutung der Quantenmechanik" in the Max Planck Festschrift, Deutscher Verlag der Wissenschaften, Berlin (1958). Fock calls quantum mechanics a "basic *extension* of the materialistic world picture."

Chapter VII:

The problem of causality is treated from a point of view compatible with this chapter by E. NAGEL, "The Causal Character of Modern Physical Theory" in *Philosophy of Science,* ed. H. Feigl and M. Brodbeck, Appleton-Century-Crofts, New York (1953).

See also E. CASSIRER, *Determinism and Indeterminism in Modern Physics,* translated by O. T. Benfey, Yale University Press, New Haven (1956).

M. BUNGE, *Causality,* Harvard University Press (1959).

V. F. LENZEN, *Causality in Natural Science,* C. C. Thomas, Springfield, (1954).

A very cautious view with respect to determinism, seemingly objective but noncommittal and somewhat irrelevant to the important problems of contemporary science, is contained in H. B. BRAITHWAITE, *Scientific Explanation,* Cambridge University Press (1953).

Important thoughts on the problems of section 5 are contained in *The History of Nature* by C. F. VON WEIZSÄCKER, University of Chicago Press (1949). See also *The Rise of Modern Physics* by C. F. VON WEIZSÄCKER and J. JUILFS, Braziller, New York (1957).

Problems closely related to this chapter are treated authoritatively in:

"Physics and Philosophy," W. HEISENBERG, *World Perspective,* Ruth Anshen, ed., Harper's (1958).

Atomic Physics and Human Knowledge, NIELS BOHR, John Wiley and Sons, New York (1958).

Natural Philosophy of Cause and Chance, MAX BORN, Oxford University Press (1949).

Albert Einstein, Philosopher-Scientist, ed. P. SCHILPP, Library of Living Philosophers, Evanston (1949).

"Quantum Mechanics, From Quality to Unity," A. LANDE, *Am. Scientist, 47,* 341 (1959).

Chapter VIII:

Suggested further readings are:

ALBERT EINSTEIN, "Science, Philosophy, and Religion." Reprinted in *Readings in Philosophy of Science,* ed. P. Wiener, Scribner's, New York (1953).

C. J. DUCASSE, *Nature, Mind, and Death,* Open Court, LaSalle, Illinois (1951).

Two Roads to Truth, E. W. SINNOTT, Viking Press, New York (1953).

Chance and Providence, W. G. POLLARD, Scribner's, New York (1958).

H. K. SCHILLING, "Teaching Reciprocal Relations between Natural Science and Religion," Chapter 5 in *Teacher Education and Religion,* American Association of Colleges for Teacher Education, Oneonta, New York (1959), p. 161.

New Knowledge in Human Values, ed. A. H. MASLOW and P. A. SOROKIN, Harper's, New York (1959). See especially the articles by J. Bronowski, R. Hartman, T. Dobzhanski, G. S. Allport and P. A. Sorokin.

E. P. WIGNER, ed., *Physical Science and Human Values,* Princeton University Press (1947). Articles by P. W. Bridgman, L. DuBridge, F.S.C. Northrop, M. Polanyi, I. I. Rabi, H. N. Russell, H. Shapley, F. T. Spaulding.

A remarkable modern treatise on values in their relation to science —but unfortunately one which overemphasizes the cleavage between science and the realm of values—is E. W. HALL, *Modern Science and Human Values,* Van Nostrand Company, New York (1956).

NAME INDEX

Allport, 248
Anshen, 247
Aristotle, 104–5

Bacon, 27
Benfey, 247
Bergmann, P. G., 245
Beringer, 245
Berkeley, 11
Bethe, 245
Biberman, 160
Black, 51
Bohr, 42, 116, 118, 142, 162, 163, 206, 246, 247
Bolyai, 61
Born, 42, 206, 246, 247
Boyle, 67–71
Brahe, 105 n.
Braithwaite, 247
Bridgman, 248
Bronowski, 248
Buber, 53 n.
Bucherer, 100
Builder, 244
Bunge, 247

Camus, 53 n.
Carnap, 52
Carnot, 51
Cassirer, 206, 247
Cavendish, 217
Caws, 246
Clausius, 51
Compton, A., 151
Comte, 50 n.
Conant, 243, 245

D'Abro, 246
D'Alembert, 95
Darwin, 49
Davidson, M., 246
Davisson, 154
Davy, 51
DeBroglie, 42, 154–56, 168, 246
DeHoffmann, 245
Descartes, 129
Dirac, 141 n., 216
Dobzhanski, 248
DuBridge, 248
Ducasse, 248

Eddington, 68, 216, 225
Einstein, 42, 61, 70, 95, 97, 99, 114, 125, 150, 154, 167, 238, 247, 248
Engels, 33
Euclid, 59

Fabrikant, 160
Faraday, 106–7
Feigl, 52, 244
Feller, 183
Fermi, 121–22, 126, 245
Finkelnburg, 245
Fizeau, 100
Fock, 247
Frank, P. G., 52, 244
Fresnel, 110

Galileo, 41, 48, 70, 89, 136, 171
Germer, 154
Ghyka, 244
Gödel, 244
Gregoir, M., 33
Grünbaum, 244

249

Hafstad, 41
Hall, 99, 248
Hammurabi, 236
Hartman, R., 248
Hayek, F. A., 211, 212
Hegel, 33
Heidegger, 54
Heisenberg, 42, 133, 168, 173, 206, 207, 212, 245, 247
Helmholtz, 49, 129
Hempel, 52, 244
Hinshaw, 246
Holton, 245
Hume, 27, 50 n.
Humphreys, 245
Husserl, 24, 25
Huygens, 145

Jaspers, 53 n.
Jeans, 64
Jefferson, 44
Jordan, P., 216, 230
Joule, 51
Juilfs, 247

Kant, 24, 25, 43, 50, 131, 206, 215, 240
Kelvin, 110–11
Kepler, 38, 43, 105 and n.
Kierkegaard, 53 n., 56
Kleene, 243

Lande, 246, 247
Laotse, 129, 161
Laplace, 206, 210
Lavoisier, 50
Leighton, 245
Lenin, 33
Lenzen, 247
Lessing, 74
Lindsay, 245
Lobatchevsky, 61
Locke, 44, 136
Lorentz, 95

MacCullagh, 110–11
McKnight, 246
Malraux, 53, 56
Marcel, 53, 56
Marx, 33
Maslow, 248
Maxwell, 107–8, 238
Mayer, 51
Michelson, 93, 113
Mill, J. S., 27
Morley, 93, 113
Moses, 236
Mould, 244

Nagel, E., 247
Newton, 16, 38, 41, 43, 48, 50, 51, 52, 62, 63, 69, 70, 105, 130, 131, 148, 156, 168, 203, 210–11
Nietzsche, 53, 209
Northrop, 243, 244, 248

Oersted, 41
Oppenheimer, 162, 243, 246
Parmenides, 104
Pascal, 245
Peyre, 56
Planck, 148–49, 154, 176
Poisson, 213
Polanyi, M., 244, 248
Pollard, W. G., 246, 248
Pythagoras, 29, 216

Rabi, 248
Raman, 245
Riemann, 61
Rosen, P., 244
Rossi, 99
Rumford, 51
Russell, H. N., 248

St. Augustine, 214, 243
St. Francis, 236
St. Thomas, 47, 142

NAME INDEX

Sartre, 53
Schilling, 248
Schilpp, 247
Schleiermacher, 234
Schrödinger, 42, 168, 174, 243, 246
Schroeber, S. S., 245
Seeger, 246
Shapley, 225, 248
Sinnott, 248
Snell, 124
Sorokin, 23, 243, 248
Spaulding, 248
Spinoza, 210
Stokes, 109
Sushkin, 160

Tarski, 244
Taylor, A. H., 243
Thomson, G. P., 155
Thomson, J. J., 145, 155

Thorndyke, 245
Tillich, 53
Trotter, 245

Unsöld, 221

Voltaire, 34
Von Neumann, 133
Von Weizsäcker, C. F., 247

Weyl, H., 244
Whitehead, 161
Whittaker, 109
Wiener, P., 244
Wigner, 243, 248

Yukawa, 122, 126

Zeno, 48

SUBJECT INDEX

Aberration, 112
Action, at a distance, 104, 115
Affirming the consequent, 49, 71
Antineutrino. *See* Particles
Antineutron. *See* Particles
Areas, law of, 105
Aristotelianism, 104
Arithmetic, 64; mean, 180
Astronomy, 198; Copernican, 13, 40; Ptolemean vs. Copernican, 13
Atom, 115–21; nucleus, 118–19; atomic number, 118; atomic weight, 120
Axioms, 59, 60–61, 65, 70

Being, 54–55
Berkeleian theory, 12, 20
Black body spectrum, 148
Bohr theory, 116–18, 142
Botany, 38
Boyle's law, 67–69
Bradley's aberration, 112

C-field, 9, 11, 15–17, 22
Capitalism, concepts of, 34
Cartesian frame, 86
Categorical imperative, 43
Cathode rays, 152
Causality, 14; and determinism, 203–14
Cavendish constant, 217
Central force, 49
Chameleon, 156
Chance, 213–14
Choice, 213–14
Chronon, 227–28

Circle, perfect, 81
Classical mechanics, 91, 103, 129–36, 195, 200
Classical physics, 131, 144, 166
Cognition, 4; cognitive component, 3–4; cognitive experience, 6, 7–9. *See also* Experience, cognitive component of
Coherence, 7, 142
Color, of electron, 19
Common sense, 137, 161
Communism, 40
Complementarity principle, 162
Compton effect, 101, 151
Concepts, 4, 5, 7
Concrete models, 129–169
Consequent, affirming the, 71
Conservation of energy, 49
Constant, Cavendish, 217
Constructs, 4, 5, 10, 11, 15, 16, 22, 181
Contact forces, 104
Continued creation of matter, 228
Continuous motion, 130 ff.
Contraction, of moving object, 99 ff.
Copenhagen interpretation, 166
Copernican theory, 13, 40
Correlational demonstration, 66, 73
Cosmogony, 230
Cosmology, 215–31
Coulomb forces, 125
Crystal, as analog of science, 36

DeBroglie: formula, 154–56; wave length, 168
Decay, radioactive, 218–21
Decision, 200

Deductive: approach, 22; demonstration, 66 ff., 73; method, 33; reasoning, 38
Definitions, 60–62
Democracy, 35
Demonstration, 66. See also Deductive, Inductive
Determinism: and causality, 203–14; reality, freedom, and, 171–214
Die, 165 ff., 189
Diffraction, of electrons, 157 ff.
Discontinuous emergence, 139
Discovery, 39
Displacements, 84
Dogmatism, 239
Doppler effect, 100, 151, 223, 225
Dualism, 144 ff.

Economy, of thought, 142
Eidetic truth, 24
Einstein, special theory of relativity, 77, 82, 83, 93–98, 114
Electromagnetic induction, 106–7
Electron: color of, 19; diffraction of, 157 ff.; existence of, 18. See also Particles
Elegance, 14, 84
Elementary particle. See Particles, elementary
Elements, man-made, 118
Emergence, discontinuous, 139
Empiricism, 50–53; empirical verification, 9, 14, 15, 17
Energy conservation, 49
Error, 179
Eschatology, 215
Essences, 54
Esthetics: invariance, a principle of, 79; and relativity, 77–101
Ether, 103–15
Ethics, and science, 231–42
Euclidean geometry, 59–62
Existence, meaning of, 18–21

Existentialism, 46, 53–58
Experience, 3, 36–38; cognitive component of, 3–4, 6, 7–9; elements of, 4–5
Experiment, 28
Explanation, scientific, 62
Extensibility, 13, 14

Facts: definition, 4; function, 5, 30; erroneous views of, 28–30; errors, 179; metaphysical requirements of, 14; methodological requirements of, 13; nature of, 26–38; proper function, 30
Faith, in science, 73–76
Feedback, 135
Fermi's pion, 121–22
Fine structure constant, 216
Firefly, 142, 176
Force: Aristotle, 106; central, 49; contact, 104; Coulomb, 125
Freedom: concept of, 34; human, 207–14; reality, determinism, and, 171–214

Galilean Transformations, 89–96
Gaussian arrangement, 160
Geiger counters, 152, 196
Genes, 197
Geography, 38
Geometry: Euclidean, 59–62; Lobatchevsky's, 61
Gravitation, 16; gravitational constant, 217. See also Newtonian

Hamiltonian quality, 18
Heisenberg's principle, 201
Historicity, 196, 198
Hodon, 227–28
Hubble constant, 222–23
Human affairs, and science, 26–58
Huygens' principle, 145
Hyperon. See Particles
Hypothesis, 15

Ionization, 13
Imperative, categorical, 43
Increase, mass, 100
Inductive: approach, 22, 23, 33; demonstration, 66 ff., 73
Inertial systems, 85–90
Interaction, 132
Interpretation, 30
Introspection, 24
Intuition, role of, in science, 21–25
Invariance, 77, 79–89, 101

Judaeo–Christian religion, 233–34

Kepler's laws, 38, 43
Knowledge, 29; elements, 4

Latent: attribute, 136; observables, 138, 141, 157
Law: of areas, 105; definition of, 82; invariance and, 84–85; of physics, 91–92; scientific, 52, 171–77. See also Newtonian
Light: motion of, 112; polarization of, 146; velocity of, 108, 126, 217; waves, 108–9, 145, 146, 152
Lightning, explanations of, 12
Linearity, 95
Lobatchevsky's geometry, 61
Logic: of scientific reasoning, 66–73; logical fertility, 11, 12, 14, 19; logical positivism, 50–53
Lorentz Transformations, 95–101, 114
Lumen naturale, 95

Marxism, 40
Mass increase, 100
Materialism, 47–50, 57, 103–27
Matter, continued creation, 228; continuous or discrete, 103–4; mean density, 217
Mechanics, 47; classical, 91, 103, 129–36, 195, 200; Newtonian, 103, 130–

31, 140; quantum, 64, 103, 144, 166, 167, 189, 190, 196, 199, 209; mechanistic materialism, 47–50
Mendelevium, 118
Meson. See Particles
Metaphysical requirements of facts, 14
Method. See Scientific method
Methodology, 13–14; methodological requirements of facts, 13
Michelson–Morley experiments, 93, 94, 113–14
Microcosm, 136–44, 177–84
Millikan's oil drop experiment, 153
Models, 193; concrete, 129–169
Modern physics. See Physics, modern
Morley. See Michelson–Morley experiments
Movement: continuous, 130 ff.; obscure, 40, 41, 43, 45; obvious, 39, 41, 42, 43, 45; relative, 92
Multiple connection, 14
Muon. See Particles

Natural history, 38
Nebulae, rate of recession, 217
Neptunium, 118
Neutrino. See Particles
Neutron. See Particles
Newtonian: doctrine, 210–11; gravitation, law of, 15, 16, 38, 43, 48, 51, 52, 62, 63, 105; mechanics, 103, 130–31, 140; motion, laws of, 203; relativity, 90–93
Nuclear physics, 120–27
Nucleon. See Particles
Nucleus, of atom, 118–19
Numerical constants, 223

Objective probabilities, 188
Observables: latent, 138, 141, 157; possessed, 136

Observation, 15
Obvious movement. *See* Movement, obvious
Ockam's razor, 111
Olber's paradox, 222
Omniscience, 211
Onta, 118, 123, 144–62, 218, 228, 230
Optics, 176
Origin of species, 49
Original sin, 241

P-data, 9. *See also* P-element
P-domain, 9
P-element, distinguished from construct, 6–9
P-experience, 7, 8, 10–12, 22, 23, 25
P-fact, 10, 11, 18
P-plane, 8, 9, 10, 13, 15–19, 21–23, 26 n.
Particles, 146, 147; elementary, 115–127, 143; antineutrino, 123; antineutron, 123; atom, 115–21; electron, 18, 19, 116–18, 122, 124, 142, 143, 145, 149, 150, 153–55, 157–61, 163, 174, 180, 190, 226; hyperon, 122–23; meson, 99, 122; motion of, 103; muon, 123; neutrino, 123; neutron, 120, 123–26, 199, 200, 226; nucleon, 126, 228; pion, 121–23, 126; positron, 121–22; proton, 119, 121, 123–26, 174, 190, 226; tauon, 122–23; theton, 122–23
Phenomenologists, 24
Philosophy, 40; of science, 41–44; influence on science, 46–47; scientific roots of modern, 46–58
Photoelectric effect, 149
Photon, 118, 126, 139, 143, 147, 148, 151, 154–55, 197
Physical sciences, 38, 50 n.
Physics, 57, 72; bankruptcy of, 191; classical, 131, 144, 166, 195; modern, 191–94; nuclear, 120–27;

quantum, *see* Quantum mechanics; teaching of, 30–32, 36
Pion. *See* Particles
Planck's: constant, 117, 149, 150, 154; law, 176
Polarization, of light, 146
Positivism, 50 and n., 57; positivist, 178
Positron. *See* Particles
Possessed observables, 136
Postulates, 72, 75; tentative nature of, 59–66
Probability: continued, 184–90; objective, 188; waves of, 162–69
Protocol, 5
Proton. *See* Particles
Psi-functions, 15
Ptolemean doctrine, 13
Pythagorean: philosophy, 216–17; theorem, 29

Quantization, 117
Quantum: mechanics, 64, 103, 144, 166, 167, 189, 190, 196, 199, 209; theory, 42, 140

Radioactive decay, 218–21
Radio waves, 107–8
Radius, of the universe, 217, 222
Random universe, 171
Rationalist, 178
Ray, cathode, 152. *See also* X-ray
Reality: determinism, freedom, and, 171–214; historical, 194–203
Reason: inner light of, 59–76
Reductio ad absurdum, 61
Relative motion, 92
Relativity: Einstein's special theory of, 77, 82, 83, 93–98, 114; esthetics and, 77–101; general theory of, 222; the inverse of invariance, 82; Newtonian, 90–93

Religion: and science, 231–42; Judaeo–Christian, 233–34
Retardation, of moving objects, 98 ff.

St. Elmo's fire, 145
Science: approach to, 2–3; basic maxims of, 14; discovery, 39; and ethics, 231–42; exact, 38, 39; of history, 203; and human affairs, 26–58; importance, 2–3; meaning of existence in, 18–21; new faith in, 73–76; observation in, 5; and philosophy, see Philosophy; influence of philosophy on, 46–47; philosophy of, 41–44, 59; physical, 38, 50 n.; and religion, 231–42; role of intuition in, 21–25; teaching of, 30. See also Scientific method
Scientific: explanation, 62; law, 52, 171–77; method, 2–18; reasoning, logic of, 66–73
Scintillations, 158
Simplicity, 14
Sin, original, 241
Singularities, 115
Snowflakes, shape of, 79
Spectrum, black body, 148
Speculation, 27
Statistical: mechanics, 52; regularity, 140
Symmetry, 78, 124
Synchronization, 88
Systems, inertial, 85–90

Tauon. See Particles

Theorems, 62
Theory, theories, 15, 27, 30, 38, 72–73; definition, 14. See also Hypothesis, Postulate
Thermodynamics, 50–53
Theton. See Particles
Transformations, and invariance, 80–89
True value, 180
Truth: a priori, 59, 62; eidetic, 24; meaning of term, 21; scientific, 74

Universe: age of, 217, 218; radius of, 222; random, 171
Uranium, half-life, 218–19

Validity, meaning of term, 21
Vedas, 115
Velocity, 98–101. See also Light, velocity of
Velocity addition, relativistic, 100
Verification, 14, 59, 142

Wave: function, 195; length, De-Broglie, 168; packet, 175. See also Waves
Waves: of probability, 162–69; radio, 107–8. See also Light
Wavicle, 156
Wesensschau, 24

X-ray, 150, 151, 154–55, 163, 164, 190, 197

Zeno's paradoxes, 48
Zoology, 38

THE YALE PAPERBOUNDS

Y-1   LIBERAL EDUCATION AND THE DEMOCRATIC IDEAL *by A. Whitney Griswold*

Y-2   A TOUCH OF THE POET *by Eugene O'Neill*

Y-3   THE FOLKLORE OF CAPITALISM *by Thurman Arnold*

Y-4   THE LOWER DEPTHS AND OTHER PLAYS *by Maxim Gorky*

Y-5   THE HEAVENLY CITY OF THE EIGHTEENTH-CENTURY PHILOSOPHERS *by Carl Becker*

Y-6   LORCA *by Roy Campbell*

Y-7   THE AMERICAN MIND *by Henry Steele Commager*

Y-8   GOD AND PHILOSOPHY *by Etienne Gilson*

Y-9   SARTRE *by Iris Murdoch*

Y-10   AN INTRODUCTION TO THE PHILOSOPHY OF LAW *by Roscoe Pound*

Y-11   THE COURAGE TO BE *by Paul Tillich*

Y-12   PSYCHOANALYSIS AND RELIGION *by Erich Fromm*

Y-13   BONE THOUGHTS *by George Starbuck*

Y-14   PSYCHOLOGY AND RELIGION *by C. G. Jung*

Y-15   EDUCATION AT THE CROSSROADS *by Jacques Maritain*

Y-16   LEGENDS OF HAWAII *by Padraic Colum*

Y-17   AN INTRODUCTION TO LINGUISTIC SCIENCE *by E. H. Sturtevant*

Y-18   A COMMON FAITH *by John Dewey*

Y-19   ETHICS AND LANGUAGE *by Charles L. Stevenson*

Y-20   BECOMING *by Gordon W. Allport*

Y-21   THE NATURE OF THE JUDICIAL PROCESS *by Benjamin N. Cardozo*

Y-22   PASSIVE RESISTANCE IN SOUTH AFRICA *by Leo Kuper*

Y-23   THE MEANING OF EVOLUTION *by George Gaylord Simpson*

Y-24   PINCKNEY'S TREATY *by Samuel Flagg Bemis*

Y-25   TRAGIC THEMES IN WESTERN LITERATURE *edited by Cleanth Brooks*

Y-26   THREE STUDIES IN MODERN FRENCH LITERATURE *by J. M. Cocking, Enid Starkie, and Martin Jarrett-Kerr*

Y-27   WAY TO WISDOM *by Karl Jaspers*

Y-28   DAILY LIFE IN ANCIENT ROME *by Jérôme Carcopino*

Y-29   THE CHRISTIAN IDEA OF EDUCATION *edited by Edmund Fuller*

Y-30   FRIAR FELIX AT LARGE *by H. F. M. Prescott*

Y-31   THE COURT AND THE CASTLE *by Rebecca West*

Y-32   SCIENCE AND COMMON SENSE *by James B. Conant*

Y-33   THE MYTH OF THE STATE *by Ernst Cassirer*

Y–34 FRUSTRATION AND AGGRESSION *by John Dollard et al.*

Y–35 THE INTEGRATIVE ACTION OF THE NERVOUS SYSTEM *by Sir Charles Sherrington*

Y–36 TOWARD A MATURE FAITH *by Erwin R. Goodenough*

Y–37 NATHANIEL HAWTHORNE *by Randall Stewart*

Y–38 POEMS *by Alan Dugan*

Y–39 GOLD AND THE DOLLAR CRISIS *by Robert Triffin*

Y–40 THE STRATEGY OF ECONOMIC DEVELOPMENT *by Albert O. Hirschman*

Y–41 THE LONELY CROWD *by David Riesman*

Y–42 LIFE OF THE PAST *by George Gaylord Simpson*

Y–43 A HISTORY OF RUSSIA *by George Vernadsky*

Y–44 THE COLONIAL BACKGROUND OF THE AMERICAN REVOLUTION *by Charles M. Andrews*

Y–45 THE FAMILY OF GOD *by W. Lloyd Warner*

Y–46 THE MAKING OF THE MIDDLE AGES *by R. W. Southern*

Y–47 THE DYNAMICS OF CULTURE CHANGE *by Bronislaw Malinowski*

Y–48 ELEMENTARY PARTICLES *by Enrico Fermi*

Y–49 SWEDEN: THE MIDDLE WAY *by Marquis W. Childs*

Y–50 JONATHAN DICKINSON'S JOURNAL *edited by Evangeline Walker Andrews and Charles McLean Andrews*

Y–51 MODERN FRENCH THEATRE *by Jacques Guicharnaud*

Y–52 AN ESSAY ON MAN *by Ernst Cassirer*

Y–53 THE FRAMING OF THE CONSTITUTION OF THE UNITED STATES *by Max Farrand*

Y–54 JOURNEY TO AMERICA *by Alexis de Tocqueville*

Y–55 THE HIGHER LEARNING IN AMERICA *by Robert M. Hutchins*

Y–56 THE VISION OF TRAGEDY *by Richard B. Sewall*

Y–57 MY EYES HAVE A COLD NOSE *by Hector Chevigny*

Y–58 CHILD TRAINING AND PERSONALITY *by John W. M. Whiting and Irvin L. Child*

Y–59 RECEPTORS AND SENSORY PERCEPTION *by Ragnar Granit*

Y–60 VIEWS OF JEOPARDY *by Jack Gilbert*

Y–61 LONG DAY'S JOURNEY INTO NIGHT *by Eugene O'Neill*

Y–62 JAY'S TREATY *by Samuel Flagg Bemis*

Y–63 SHAKESPEARE: A BIOGRAPHICAL HANDBOOK *by Gerald Eades Bentley*

Y–64 THE POETRY OF MEDITATION *by Louis L. Martz*

Y–65 SOCIAL LEARNING AND IMITATION *by Neal E. Miller and John Dollard*

Y–66 LINCOLN AND HIS PARTY IN THE SECESSION CRISIS *by David M. Potter*

Y–67   SCIENCE SINCE BABYLON *by Derek J. de Solla Price*
Y–68   PLANNING FOR FREEDOM *by Eugene V. Rostow*
Y–69   BUREAUCRACY *by Ludwig von Mises*
Y–70   JOSIAH WILLARD GIBBS *by Lynde Phelps Wheeler*
Y–71   HOW TO BE FIT *by Robert Kiphuth*
Y–72   YANKEE CITY *by W. Lloyd Warner*
Y–73   WHO GOVERNS? *by Robert A. Dahl*
Y–74   THE SOVEREIGN PREROGATIVE *by Eugene V. Rostow*
Y–75   THE PSYCHOLOGY OF C. G. JUNG *by Jolande Jacobi*
Y–76   COMMUNICATION AND PERSUASION *by Carl I. Hovland, Irving L. Janis, and Harold H. Kelley*
Y–77   IDEOLOGICAL DIFFERENCES AND WORLD ORDER *edited by F. S. C. Northrop*
Y–78   THE ECONOMICS OF LABOR *by E. H. Phelps Brown*
Y–79   FOREIGN TRADE AND THE NATIONAL ECONOMY *by Charles P. Kindleberger*
Y–80   VOLPONE *edited by Alvin B. Kernan*
Y–81   TWO EARLY TUDOR LIVES *edited by Richard S. Sylvester and Davis P. Harding*
Y–82   DIMENSIONAL ANALYSIS *by P. W. Bridgman*
Y–83   ORIENTAL DESPOTISM *by Karl A. Wittfogel*
Y–84   THE COMPUTER AND THE BRAIN *by John von Neumann*
Y–85   MANHATTAN PASTURES *by Sandra Hochman*
Y–86   CONCEPTS OF CRITICISM *by René Wellek*
Y–87   THE HIDDEN GOD *by Cleanth Brooks*
Y–88   THE GROWTH OF THE LAW *by Benjamin N. Cardozo*
Y–89   THE DEVELOPMENT OF CONSTITUTIONAL GUARANTEES OF LIBERTY *by Roscoe Pound*
Y–90   POWER AND SOCIETY *by Harold D. Lasswell and Abraham Kaplan*
Y–91   JOYCE AND AQUINAS *by William T. Noon, S.J.*
Y–92   HENRY ADAMS: SCIENTIFIC HISTORIAN *by William Jordy*
Y–93   THE PROSE STYLE OF SAMUEL JOHNSON *by William K. Wimsatt, Jr.*
Y–94   BEYOND THE WELFARE STATE *by Gunnar Myrdal*
Y–95   THE POEMS OF EDWARD TAYLOR *edited by Donald E. Stanford*
Y–96   ORTEGA Y GASSET *by José Ferrater Mora*
Y–97   NAPOLEON: FOR AND AGAINST *by Pieter Geyl*
Y–98   THE MEANING OF GOD IN HUMAN EXPERIENCE *by William Ernest Hocking*
Y–99   THE VICTORIAN FRAME OF MIND *by Walter E. Houghton*
Y–100 POLITICS, PERSONALITY, AND NATION BUILDING *by Lucian W. Pye*